KICK-ASS

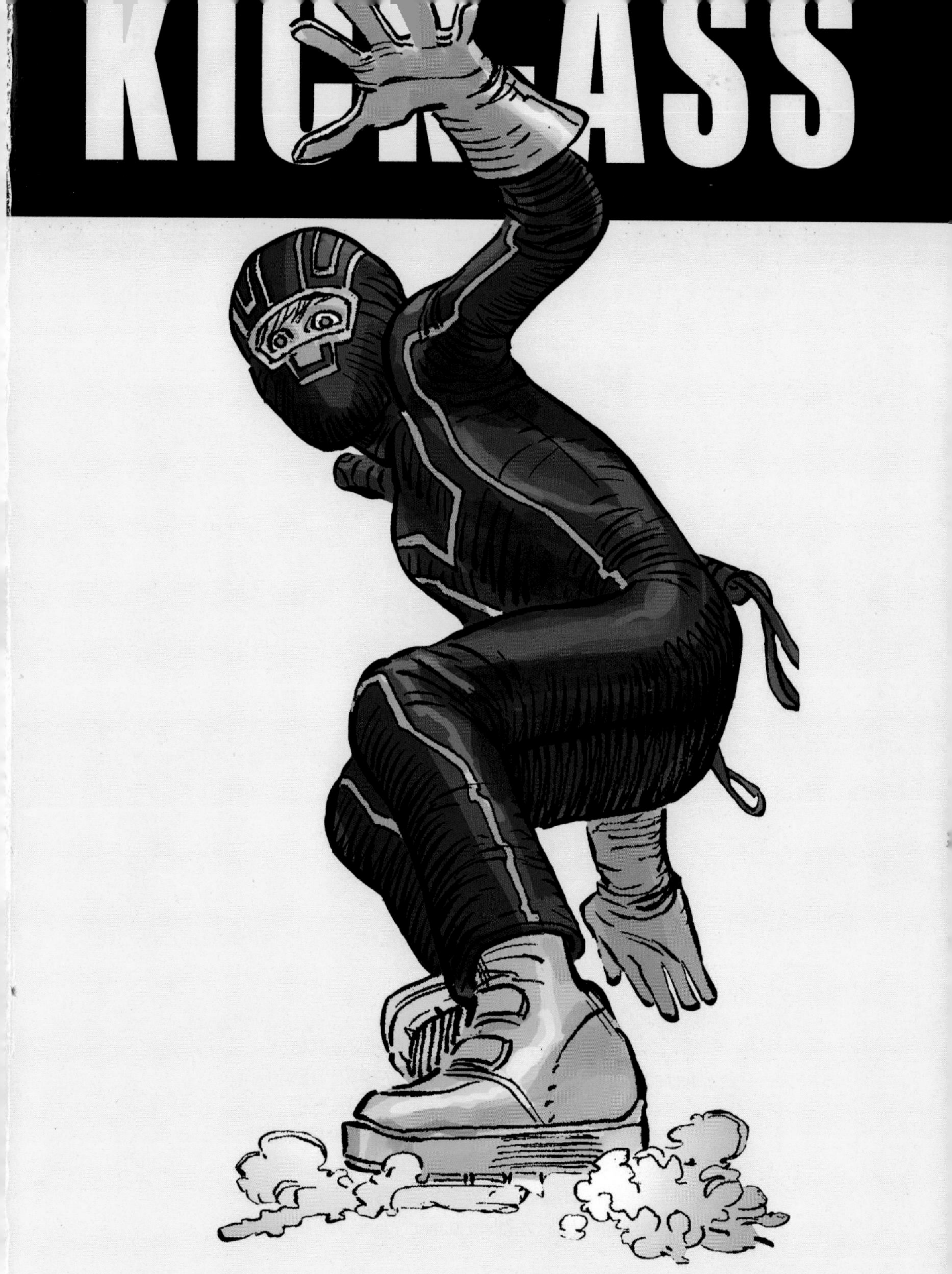

KICK-ASS. Contains material originally published in magazine form as KICK-ASS #1-8. First printing 2010. ISBN# 978-0-7851-3435-0. Published by MARVEL PUBLISHING, INC., a subsidiary of MARVEL ENTERTAINMENT, INC. OFFICE OF PUBLICATION: 417 5th Avenue, New York, NY 10016. $24.99 per copy in the U.S. (GST #R127032852); Canadian Agreement #40668537. **Printed in the U.S.A. Manufactured between 12/28/09 and 1/27/10 by R.R. DONNELLEY, INC., SALEM, VA, USA.**

10 9 8 7 6 5 4 3 2 1

KICK-ASS

Writer & Co-Creator
MARK MILLAR

Penciler & Co-Creator
JOHN ROMITA JR.

Inker
TOM PALMER

Colorist
DEAN WHITE

Letterer
CHRIS ELIOPOULOS

Assistant Editor
MICHAEL HORWITZ

Editor
JOHN BARBER

Collection Editor: JENNIFER GRÜNWALD
Assistant Editors: ALEX STARBUCK & JOHN DENNING
Editor, Special Projects: MARK D. BEAZLEY
Senior Editor, Special Projects: JEFF YOUNGQUIST
Senior Vice President of Sales: DAVID GABRIEL
Book Designer: SPRING HOTELING
SVP of Business Affairs & Talent Management: DAVID BOGART

Editor in Chief: JOE QUESADA
Publisher: DAN BUCKLEY
Executive Producer: ALAN FINE

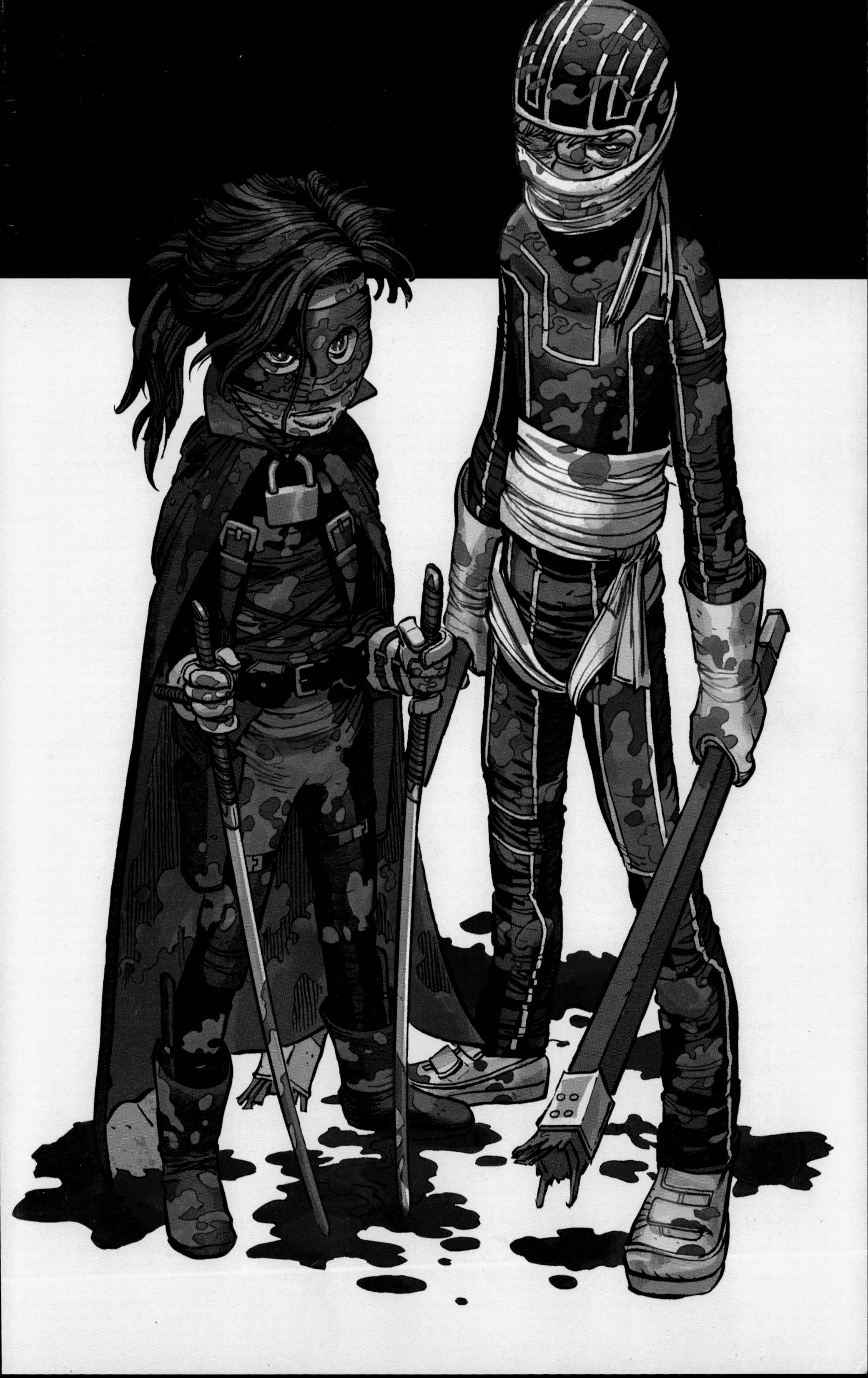

"KICK-ASS?"

Yup.

"KICK-ASS??"

That's it.

"KICK-ASS????"

So this is how the best-selling author in comics is going to follow up *Wanted* and *Civil War*? The guy that brought us Angelina Jolie as a naked, ruthless assassin dripping in wax, the guy who gave us Captain America versus Iron Man for all the marbles in the Marvel Universe? His next work was *Kick-Ass*???

My reaction to the title of Mark Millar's latest, greatest magnum opus was less than stellar. But he just smiled. Because Mark Millar gets it.

As a matter of fact, Mark got it way before the rest of us. See, If you're gonna do a book featuring the most Kick-Ass writing, the most Kick-Ass art, the most Kick-Ass action, then you can't afford to be shy, you just call it the way you see it. And in this case, with this concept and these creators, there was no doubt this comic would be Kick-Ass in every way.

Here's a story about a kid who imagines himself as a real life crime-fighter, combating evil with homemade weapons and devices available at your local Wal-Mart. What kid hasn't imagined himself grabbing a trash can lid and a baseball bat and wandering the mean streets Kickin' Ass and taking names? Dave Lizewski IS THAT KID! That kid in all of us, the kid who sought to live out his dreams and bust some bad guy ass in real-life-wannabe-superhero fashion.

The minute Dave Lizewski becomes Kick-Ass and steps into the neighborhood, your heart leaps with hope as he confronts local gang members. Your heart subsequently falls and is crushed as Dave receives his first serious beat down at the hands of same gangstas. The blood, the grit, the bloody failure. It drew us in, we couldn't look away.

And as Dave Lizewski rises again with renewed determination, so do our hopes and dreams. If Dave Lizewski can overcome, than so can I! Dave has no super powers, no Adamantium claws, no spider webbing, no gamma charged super strength. He just has a heart twice as big as yours and the guts to see it through no matter what. This is the heart of Kick-Ass!

But with courage comes the inevitable Mark Millar-imagined hyper-real super-violence. It's brutal, it's messy and it's so far over the top it has to be seen to be believed and no one on planet earth can depict it the way John Romita Jr. can.

John Romita Jr. has drawn every Marvel character imaginable. He's the ace, the closer, the go-to guy. He's the closest thing to clutch that exists in the comics biz. A few years back, he and Millar combined for the first time to bring us the super-charged epic *Wolverine: Enemy of the State*. Sales soared and fans demanded that these two team up again as often as possible. When they answered the call, was there any doubt it would be as Kick-Ass as possible?

Romita Jr's. storytelling in *Kick-Ass* is the most cinematic, widescreen, high-def he's ever attempted. The pacing, the drama, the violence in these pages is as brutal as any you will ever find. It makes you cringe and wince and ultimately leaves you with your slack-jawed mouth scraping the bottom of the floor. John Romita Jr. leaves it all on the page, he holds nothing back here and in doing so produces the seminal work of his career. Millar and Romita Jr. are peas and carrots, bees and honey, cookies and cream. Simply put, they are irresistible.

HIT-GIRL! RED MIST! BIG DADDY! It's all KICK-ASS, all the time, as only two of the brightest stars in the history of graphic novels could depict it.

When *Kick-Ass* hit the stands, fans hit the streets talking about the best damn comic to come down the pike in a long damn time. *Kick-Ass* is courageous. *Kick-Ass* is contagious. You had to get *Kick-Ass*!

It used to be that you had to be grim and gritty in order to grab everyone's attention. Now you most definitely have to Kick-Ass.

So what the hell are you waiting for? Turn the page and prepare to go KICK some ASS!

Rob Liefeld
January 2010

Rob Liefeld was one of the forefathers of the 1990s comics revolution — co-creating Cable *and* Deadpool, *and transforming* New Mutants *into* X-Force *before helping found Image Comics with his original property* Youngblood. *In 2007, Liefeld returned to Marvel to pencil the* Onslaught Reborn *miniseries.*

ONE

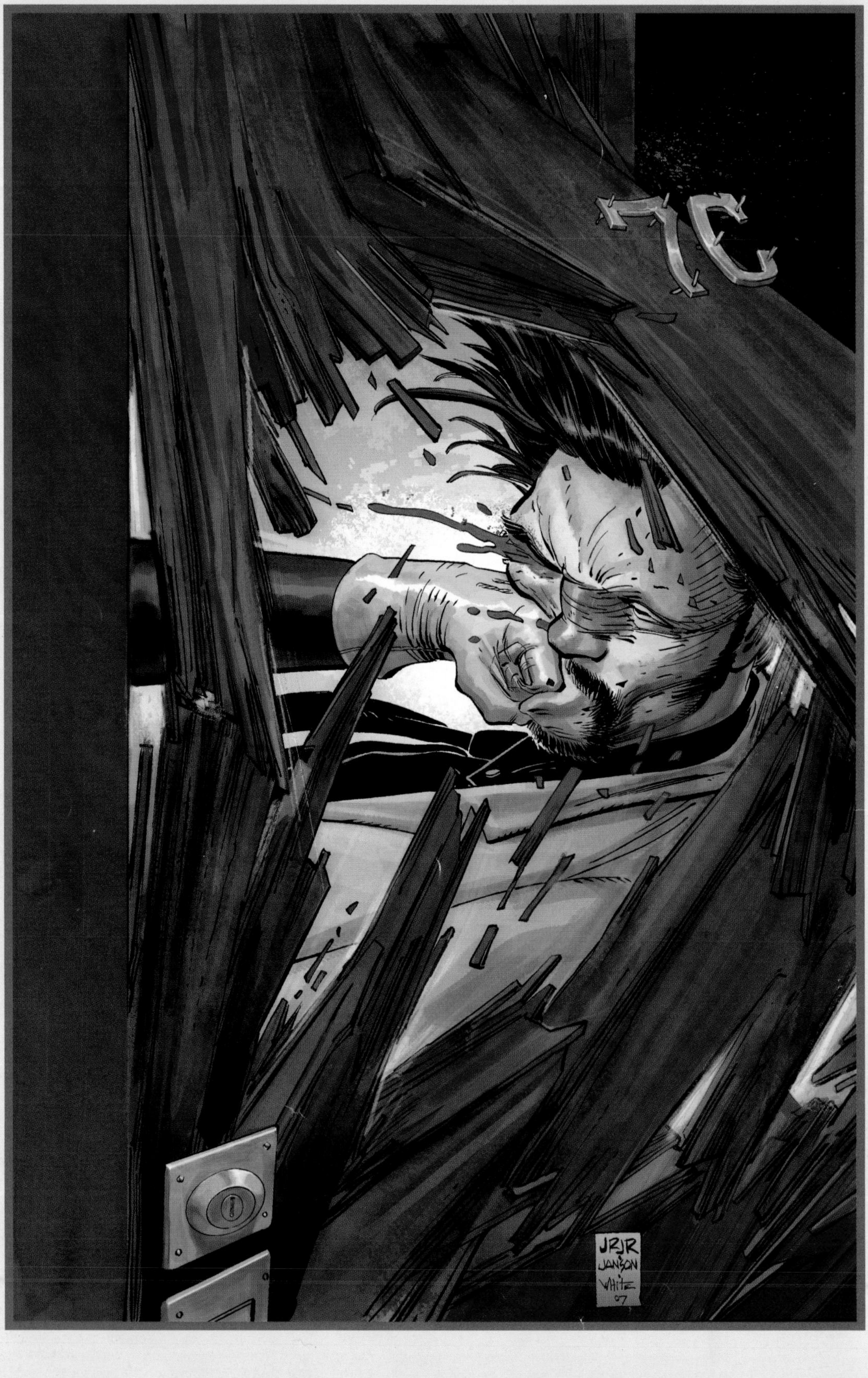
7C
JRJR
JANSON
WHITE
07

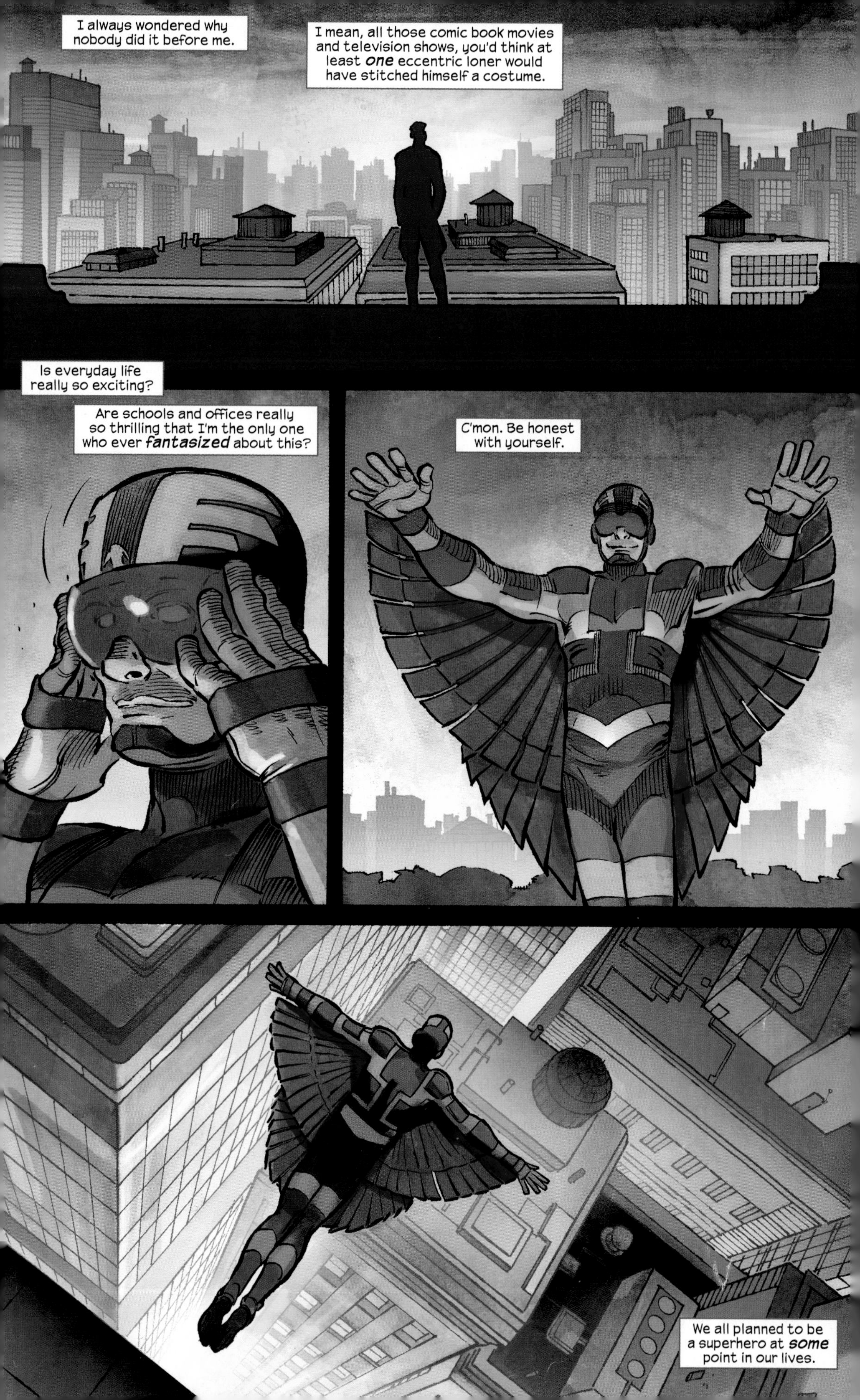
I always wondered why nobody did it before me.
I mean, all those comic book movies and television shows, you'd think at least *one* eccentric loner would have stitched himself a costume.
Is everyday life really so exciting?
Are schools and offices really so thrilling that I'm the only one who ever *fantasized* about this?
C'mon. Be honest with yourself.
We all planned to be a superhero at *some* point in our lives.

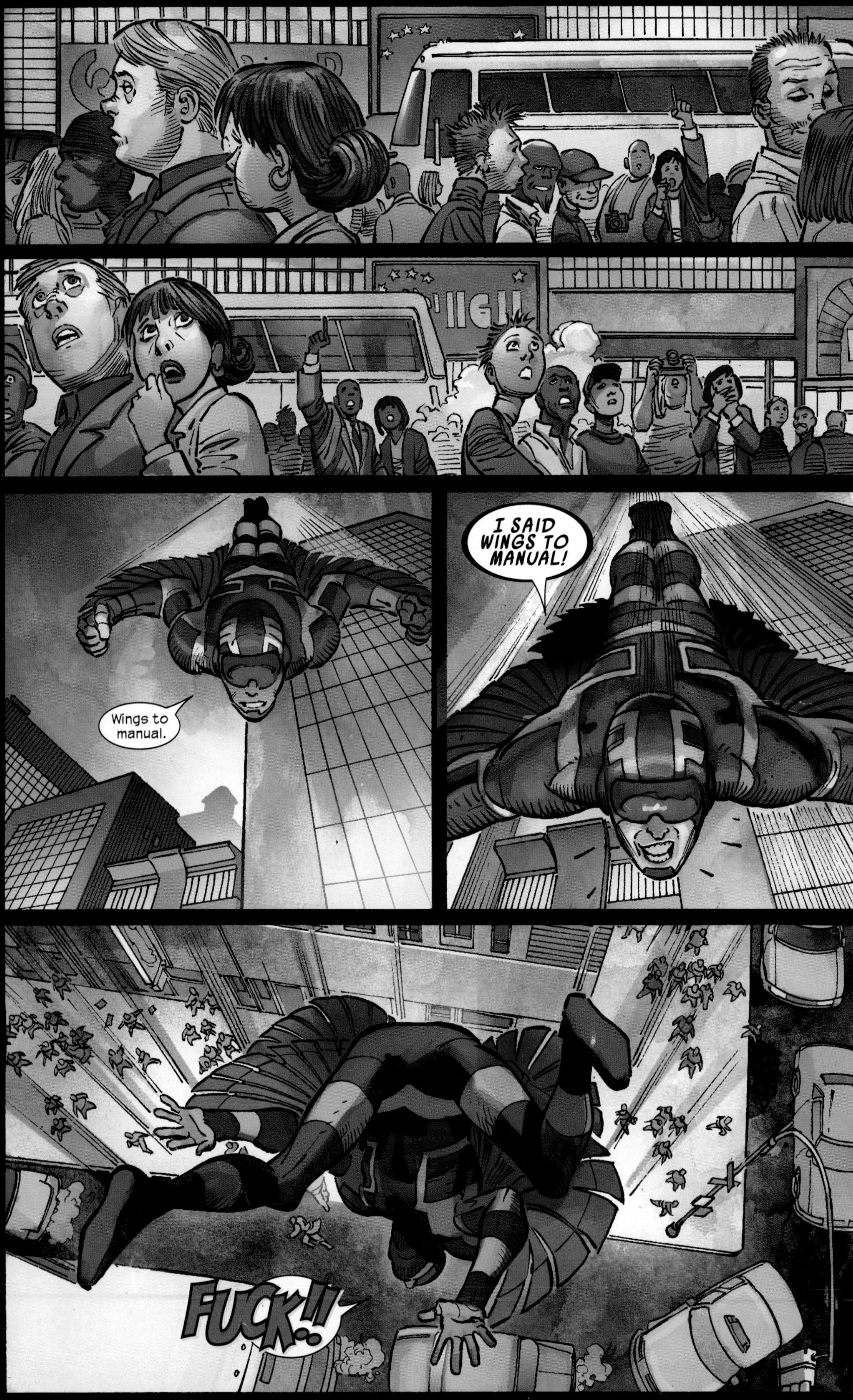
Wings to manual.
I SAID WINGS TO MANUAL!
FUCK!!

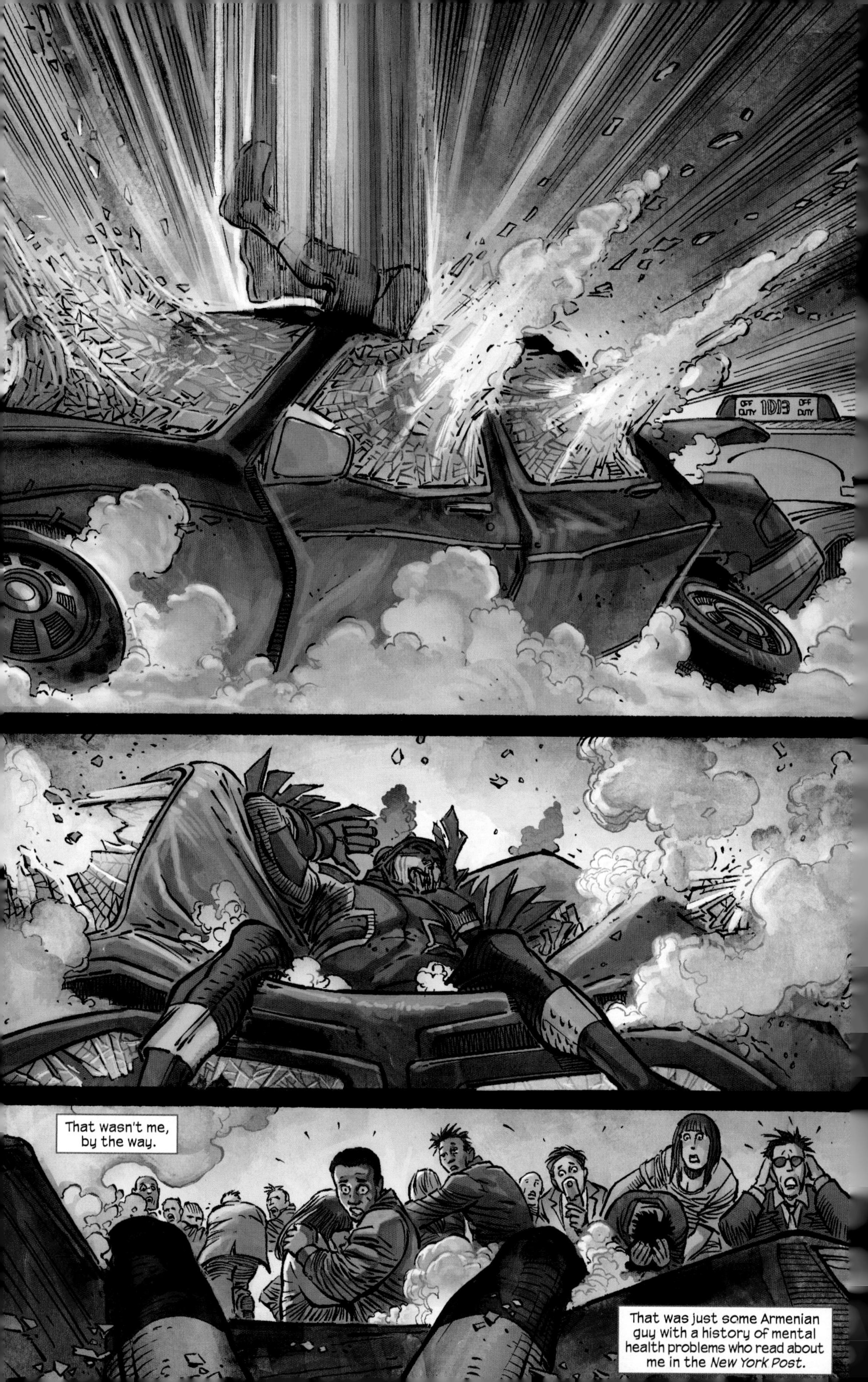
OFF DUTY 1D13 OFF DUTY
That wasn't me, by the way.
That was just some Armenian guy with a history of mental health problems who read about me in the *New York Post*.

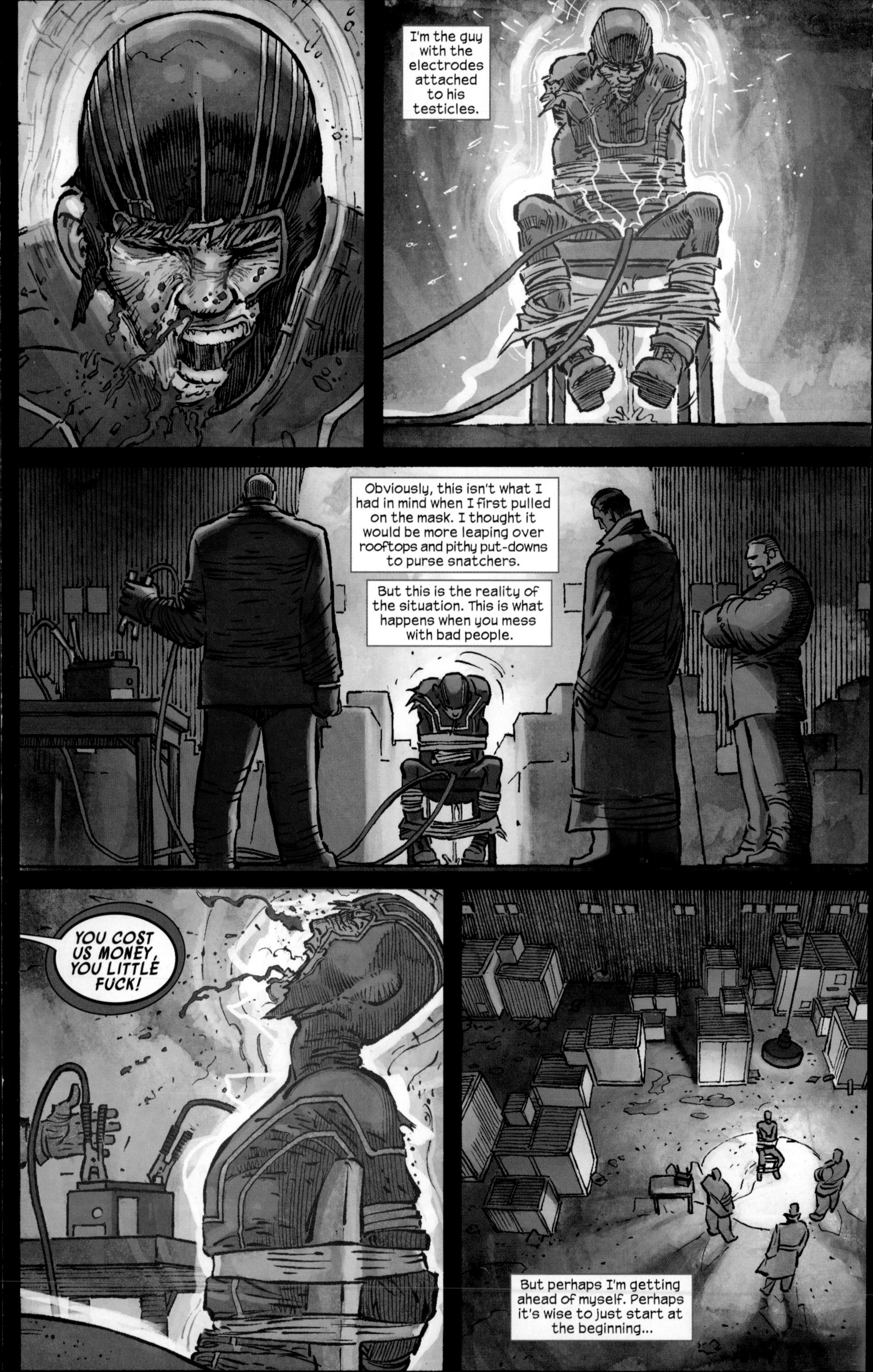
I'm the guy with the electrodes attached to his testicles.
Obviously, this isn't what I had in mind when I first pulled on the mask. I thought it would be more leaping over rooftops and pithy put-downs to purse snatchers.
But this is the reality of the situation. This is what happens when you mess with bad people.
YOU COST US MONEY, YOU LITTLE FUCK!
But perhaps I'm getting ahead of myself. Perhaps it's wise to just start at the beginning...

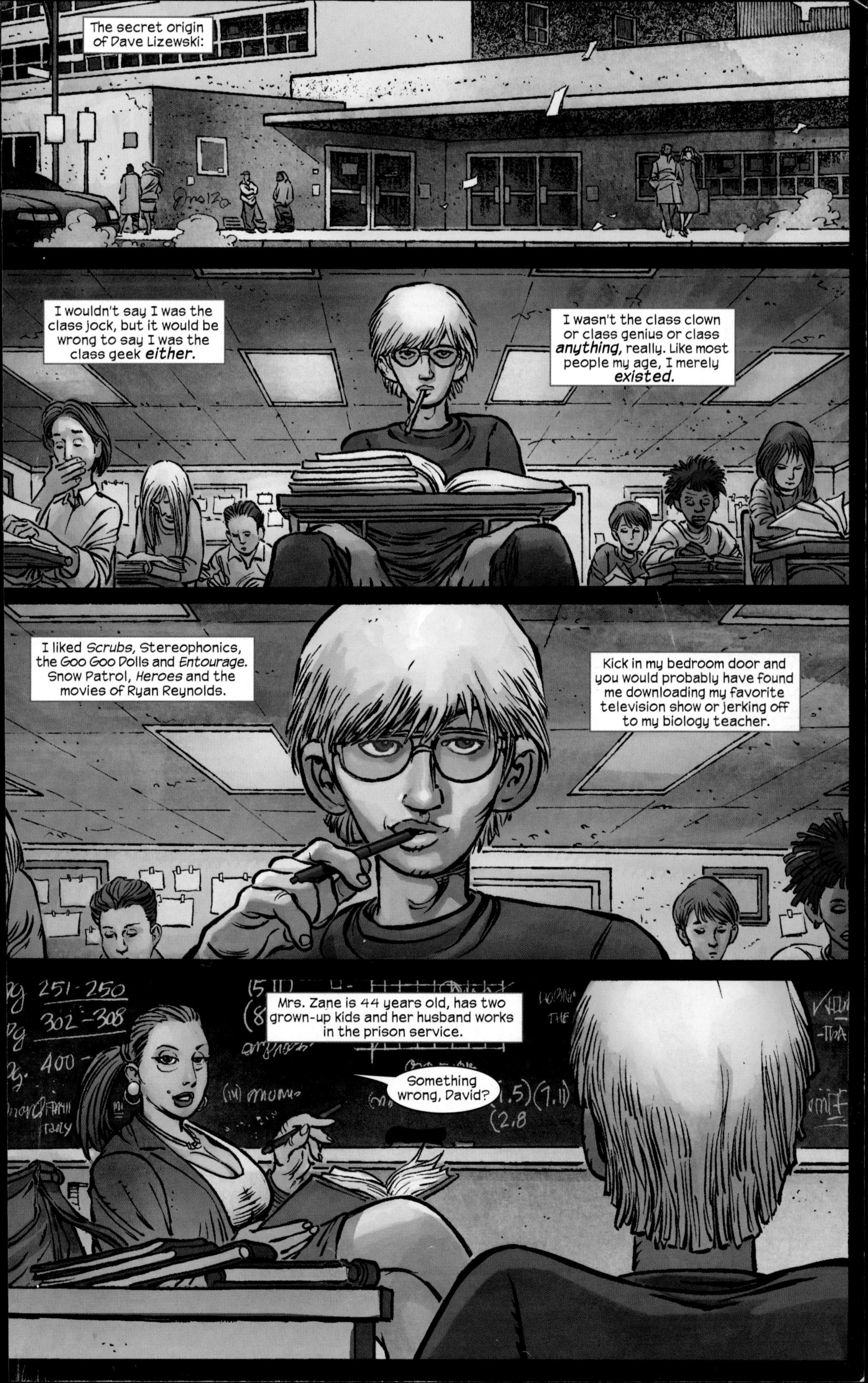
The secret origin of Dave Lizewski:
I wouldn't say I was the class jock, but it would be wrong to say I was the class geek *either.*
I wasn't the class clown or class genius or class *anything,* really. Like most people my age, I merely *existed.*
I liked *Scrubs,* Stereophonics, the *Goo Goo Dolls* and *Entourage.* Snow Patrol, *Heroes* and the movies of Ryan Reynolds.
Kick in my bedroom door and you would probably have found me downloading my favorite television show or jerking off to my biology teacher.
Mrs. Zane is 44 years old, has two grown-up kids and her husband works in the prison service.
Something wrong, David?

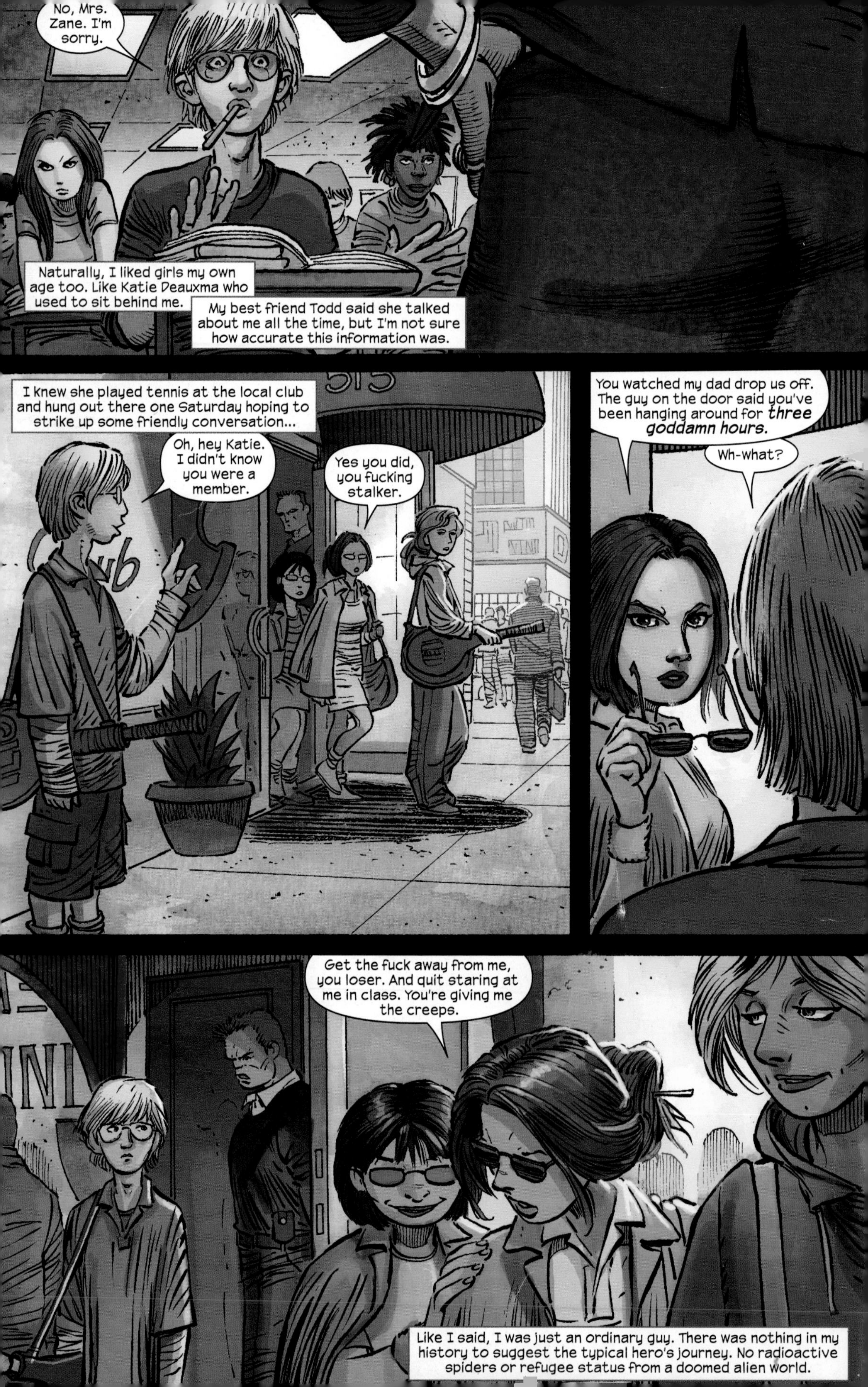
No, Mrs. Zane. I'm sorry.
Naturally, I liked girls my own age too. Like Katie Deauxma who used to sit behind me.
My best friend Todd said she talked about me all the time, but I'm not sure how accurate this information was.
I knew she played tennis at the local club and hung out there one Saturday hoping to strike up some friendly conversation...
Oh, hey Katie. I didn't know you were a member.
Yes you did, you fucking stalker.
You watched my dad drop us off. The guy on the door said you've been hanging around for *three goddamn hours.*
Wh-what?
Get the fuck away from me, you loser. And quit staring at me in class. You're giving me the creeps.
Like I said, I was just an ordinary guy. There was nothing in my history to suggest the typical hero's journey. No radioactive spiders or refugee status from a doomed alien world.

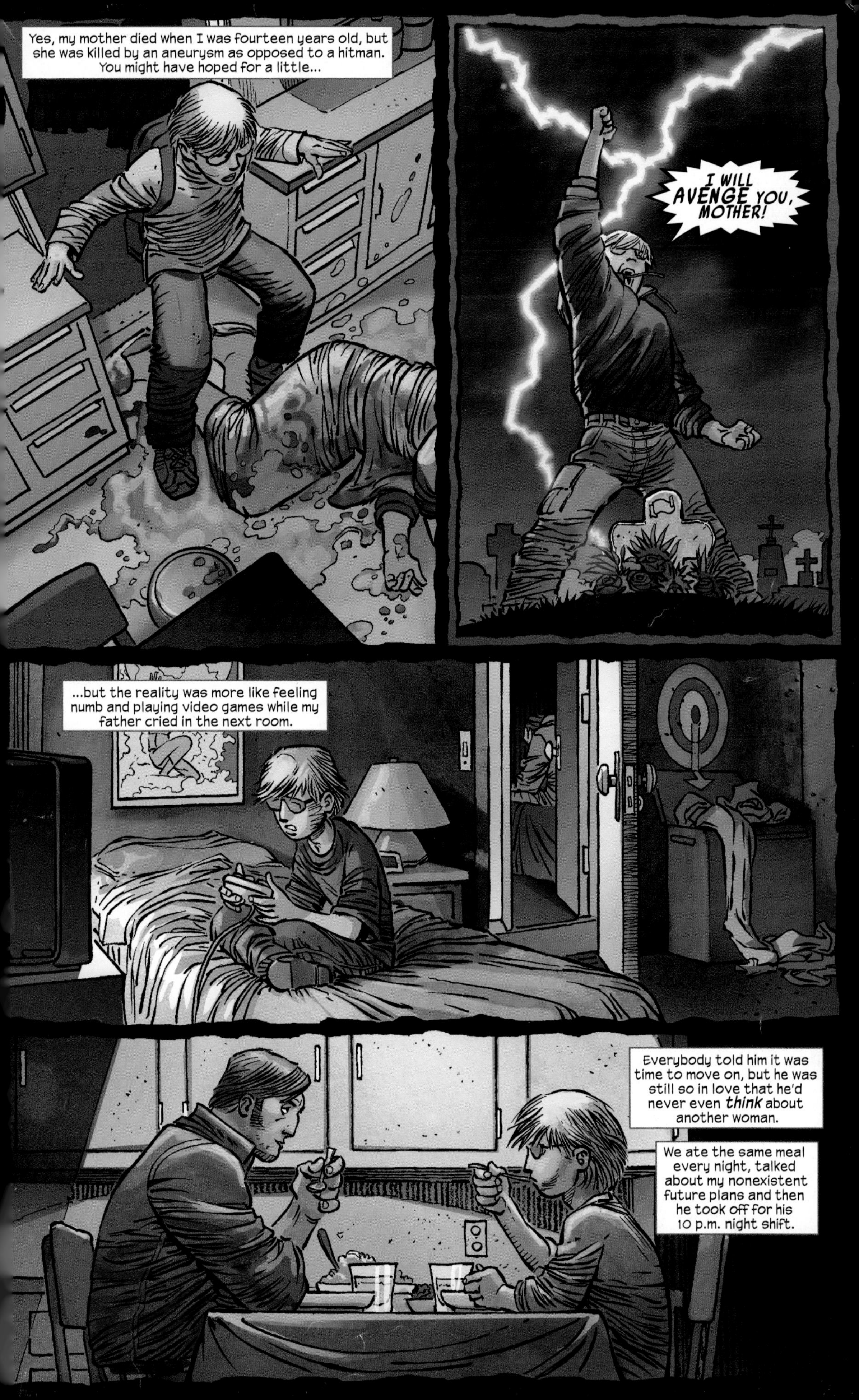
Yes, my mother died when I was fourteen years old, but she was killed by an aneurysm as opposed to a hitman. You might have hoped for a little...
I WILL AVENGE YOU, MOTHER!
...but the reality was more like feeling numb and playing video games while my father cried in the next room.
Everybody told him it was time to move on, but he was still so in love that he'd never even *think* about another woman.
We ate the same meal every night, talked about my nonexistent future plans and then he took off for his 10 p.m. night shift.

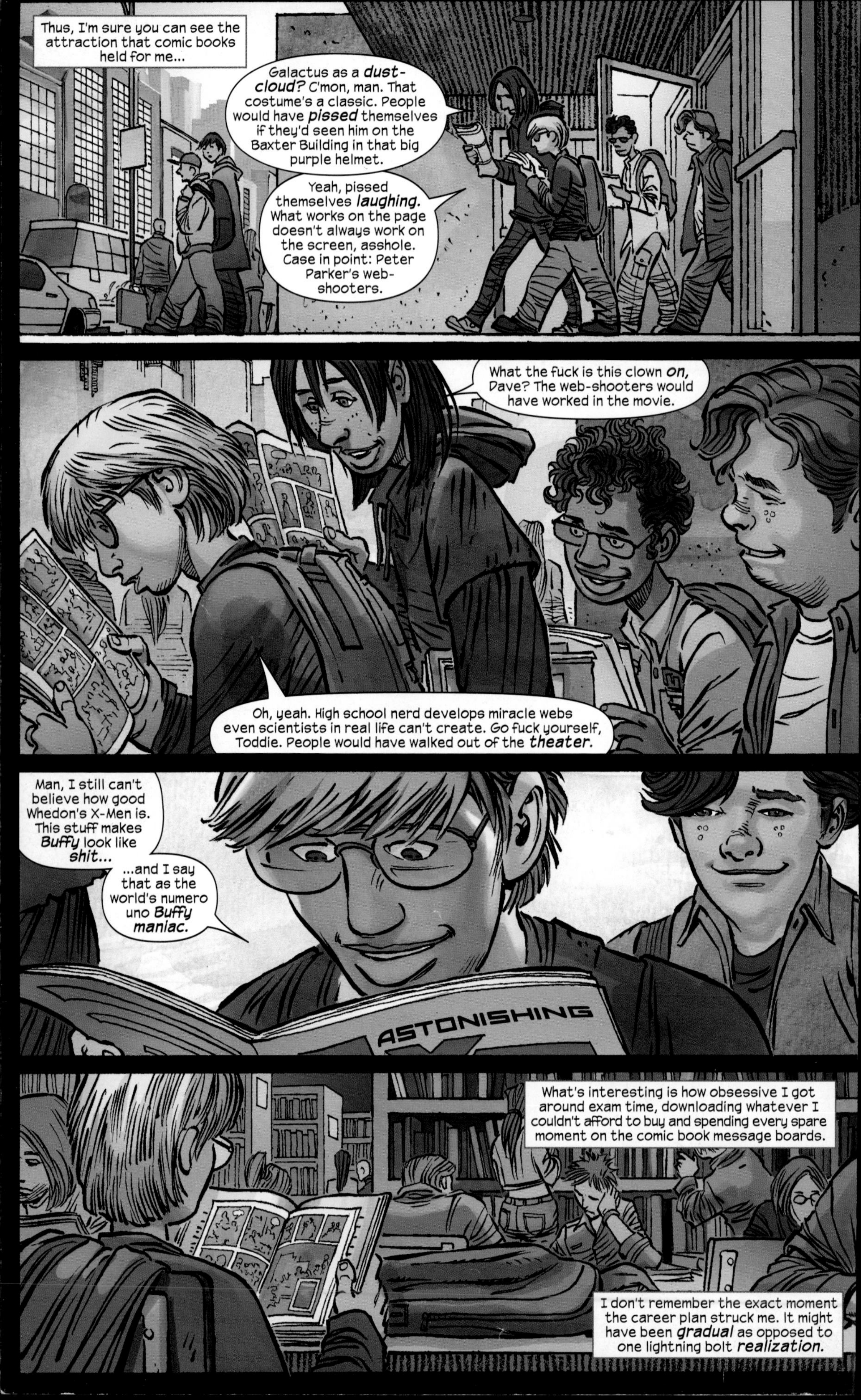
Thus, I'm sure you can see the attraction that comic books held for me...
Galactus as a dust-cloud? C'mon, man. That costume's a classic. People would have pissed themselves if they'd seen him on the Baxter Building in that big purple helmet.
Yeah, pissed themselves laughing. What works on the page doesn't always work on the screen, asshole. Case in point: Peter Parker's web-shooters.
What the fuck is this clown on, Dave? The web-shooters would have worked in the movie.
Oh, yeah. High school nerd develops miracle webs even scientists in real life can't create. Go fuck yourself, Toddie. People would have walked out of the theater.
Man, I still can't believe how good Whedon's X-Men is. This stuff makes Buffy look like shit...
...and I say that as the world's numero uno Buffy maniac.
ASTONISHING
What's interesting is how obsessive I got around exam time, downloading whatever I couldn't afford to buy and spending every spare moment on the comic book message boards.
I don't remember the exact moment the career plan struck me. It might have been gradual as opposed to one lightning bolt realization.

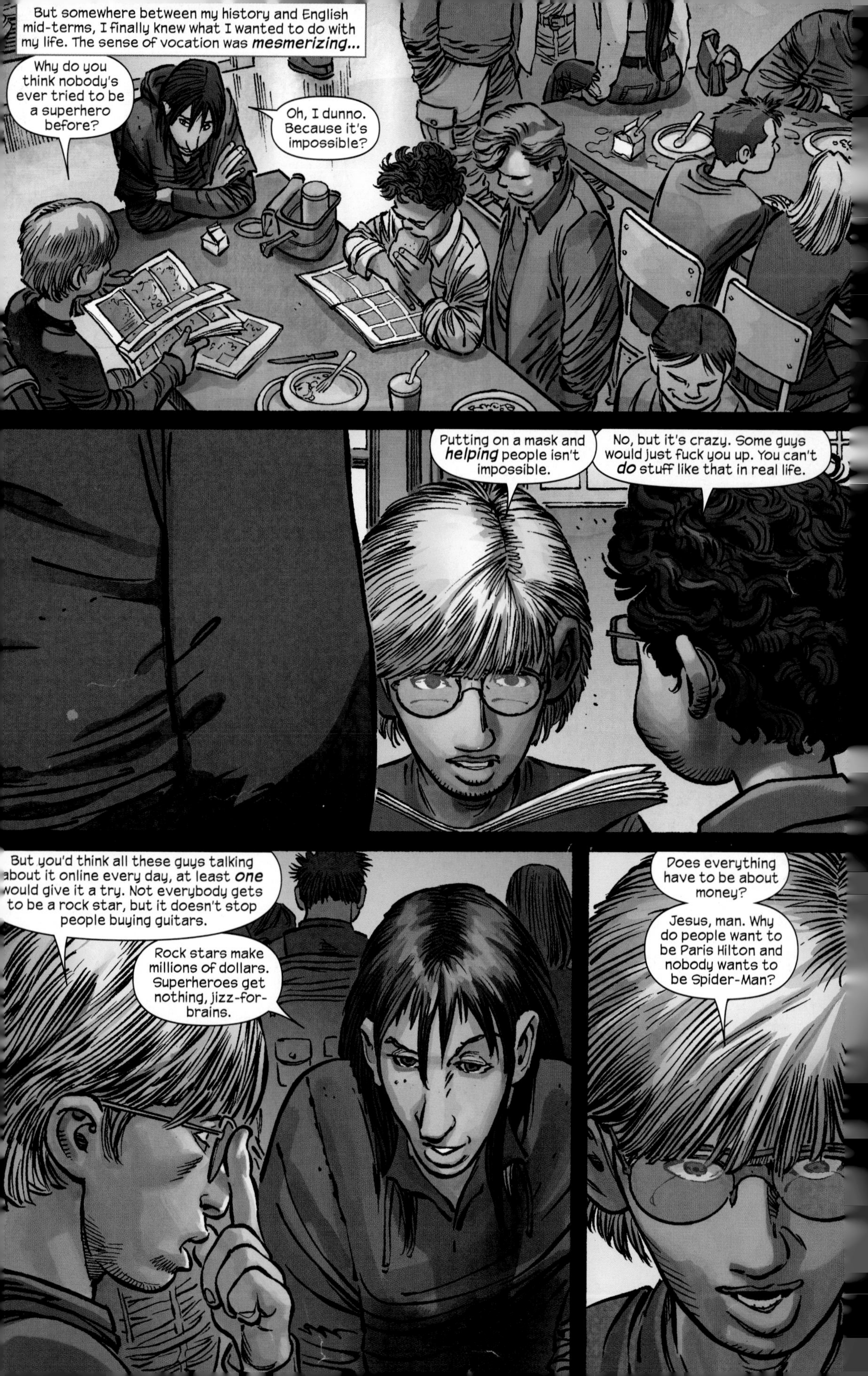
But somewhere between my history and English mid-terms, I finally knew what I wanted to do with my life. The sense of vocation was *mesmerizing...*
Why do you think nobody's ever tried to be a superhero before?
Oh, I dunno. Because it's impossible?
Putting on a mask and *helping* people isn't impossible.
No, but it's crazy. Some guys would just fuck you up. You can't *do* stuff like that in real life.
But you'd think all these guys talking about it online every day, at least *one* would give it a try. Not everybody gets to be a rock star, but it doesn't stop people buying guitars.
Rock stars make millions of dollars. Superheroes get nothing, jizz-for-brains.
Does everything have to be about money?
Jesus, man. Why do people want to be Paris Hilton and nobody wants to be Spider-Man?

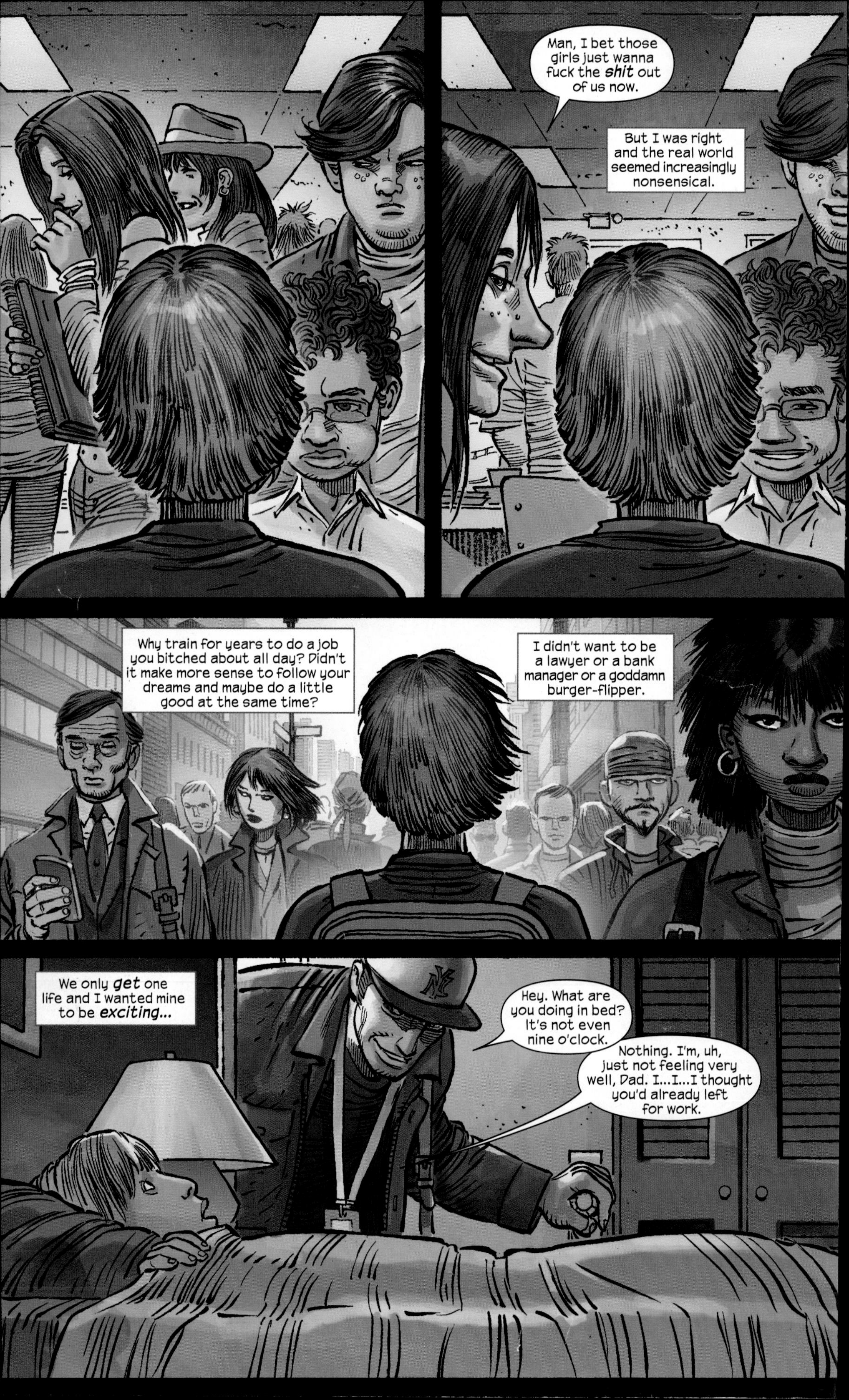
Man, I bet those girls just wanna fuck the *shit* out of us now.
But I was right and the real world seemed increasingly nonsensical.
Why train for years to do a job you bitched about all day? Didn't it make more sense to follow your dreams and maybe do a little good at the same time?
I didn't want to be a lawyer or a bank manager or a goddamn burger-flipper.
We only *get* one life and I wanted mine to be *exciting...*
Hey. What are you doing in bed? It's not even nine o'clock.
Nothing. I'm, uh, just not feeling very well, Dad. I...I...I thought you'd already left for work.

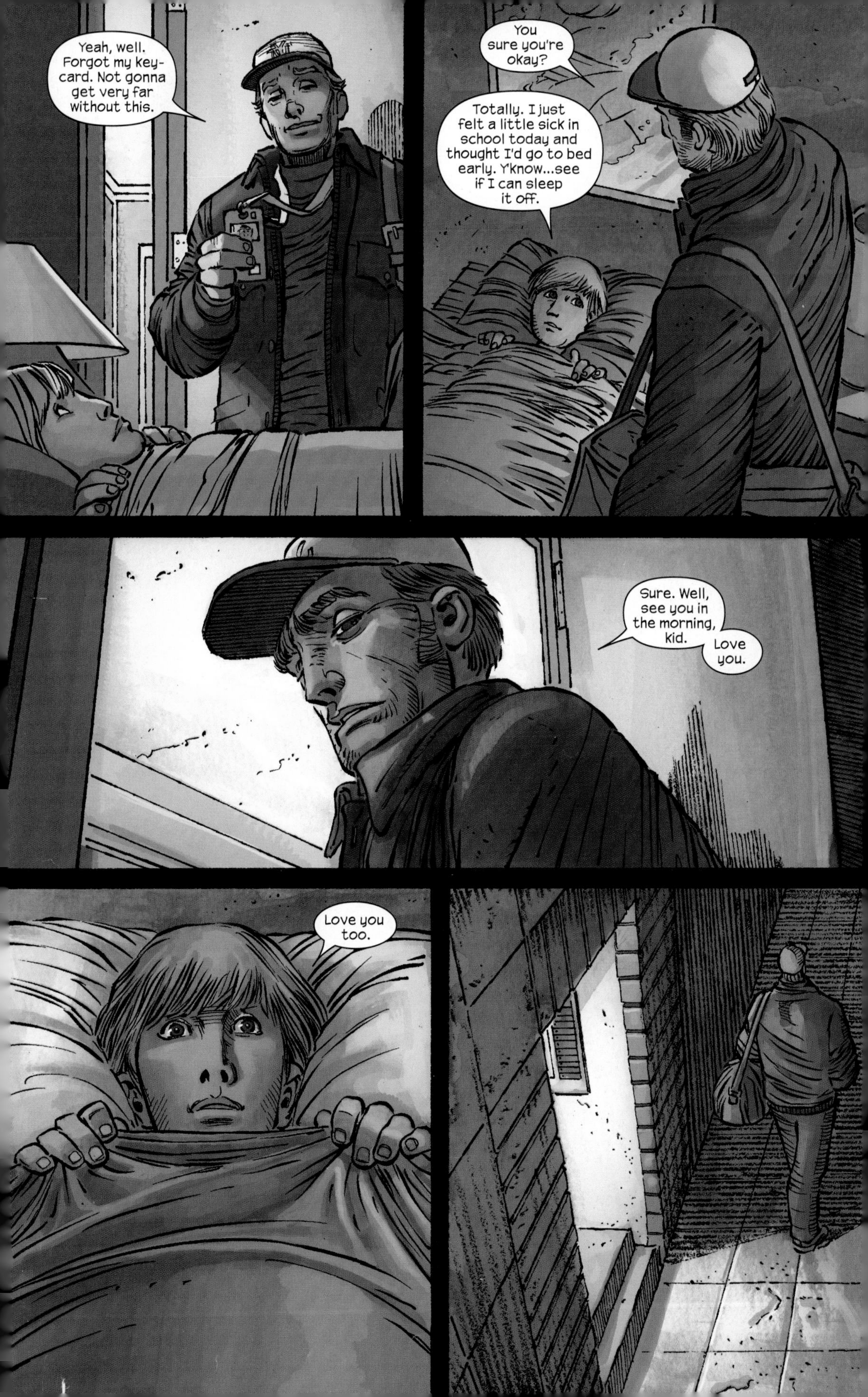
Yeah, well. Forgot my key-card. Not gonna get very far without this.
You sure you're okay?
Totally. I just felt a little sick in school today and thought I'd go to bed early. Y'know...see if I can sleep it off.
Sure. Well, see you in the morning, kid.
Love you.
Love you too.

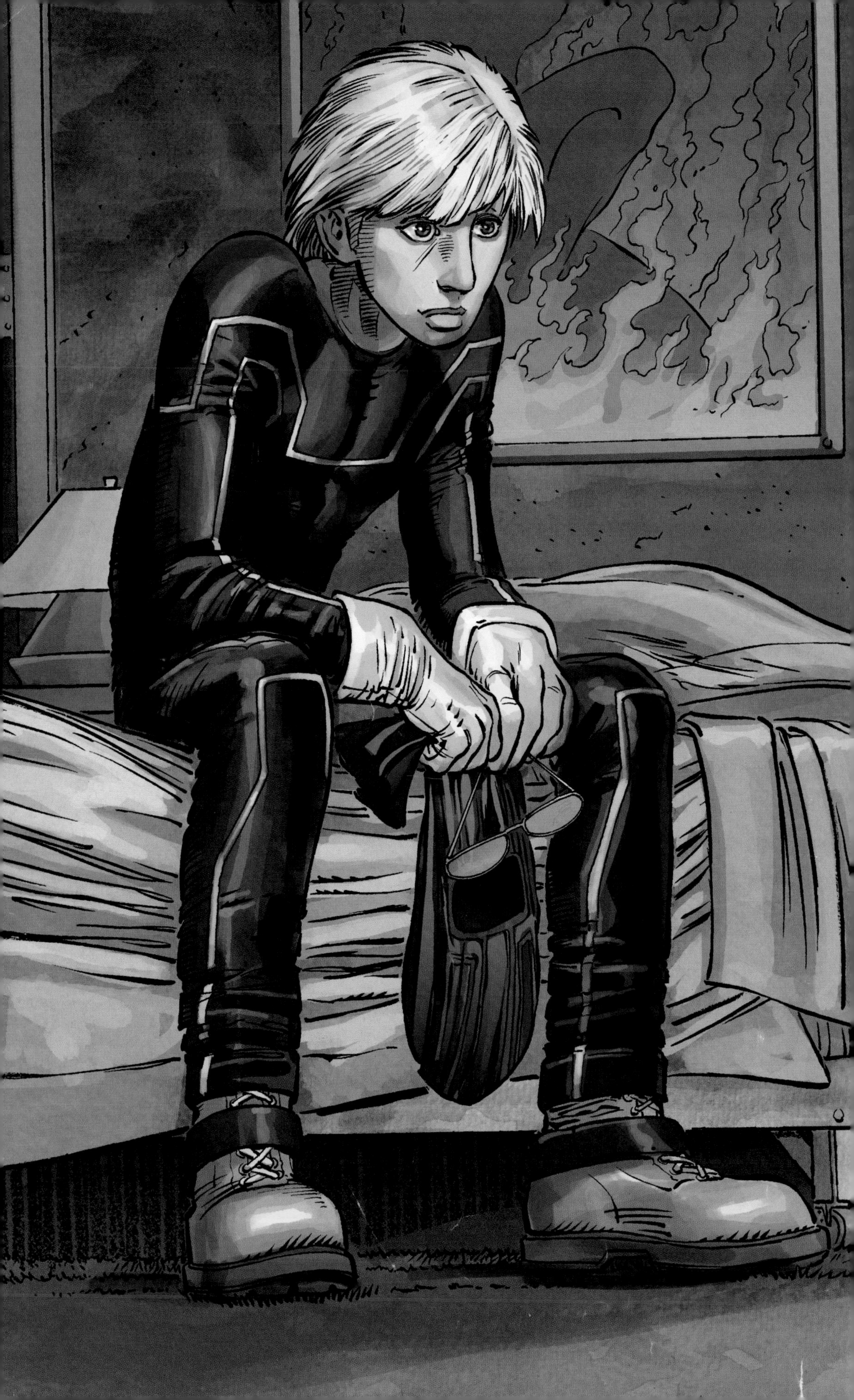

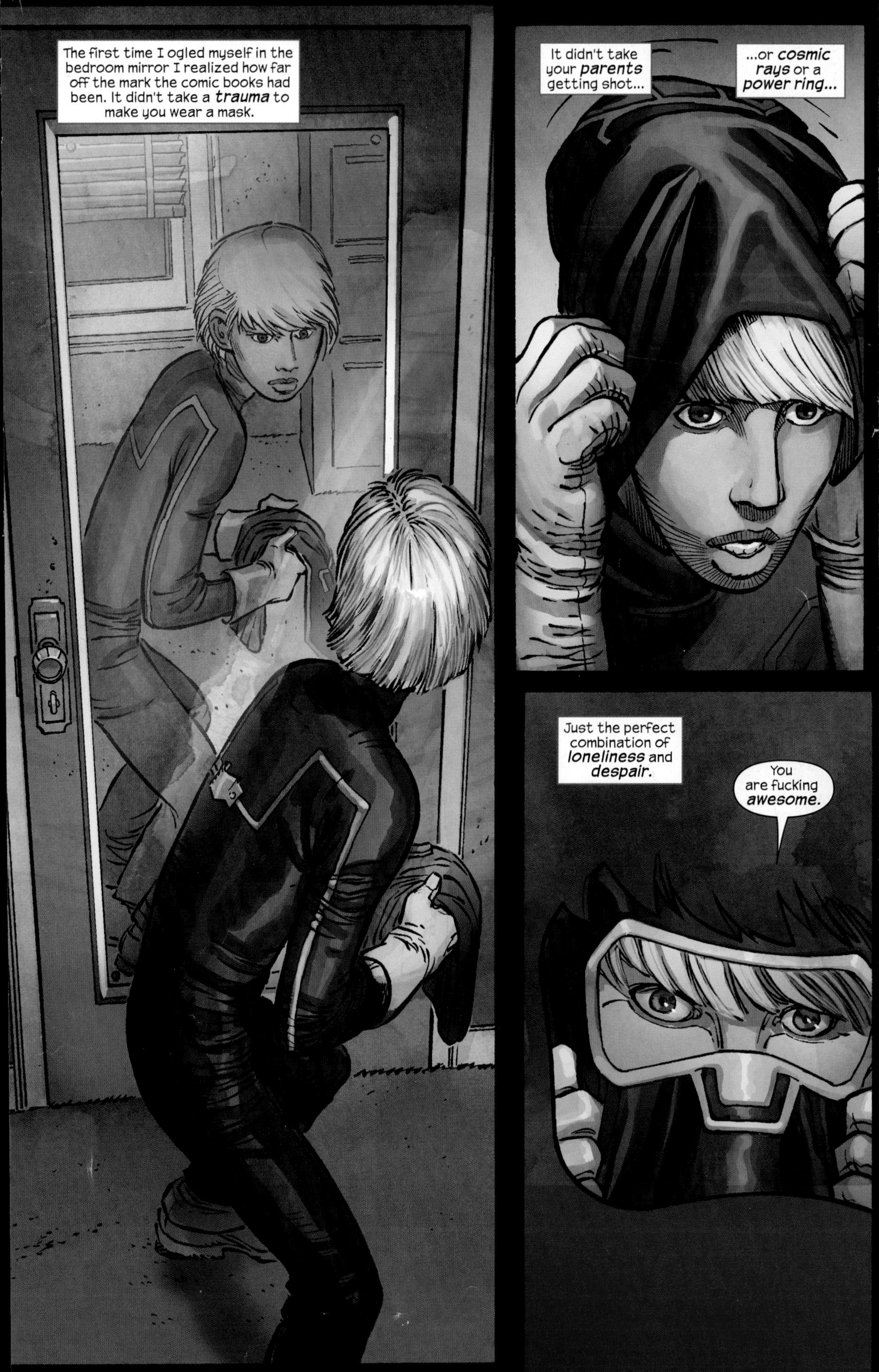
The first time I ogled myself in the bedroom mirror I realized how far off the mark the comic books had been. It didn't take a *trauma* to make you wear a mask.
It didn't take your *parents* getting shot...
...or *cosmic rays* or a *power ring...*
Just the perfect combination of *loneliness* and *despair*.
You are fucking *awesome.*

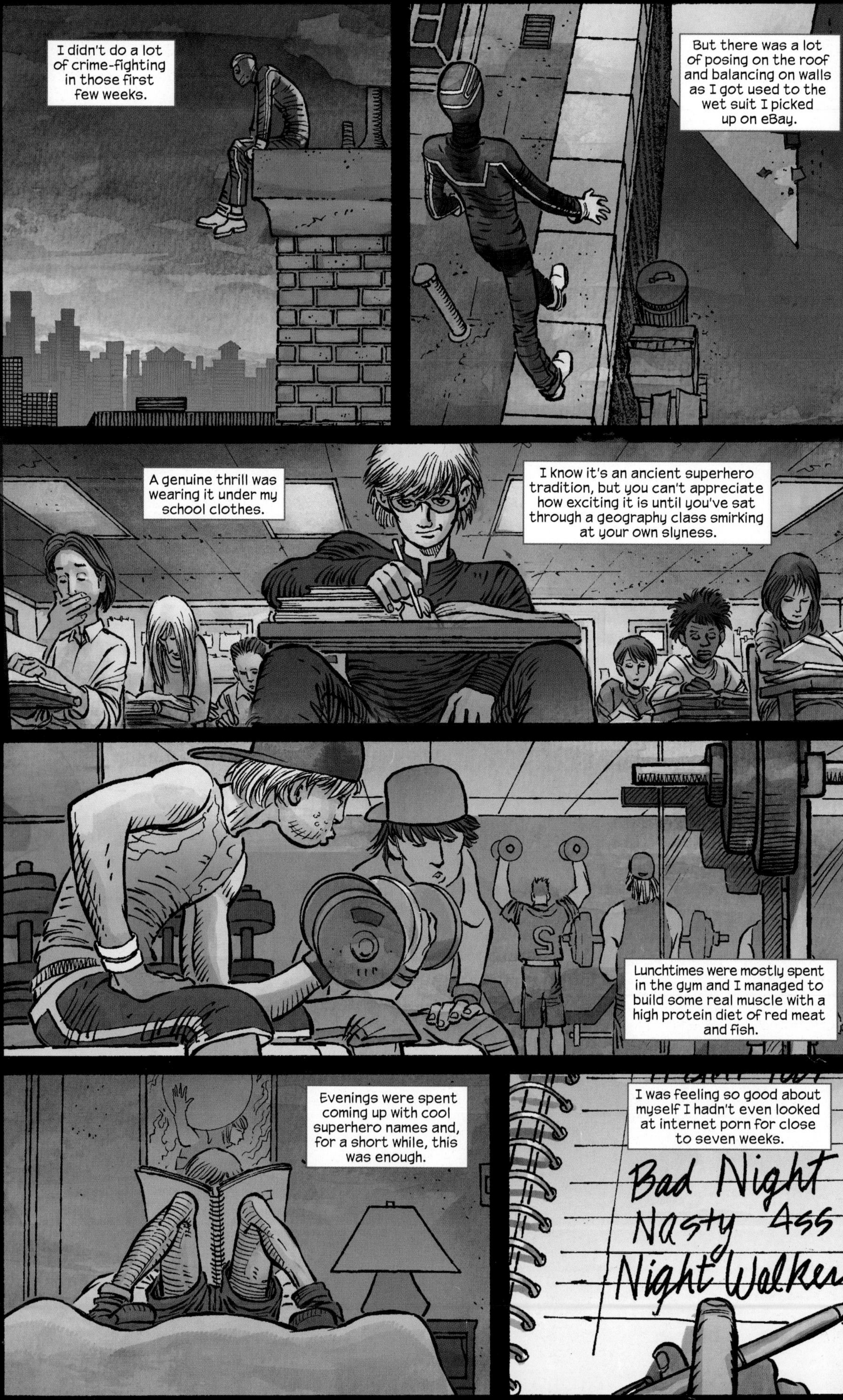
I didn't do a lot of crime-fighting in those first few weeks.
But there was a lot of posing on the roof and balancing on walls as I got used to the wet suit I picked up on eBay.
A genuine thrill was wearing it under my school clothes.
I know it's an ancient superhero tradition, but you can't appreciate how exciting it is until you've sat through a geography class smirking at your own slyness.
Lunchtimes were mostly spent in the gym and I managed to build some real muscle with a high protein diet of red meat and fish.
Evenings were spent coming up with cool superhero names and, for a short while, this was enough.
I was feeling so good about myself I hadn't even looked at internet porn for close to seven weeks.
Bad Night
Nasty Ass
Night Walker

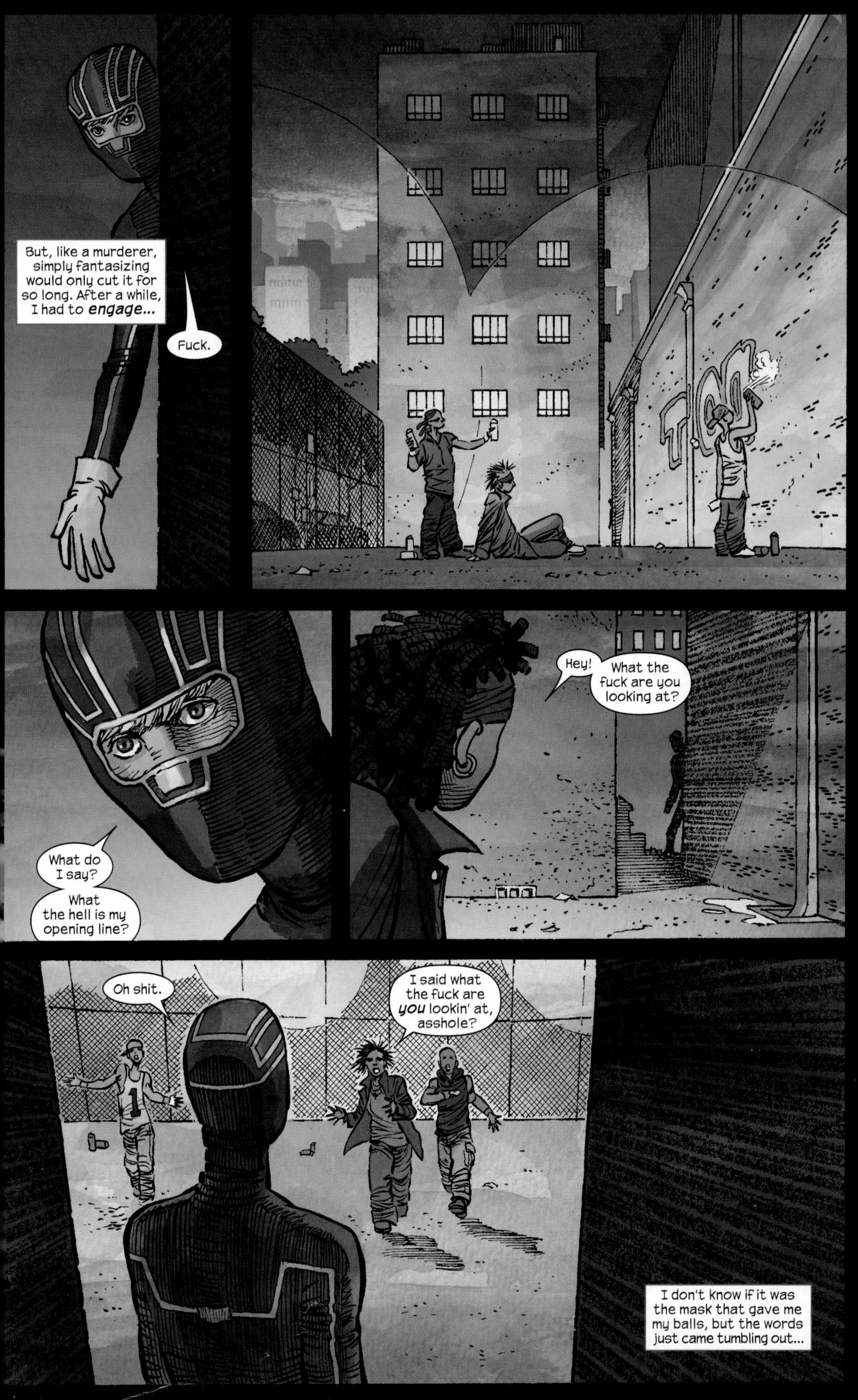
But, like a murderer, simply fantasizing would only cut it for so long. After a while, I had to ***engage...***
Fuck.
What do I say?
What the hell is my opening line?
Hey!
What the fuck are you looking at?
Oh shit.
I said what the fuck are ***you*** lookin' at, asshole?
I don't know if it was the mask that gave me my balls, but the words just came tumbling out...

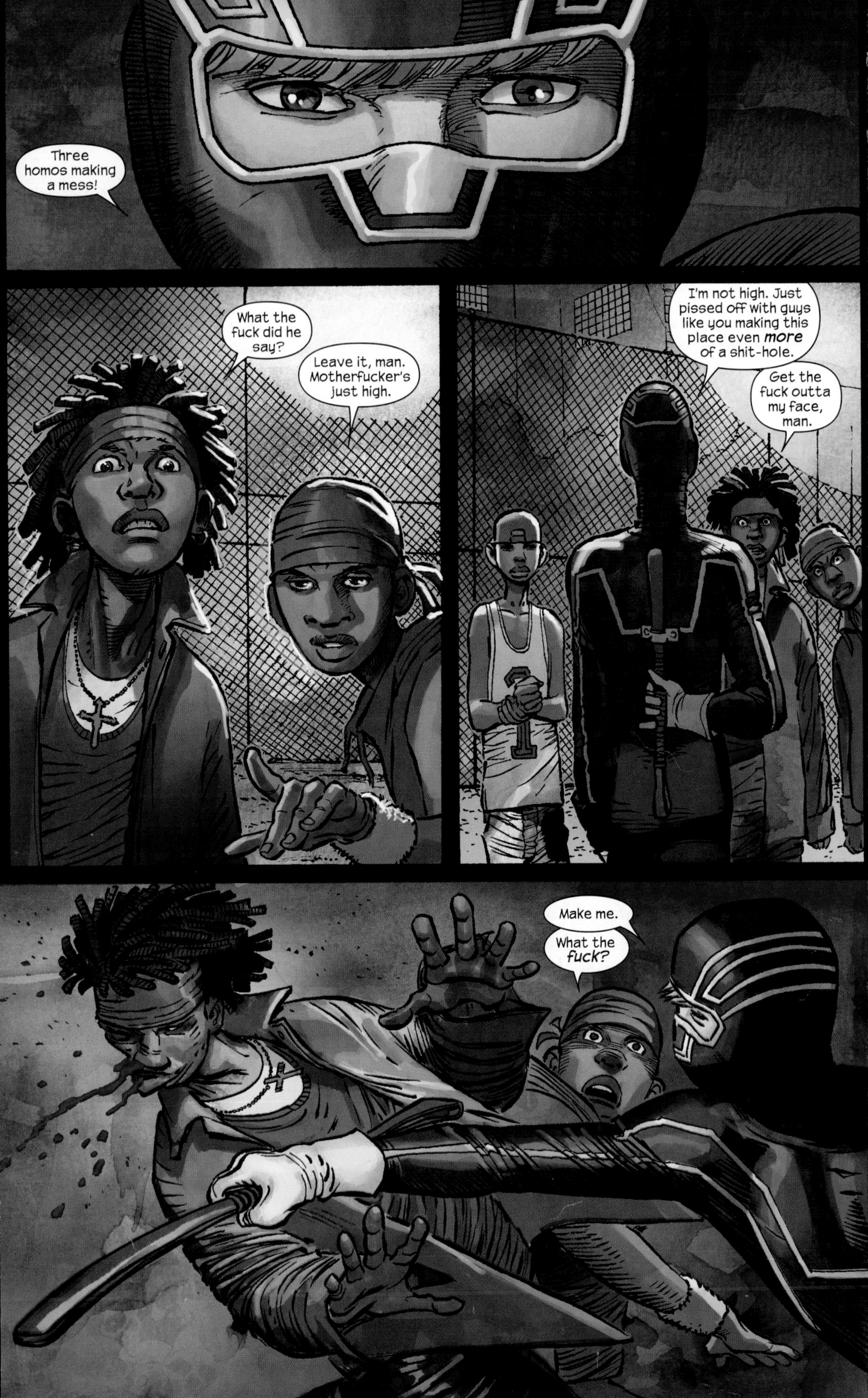
Three homos making a mess!
What the fuck did he say?
Leave it, man. Motherfucker's just high.
I'm not high. Just pissed off with guys like you making this place even *more* of a shit-hole.
Get the fuck outta my face, man.
Make me.
What the *fuck?*

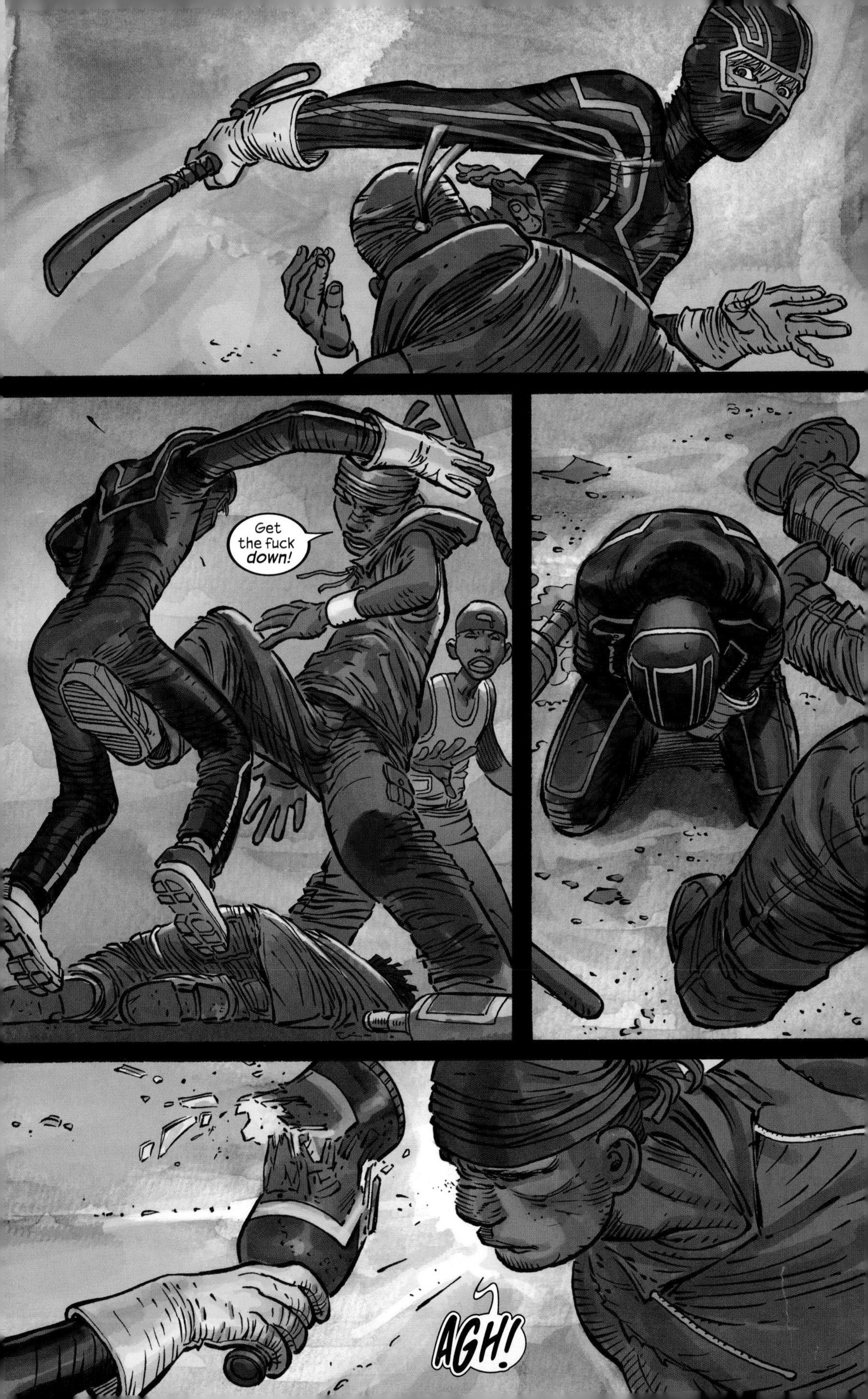
Get the fuck down!
AGH!

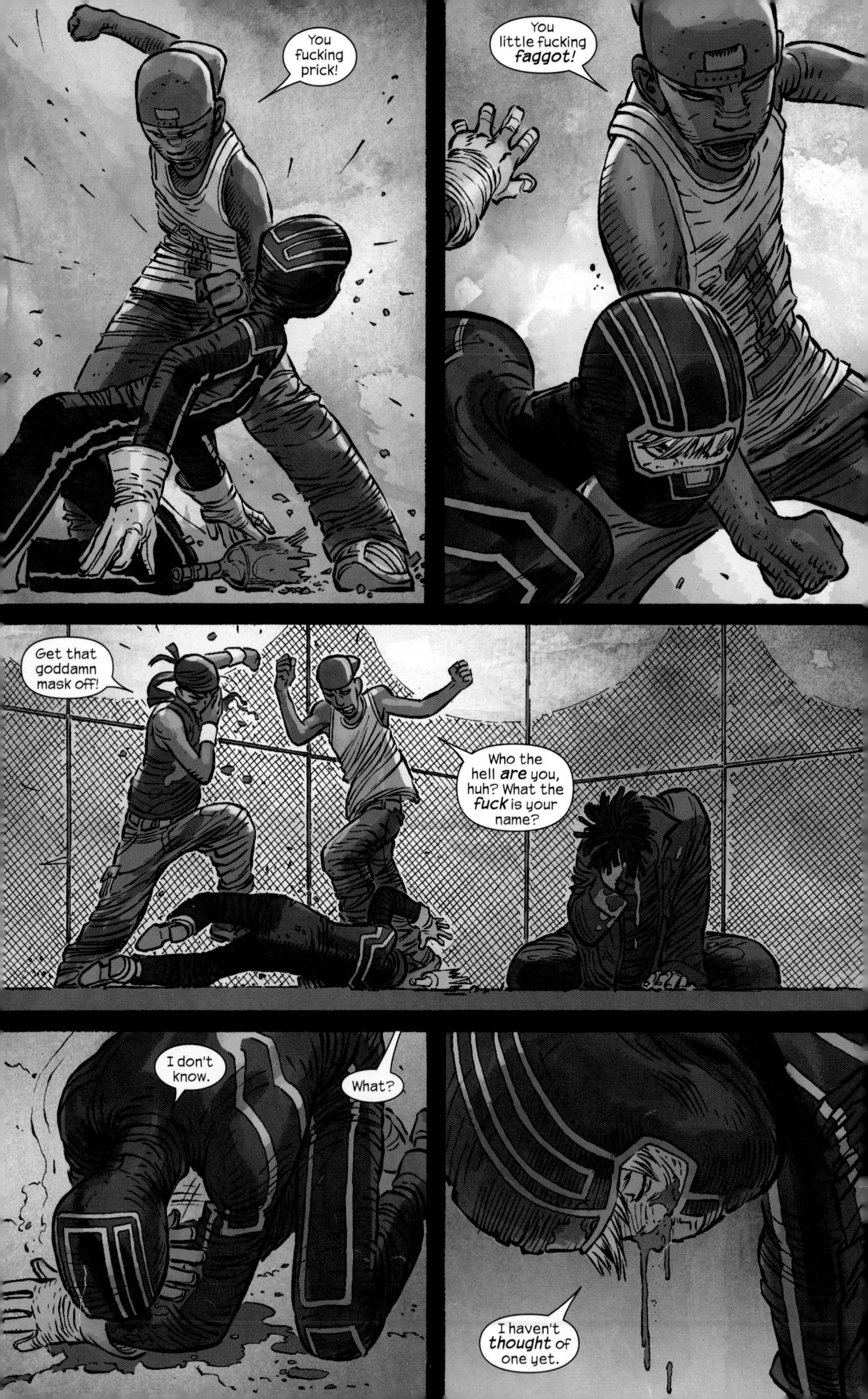
You fucking prick!
You little fucking *faggot!*
Get that goddamn mask off!
Who the hell *are* you, huh? What the *fuck* is your name?
I don't know.
What?
I haven't *thought* of one yet.

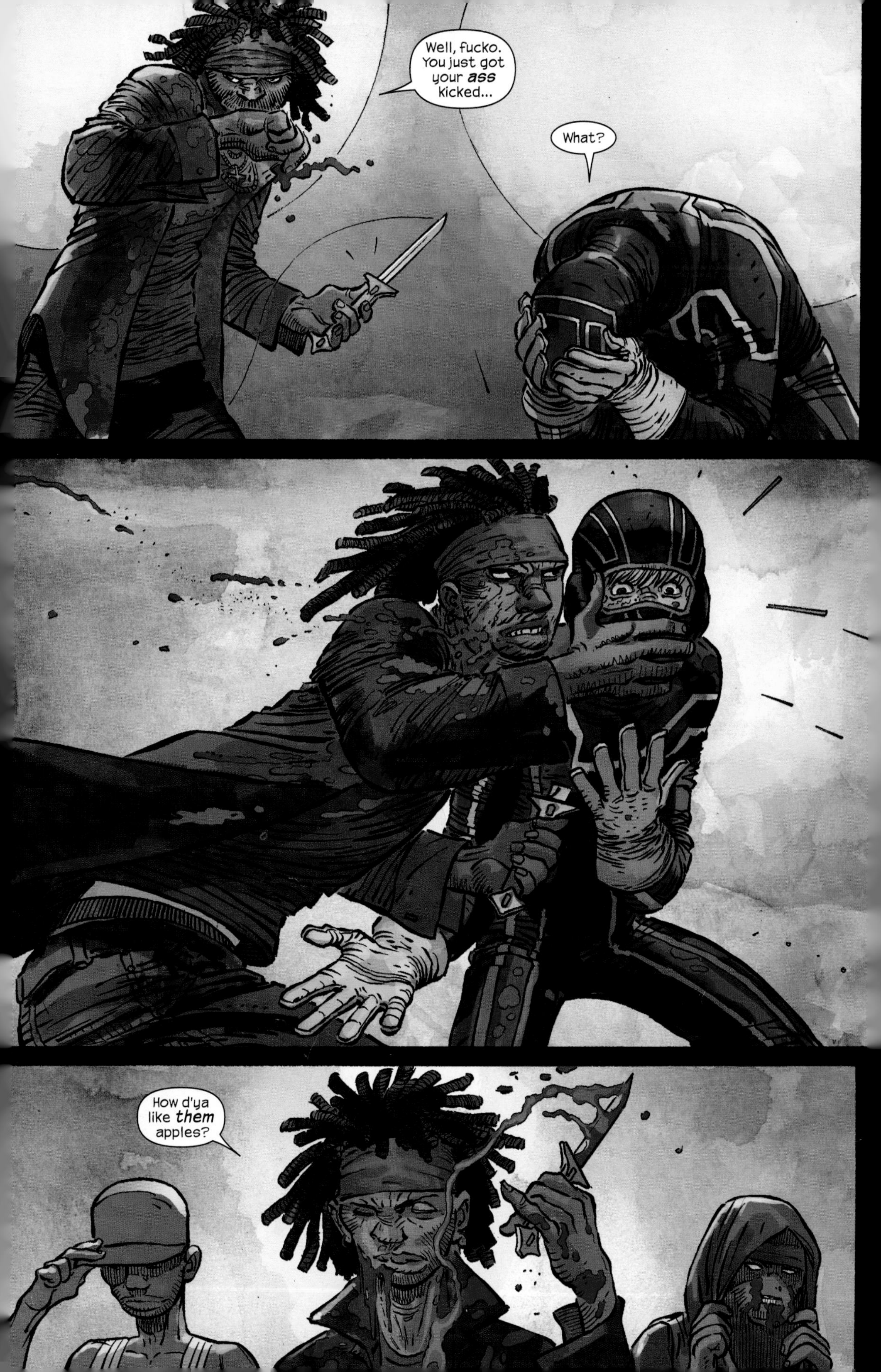
Well, fucko. You just got your *ass* kicked...
What?
How d'ya like *them* apples?

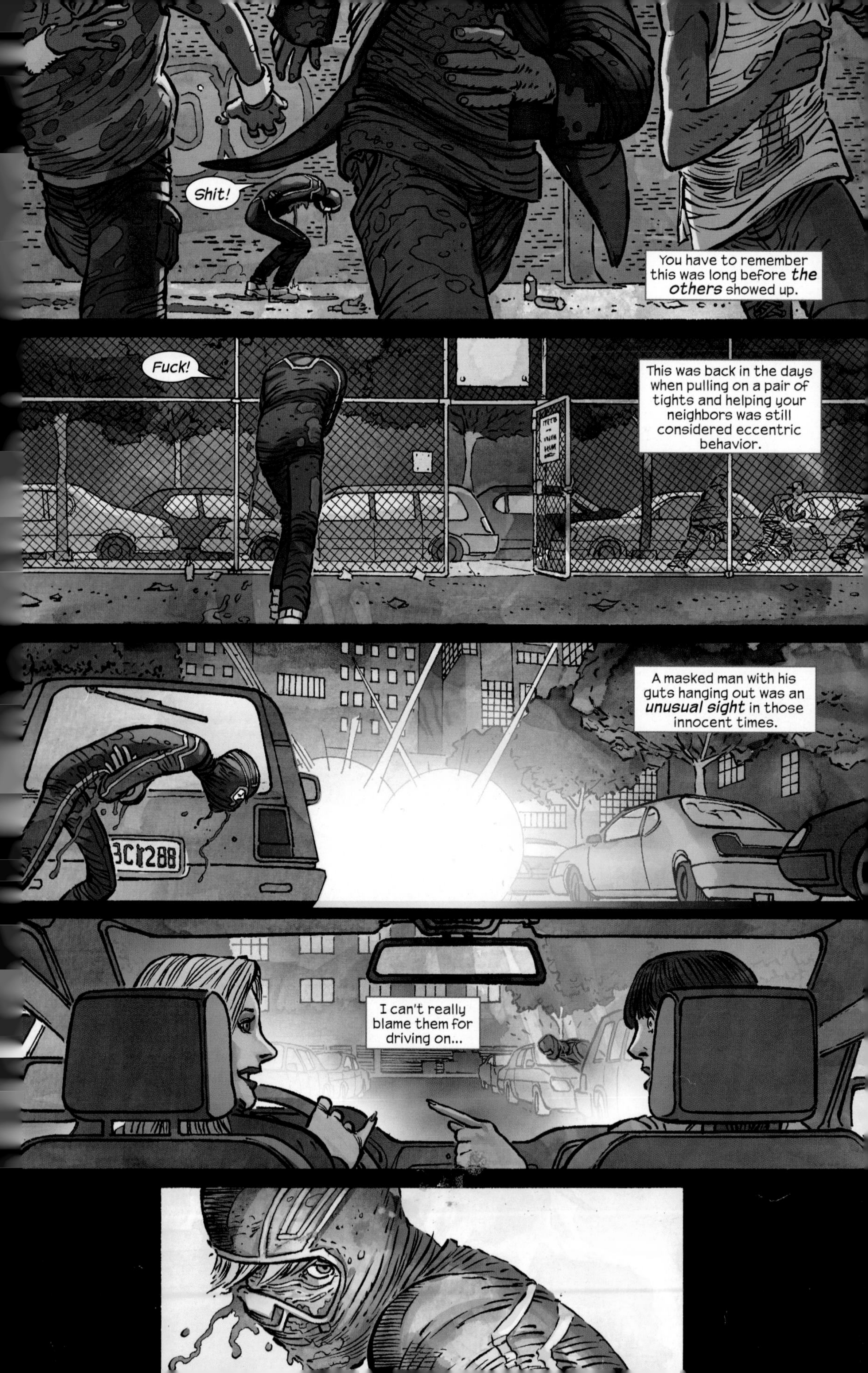
Shit!
You have to remember this was long before the others showed up.
Fuck!
This was back in the days when pulling on a pair of tights and helping your neighbors was still considered eccentric behavior.
A masked man with his guts hanging out was an unusual sight in those innocent times.
I can't really blame them for driving on...

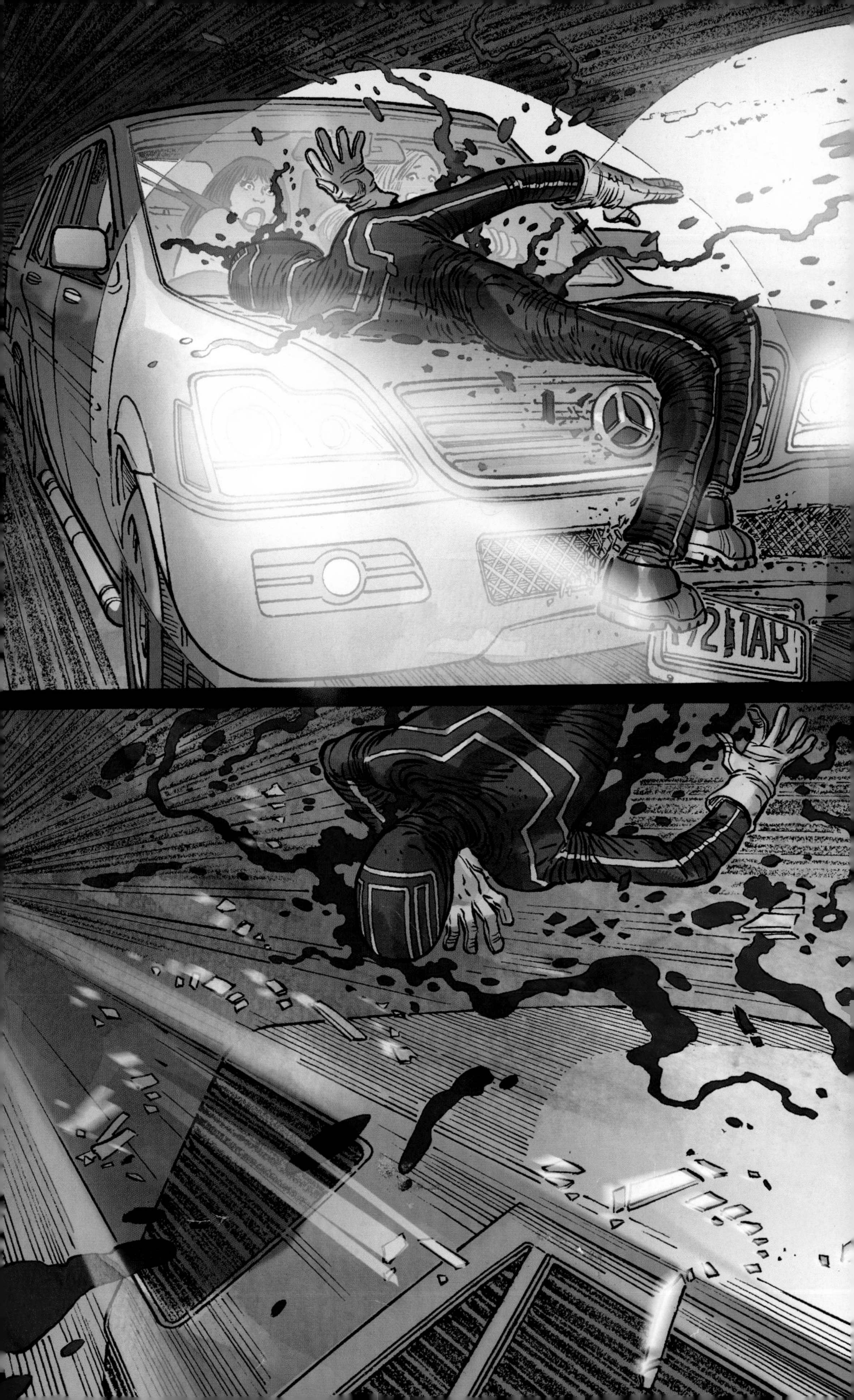

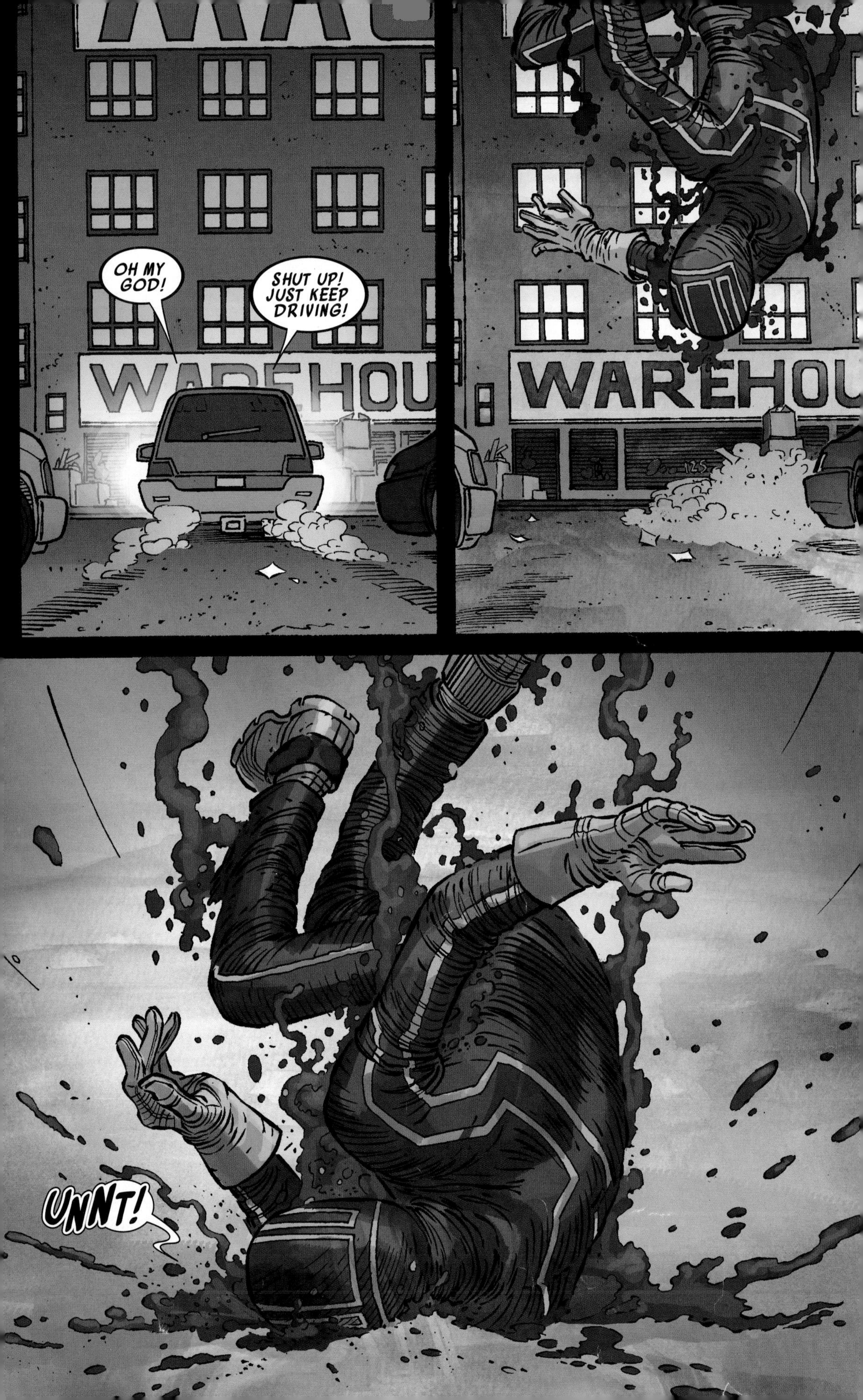
OH MY GOD!
SHUT UP! JUST KEEP DRIVING!
WAREHOU
WAREHOU
UNNT!

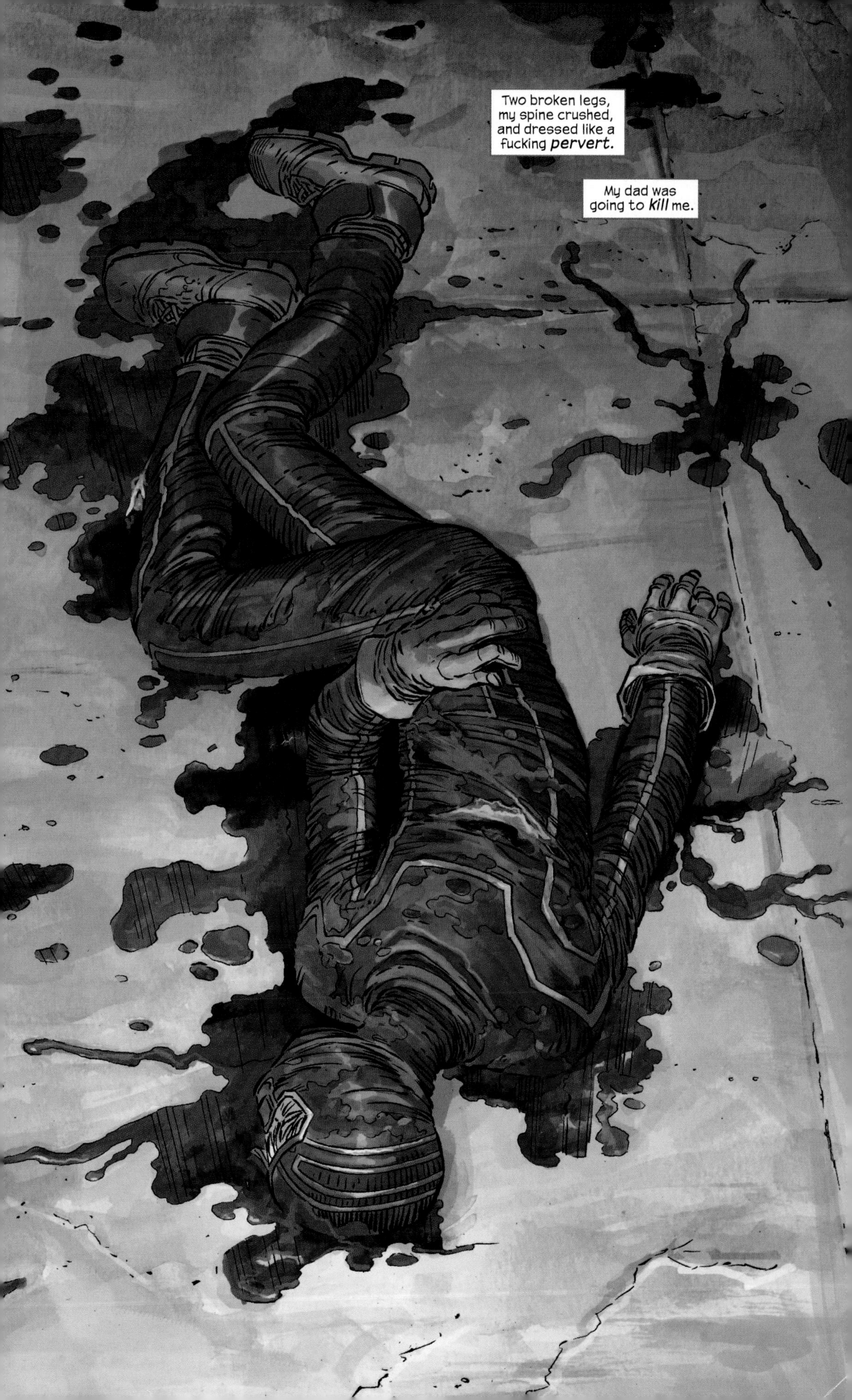
Two broken legs, my spine crushed, and dressed like a fucking *pervert.*
My dad was going to *kill* me.

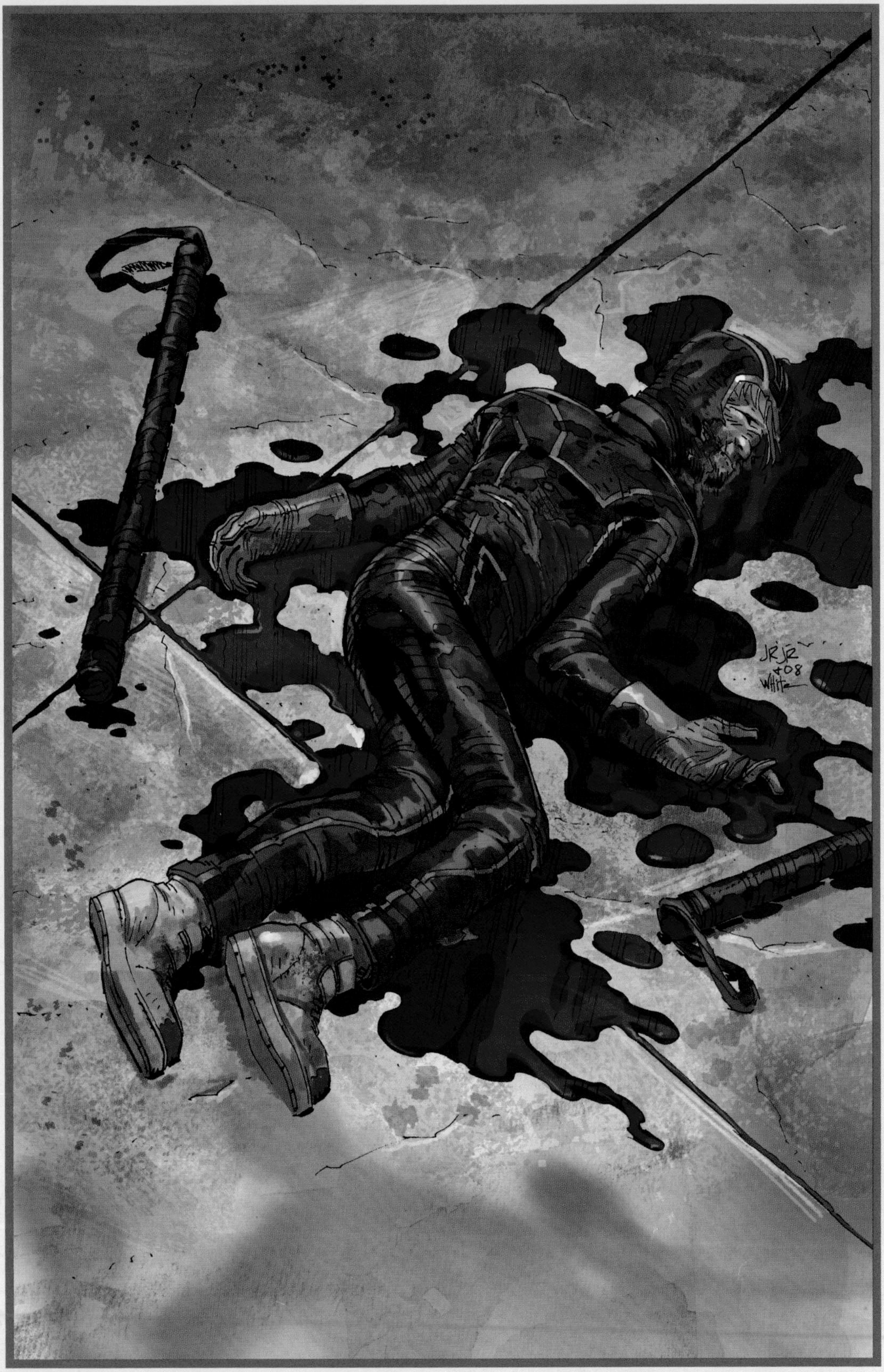

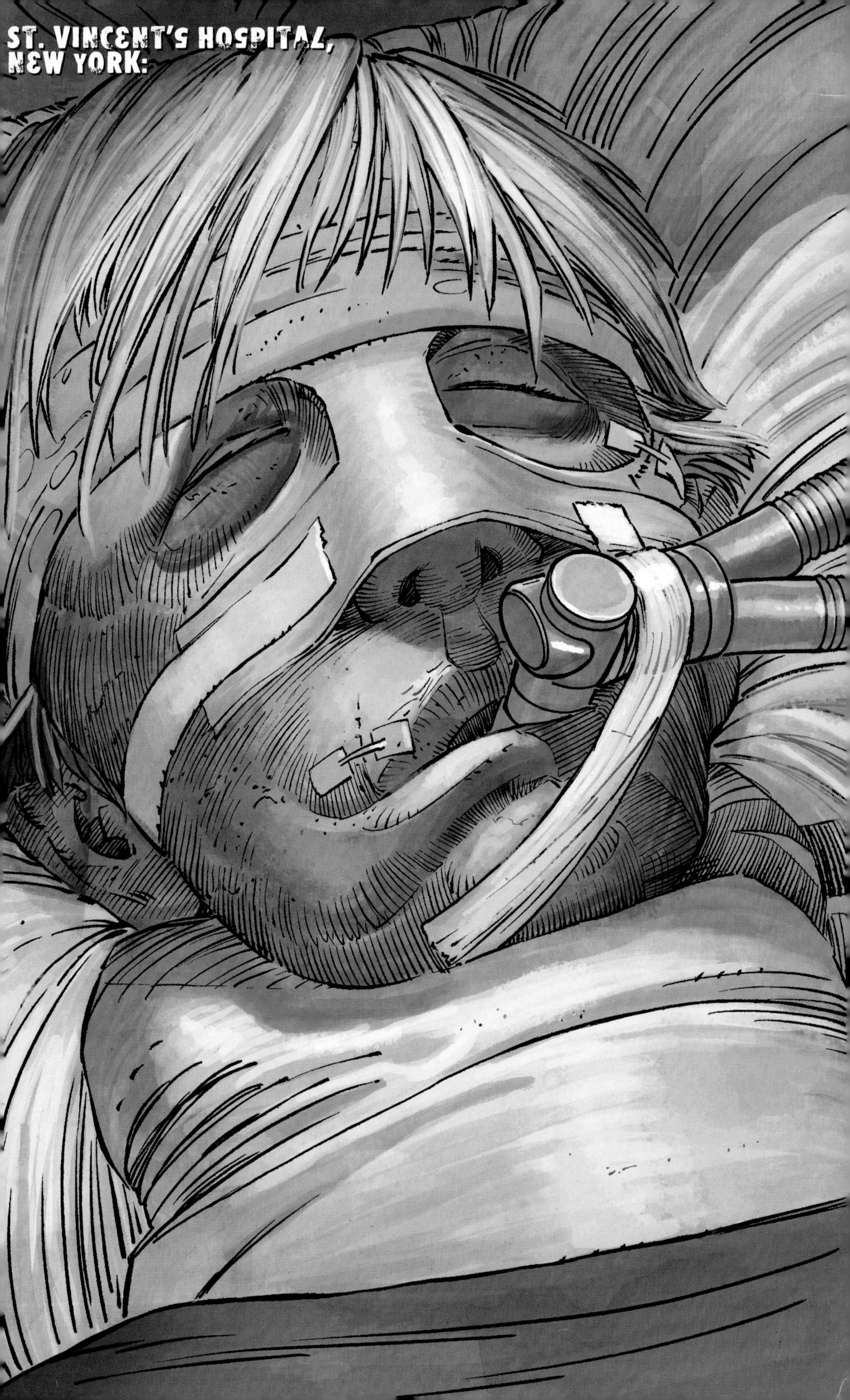
ST. VINCENT'S HOSPITAL, NEW YORK:

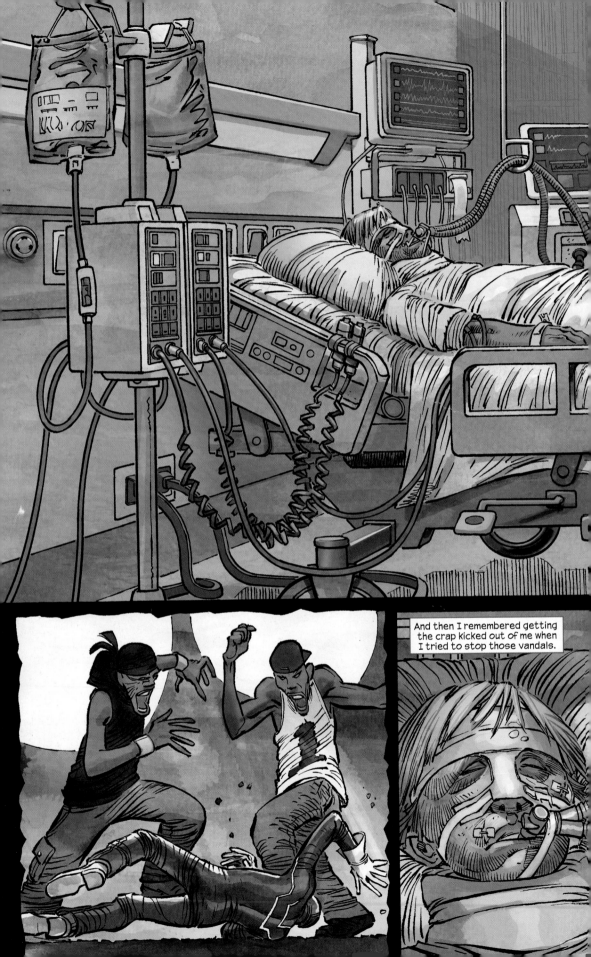

And then I remembered getting the crap kicked out of me when I tried to stop those vandals.

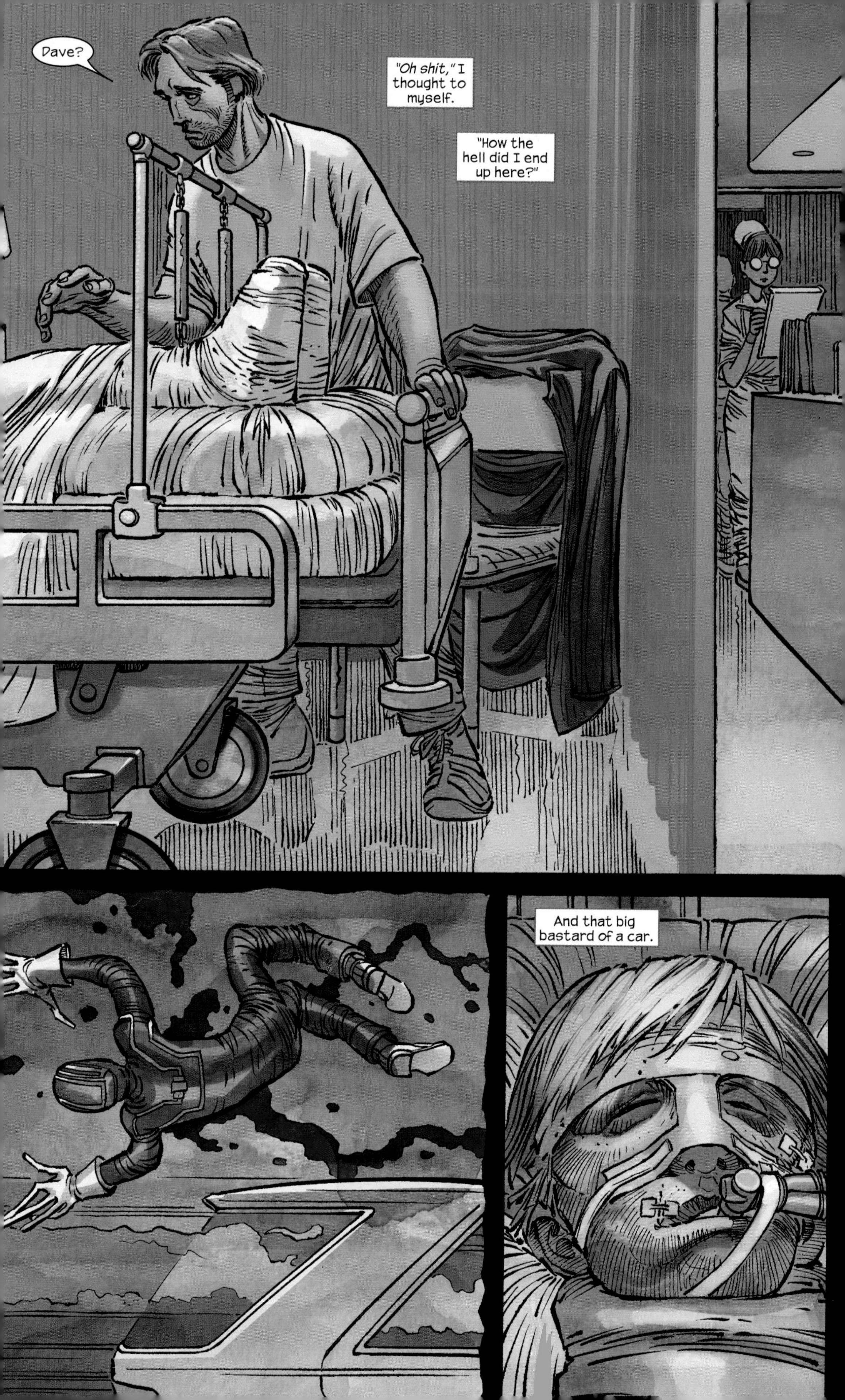
Dave?
"Oh shit," I thought to myself.
"How the hell did I end up here?"
And that big bastard of a car.

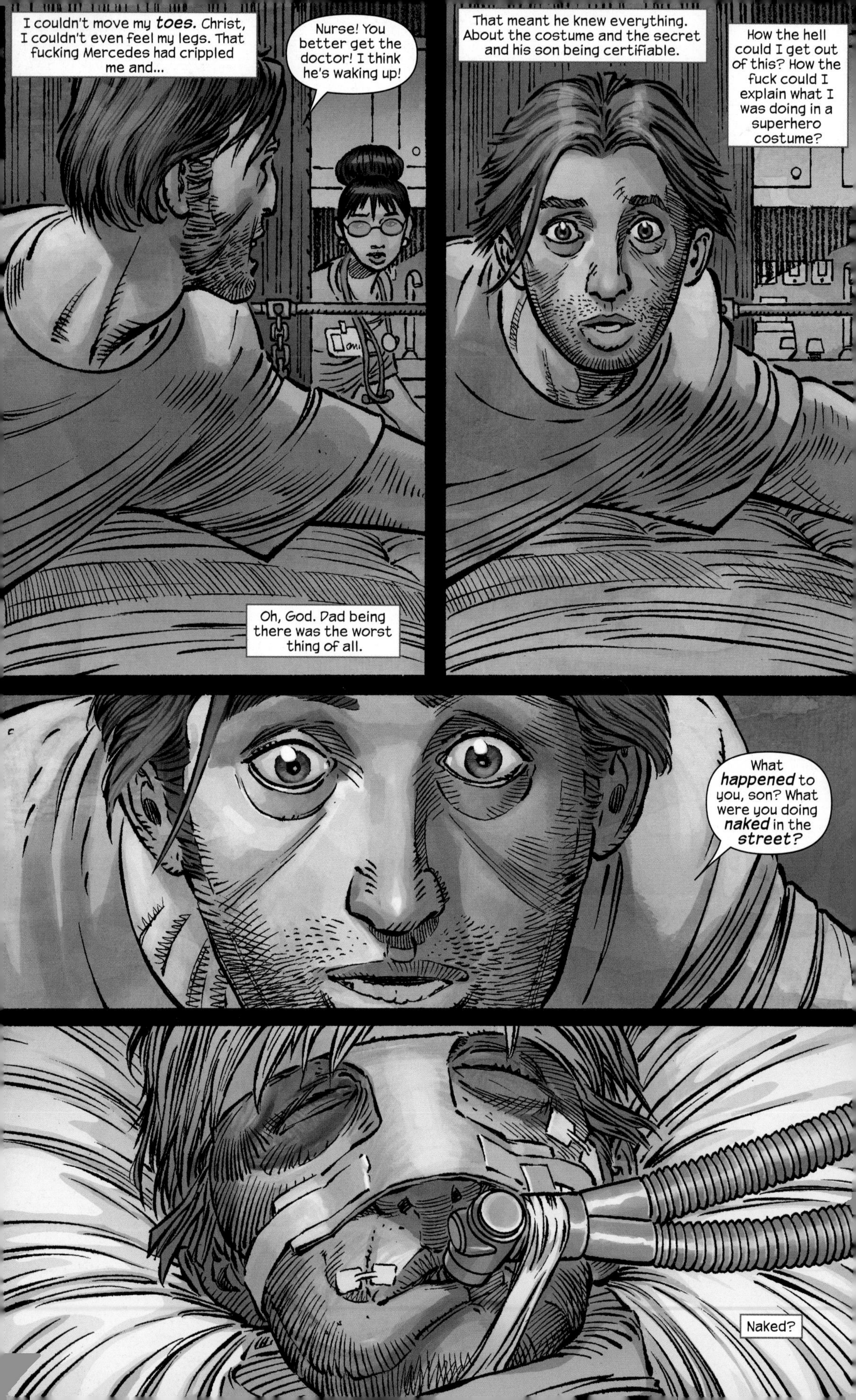

I couldn't move my *toes.* Christ, I couldn't even feel my legs. That fucking Mercedes had crippled me and...
Nurse! You better get the doctor! I think he's waking up!
Oh, God. Dad being there was the worst thing of all.
That meant he knew everything. About the costume and the secret and his son being certifiable.
How the hell could I get out of this? How the fuck could I explain what I was doing in a superhero costume?
What *happened* to you, son? What were you doing *naked* in the *street?*
Naked?

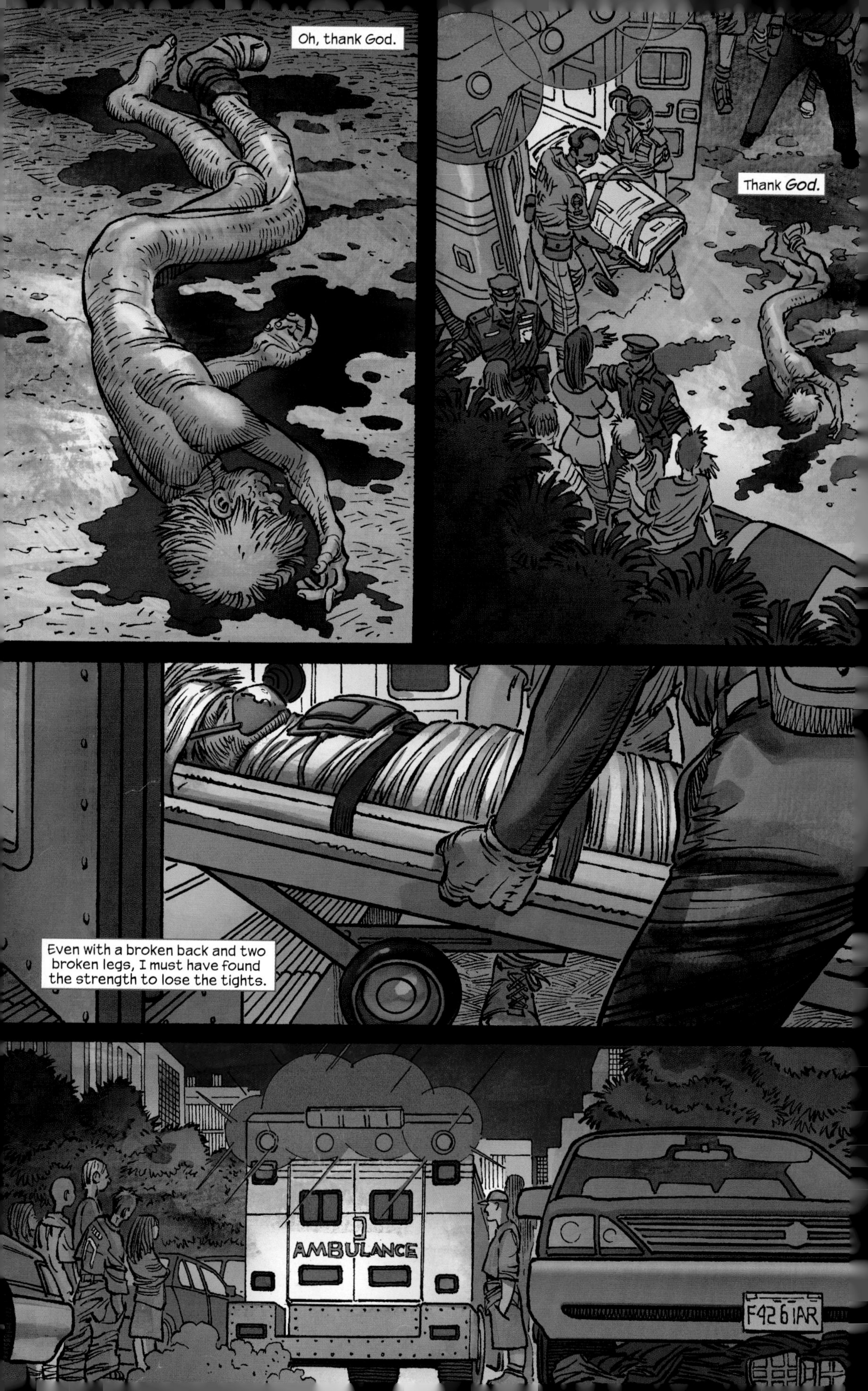
Oh, thank God.
Thank God.
Even with a broken back and two broken legs, I must have found the strength to lose the tights.
AMBULANCE
F4261AR

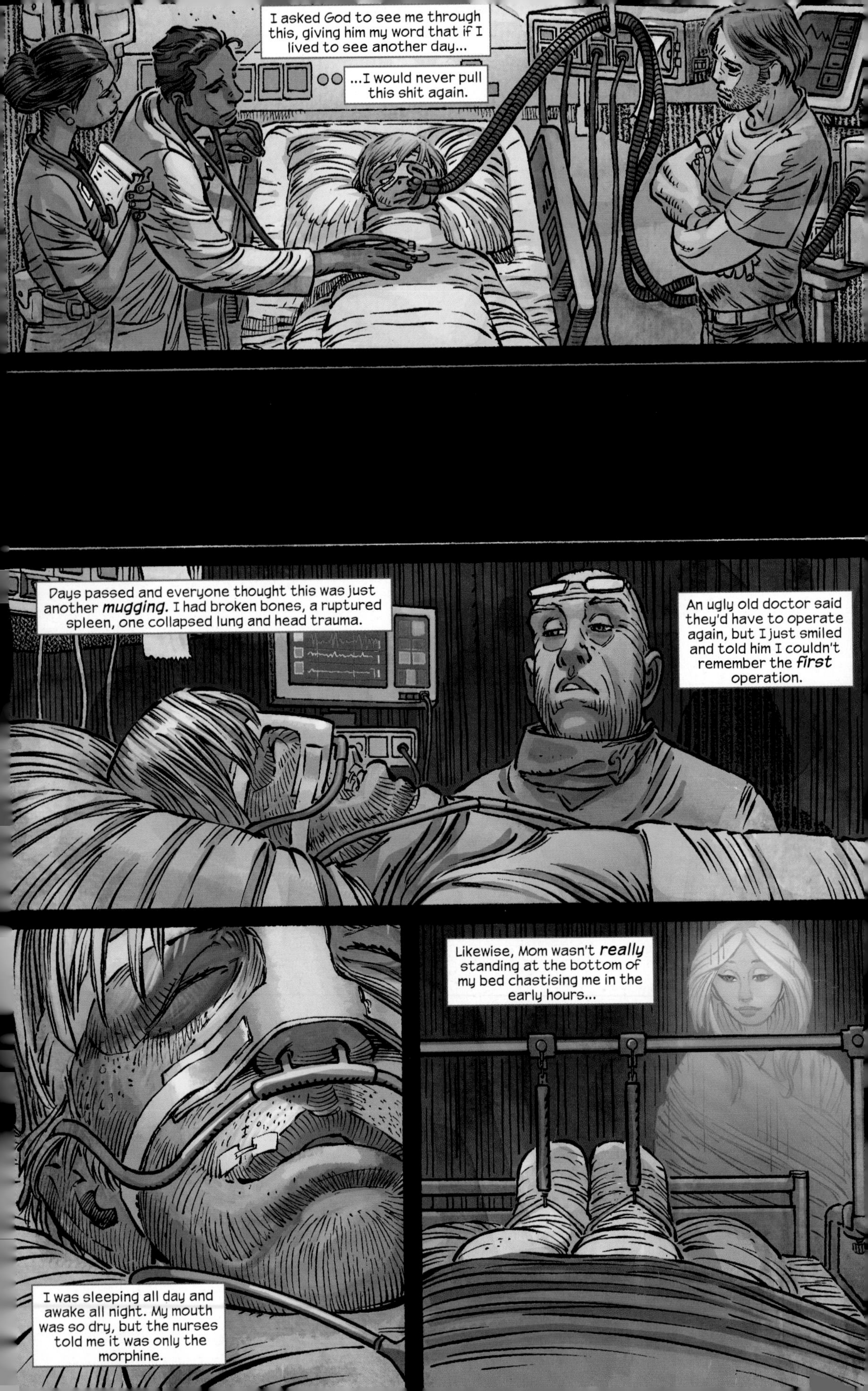
I asked God to see me through this, giving him my word that if I lived to see another day...
...I would never pull this shit again.
Days passed and everyone thought this was just another *mugging*. I had broken bones, a ruptured spleen, one collapsed lung and head trauma.
An ugly old doctor said they'd have to operate again, but I just smiled and told him I couldn't remember the *first* operation.
I was sleeping all day and awake all night. My mouth was so dry, but the nurses told me it was only the morphine.
Likewise, Mom wasn't *really* standing at the bottom of my bed chastising me in the early hours...

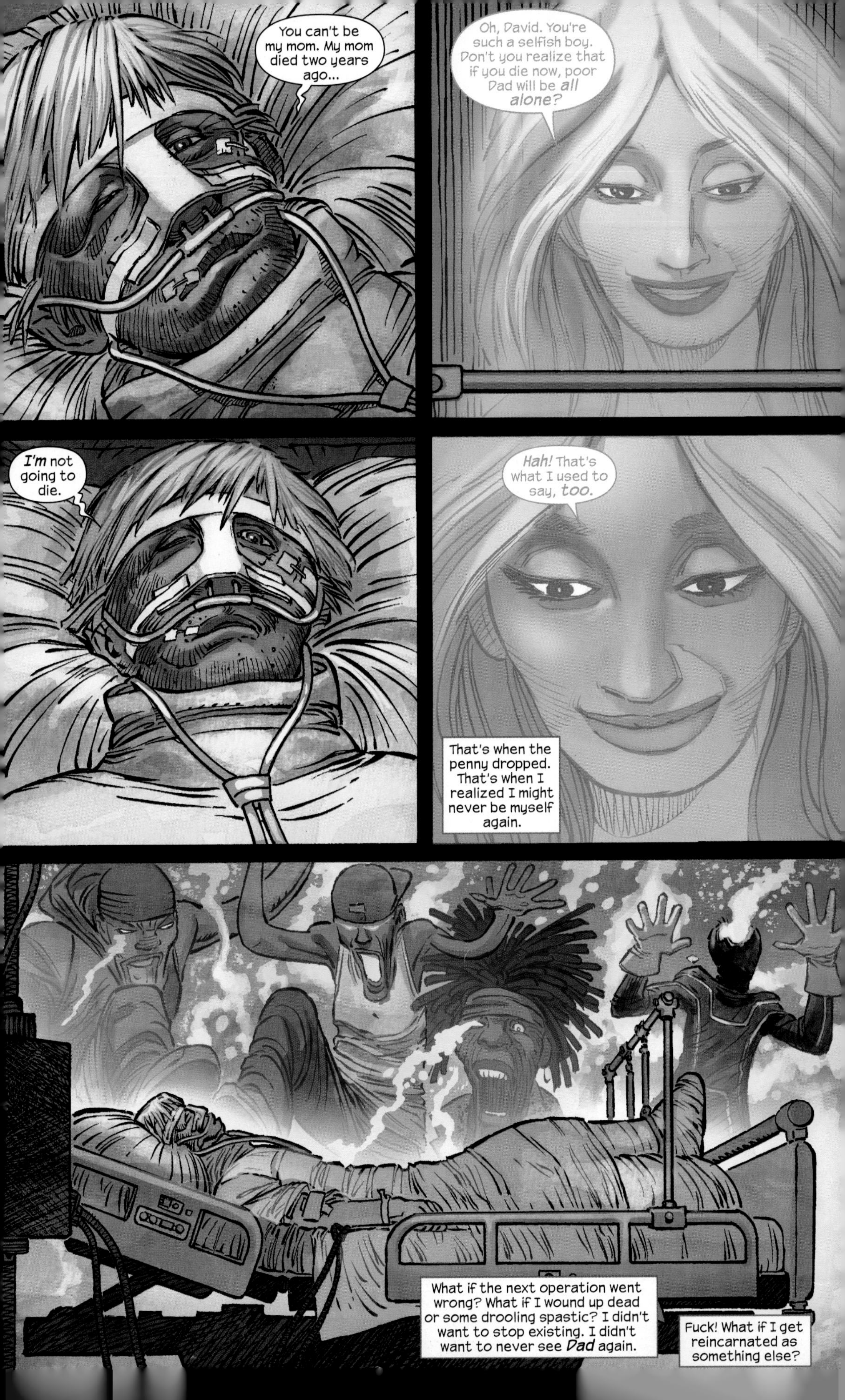
You can't be my mom. My mom died two years ago...
Oh, David. You're such a selfish boy. Don't you realize that if you die now, poor Dad will be *all alone*?
I'm not going to die.
Hah! That's what I used to say, *too.*
That's when the penny dropped. That's when I realized I might never be myself again.
What if the next operation went wrong? What if I wound up dead or some drooling spastic? I didn't want to stop existing. I didn't want to never see *Dad* again.
Fuck! What if I get reincarnated as something else?

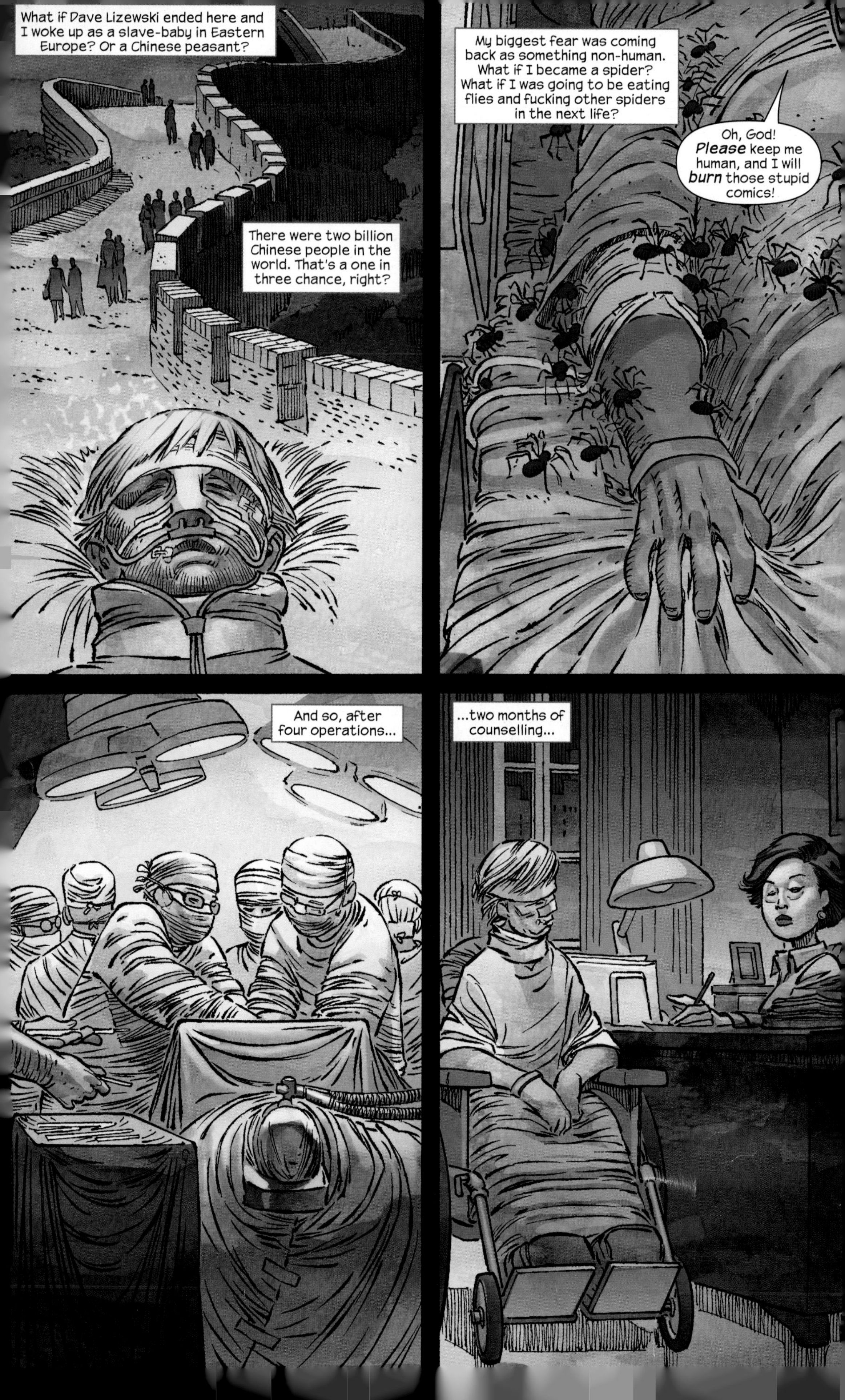
What if Dave Lizewski ended here and I woke up as a slave-baby in Eastern Europe? Or a Chinese peasant?
There were two billion Chinese people in the world. That's a one in three chance, right?
My biggest fear was coming back as something non-human. What if I became a spider? What if I was going to be eating flies and fucking other spiders in the next life?
Oh, God! *Please* keep me human, and I will *burn* those stupid comics!
And so, after four operations...
...two months of counselling...

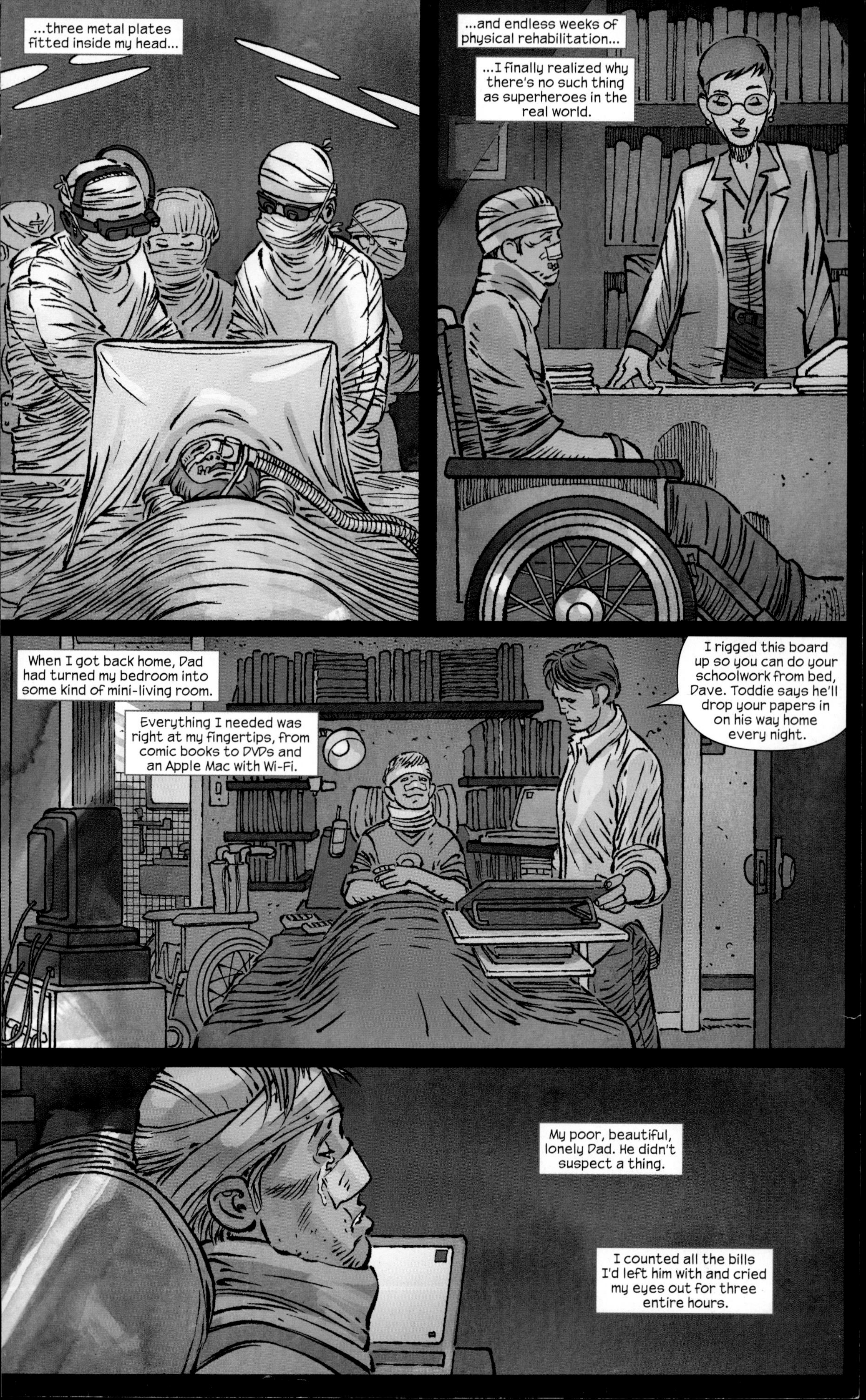
...three metal plates fitted inside my head...
...and endless weeks of physical rehabilitation...
...I finally realized why there's no such thing as superheroes in the real world.
When I got back home, Dad had turned my bedroom into some kind of mini-living room.
Everything I needed was right at my fingertips, from comic books to DVDs and an Apple Mac with Wi-Fi.
I rigged this board up so you can do your schoolwork from bed, Dave. Toddie says he'll drop your papers in on his way home every night.
My poor, beautiful, lonely Dad. He didn't suspect a thing.
I counted all the bills I'd left him with and cried my eyes out for three entire hours.

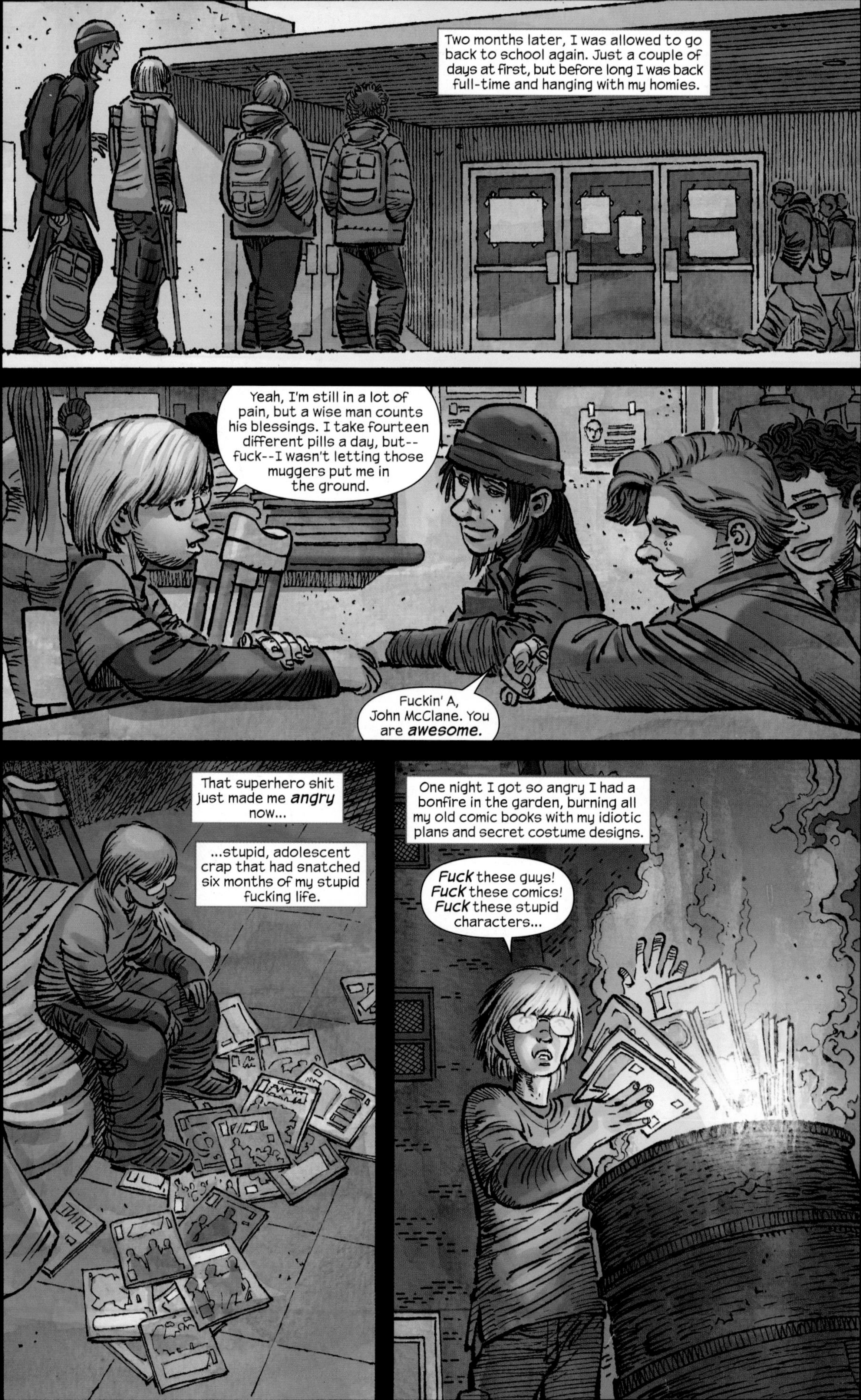
Two months later, I was allowed to go back to school again. Just a couple of days at first, but before long I was back full-time and hanging with my homies.
Yeah, I'm still in a lot of pain, but a wise man counts his blessings. I take fourteen different pills a day, but--fuck--I wasn't letting those muggers put me in the ground.
Fuckin' A, John McClane. You are *awesome.*
That superhero shit just made me *angry* now...
...stupid, adolescent crap that had snatched six months of my stupid fucking life.
One night I got so angry I had a bonfire in the garden, burning all my old comic books with my idiotic plans and secret costume designs.
Fuck these guys! *Fuck* these comics! *Fuck* these stupid characters...

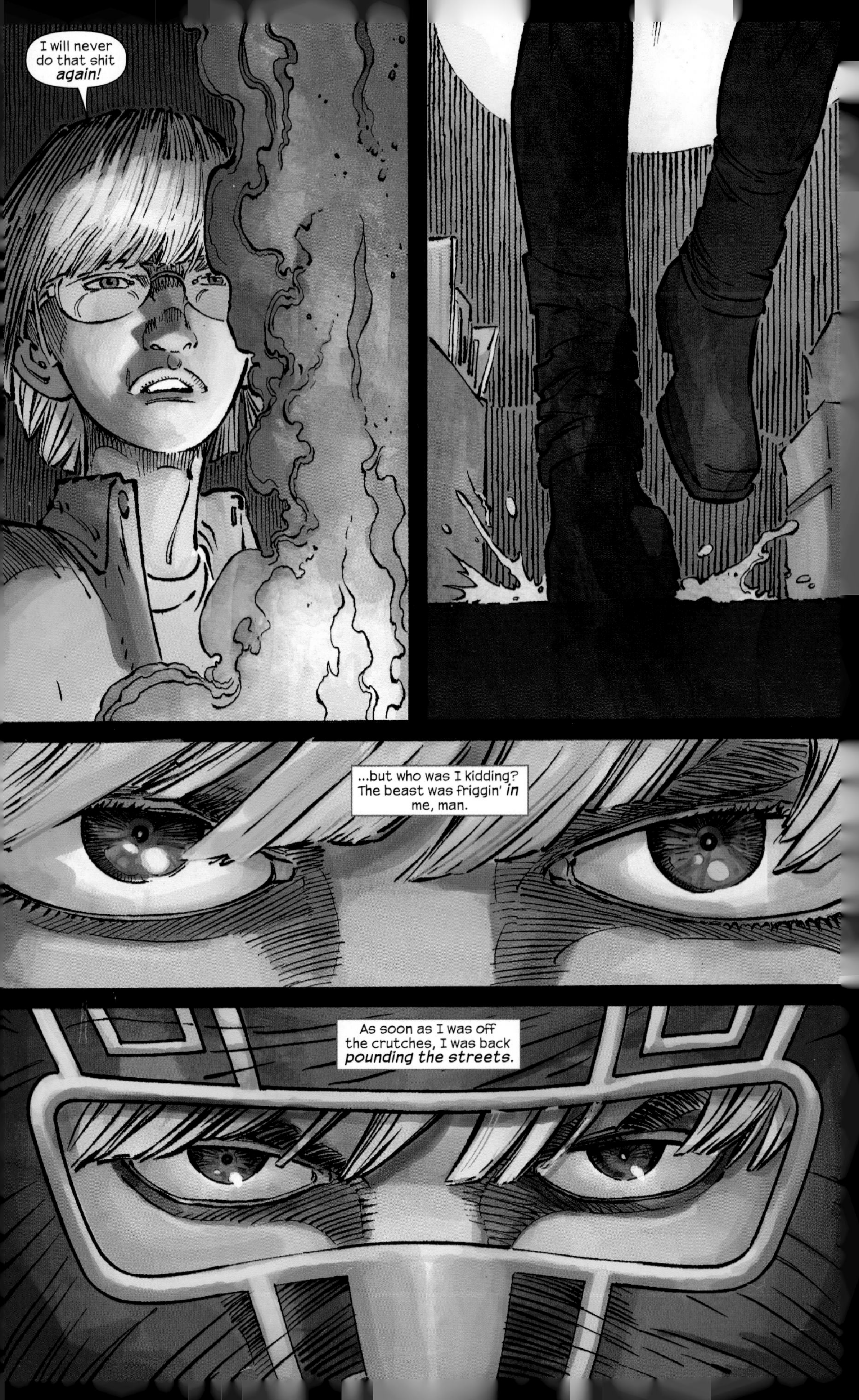
I will never do that shit *again!*
...but who was I kidding? The beast was friggin' *in* me, man.
As soon as I was off the crutches, I was back **pounding the streets.**

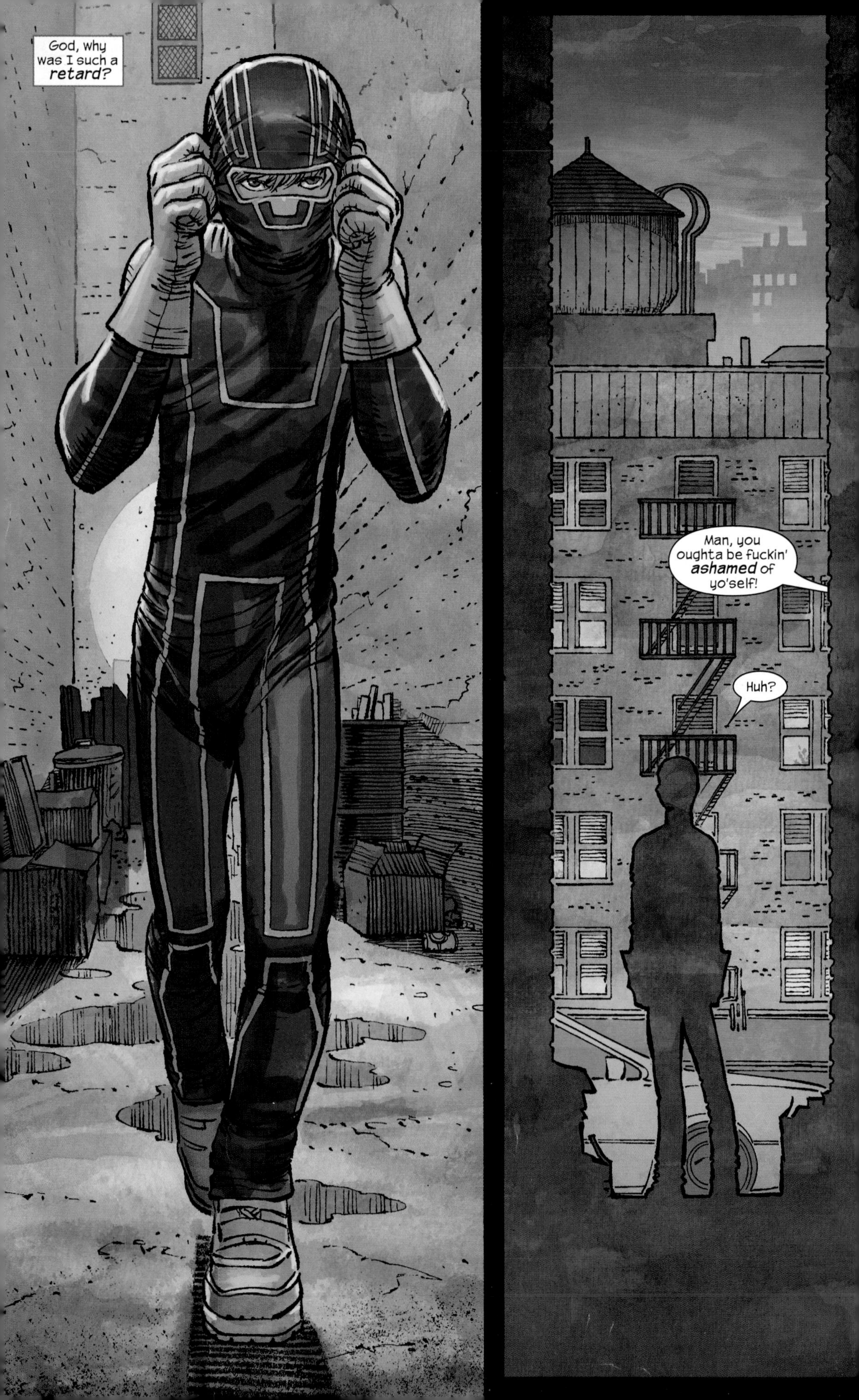
God, why was I such a *retard?*
Man, you oughta be fuckin' ***ashamed*** of yo'self!
Huh?

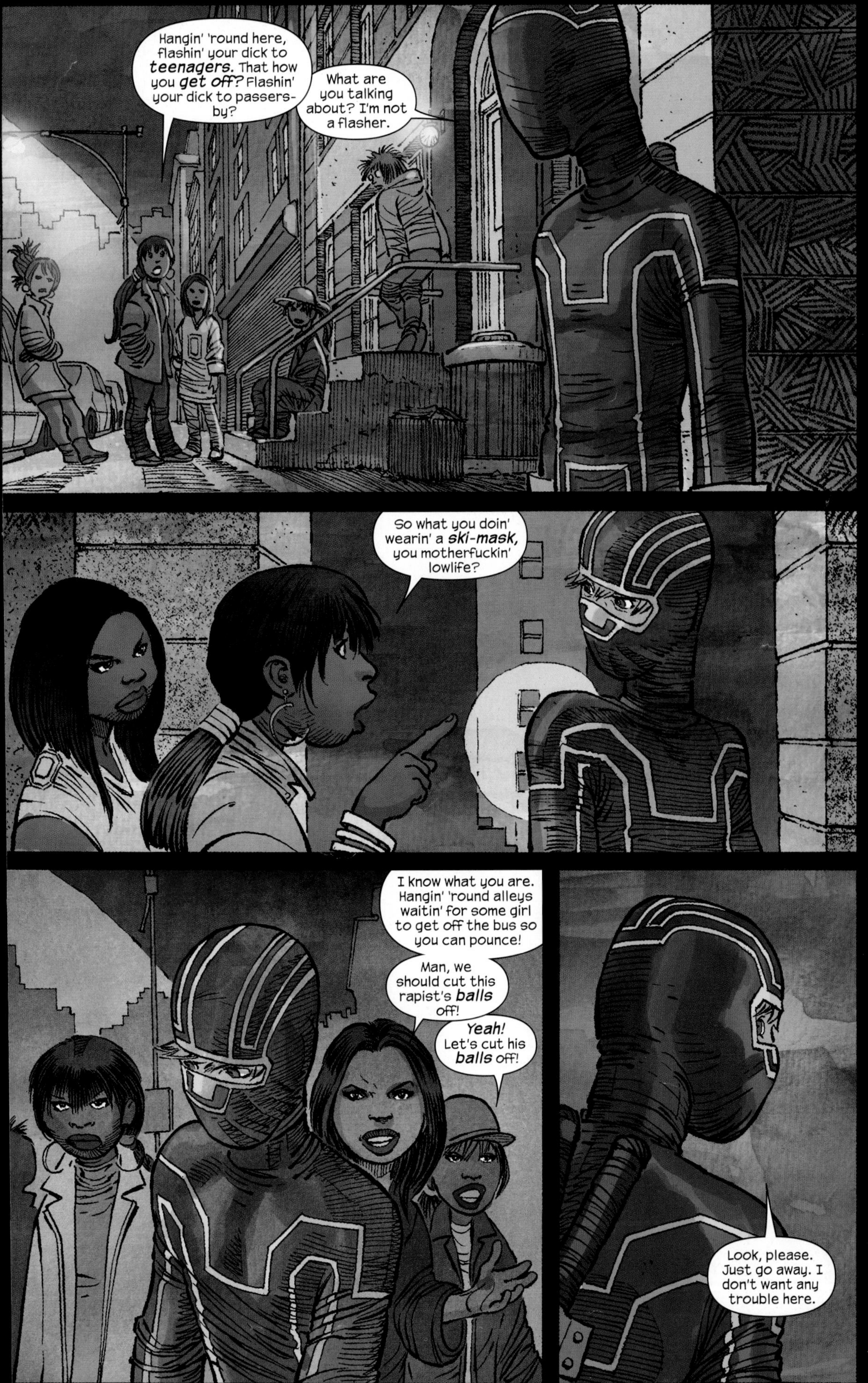
Hangin' 'round here, flashin' your dick to teenagers. That how you get off? Flashin' your dick to passers-by?
What are you talking about? I'm not a flasher.
So what you doin' wearin' a ski-mask, you motherfuckin' lowlife?
I know what you are. Hangin' 'round alleys waitin' for some girl to get off the bus so you can pounce!
Man, we should cut this rapist's balls off!
Yeah! Let's cut his balls off!
Look, please. Just go away. I don't want any trouble here.

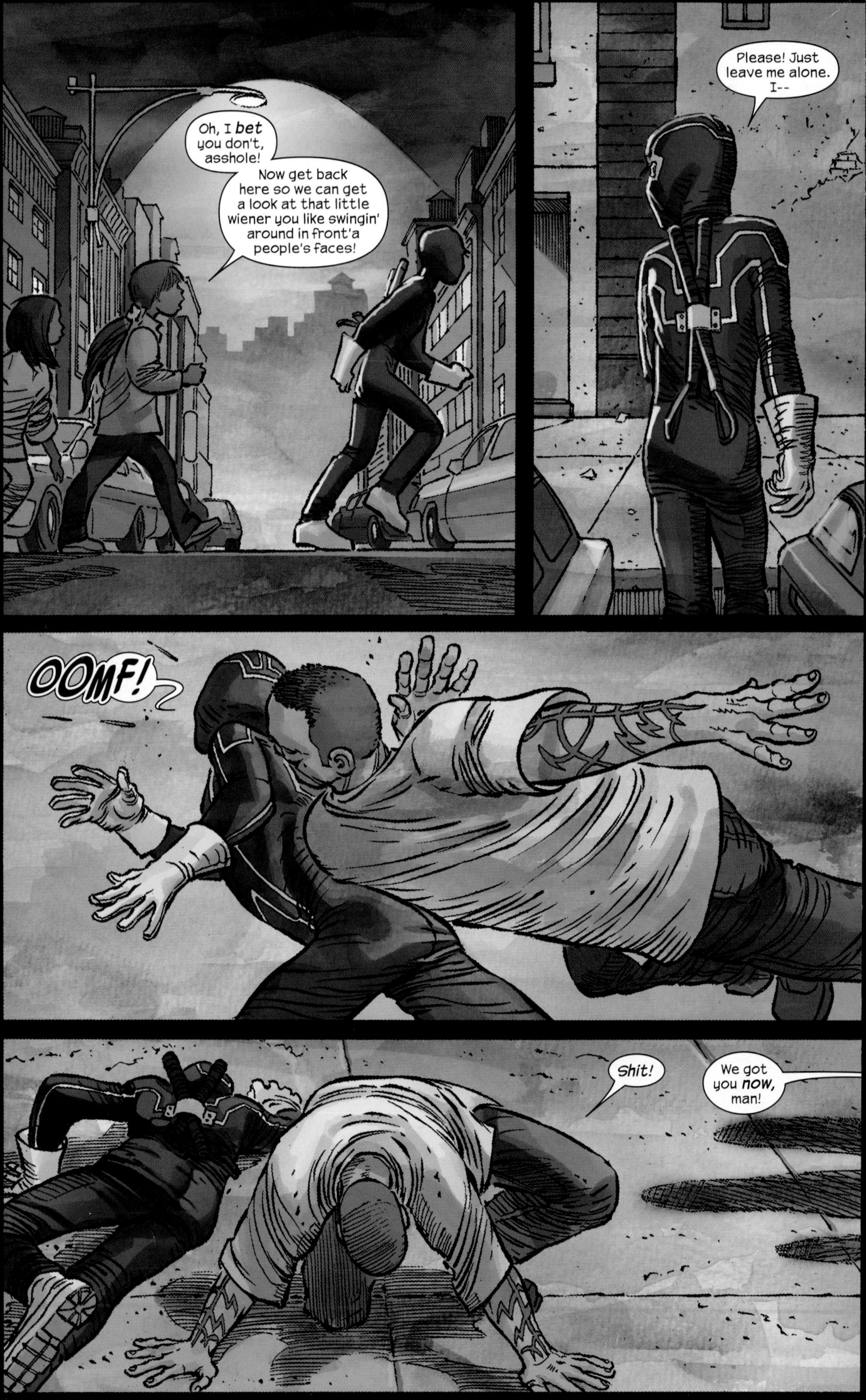
Oh, I bet you don't, asshole!
Now get back here so we can get a look at that little wiener you like swingin' around in front'a people's faces!
Please! Just leave me alone. I--
OOMF!
Shit!
We got you NOW, man!

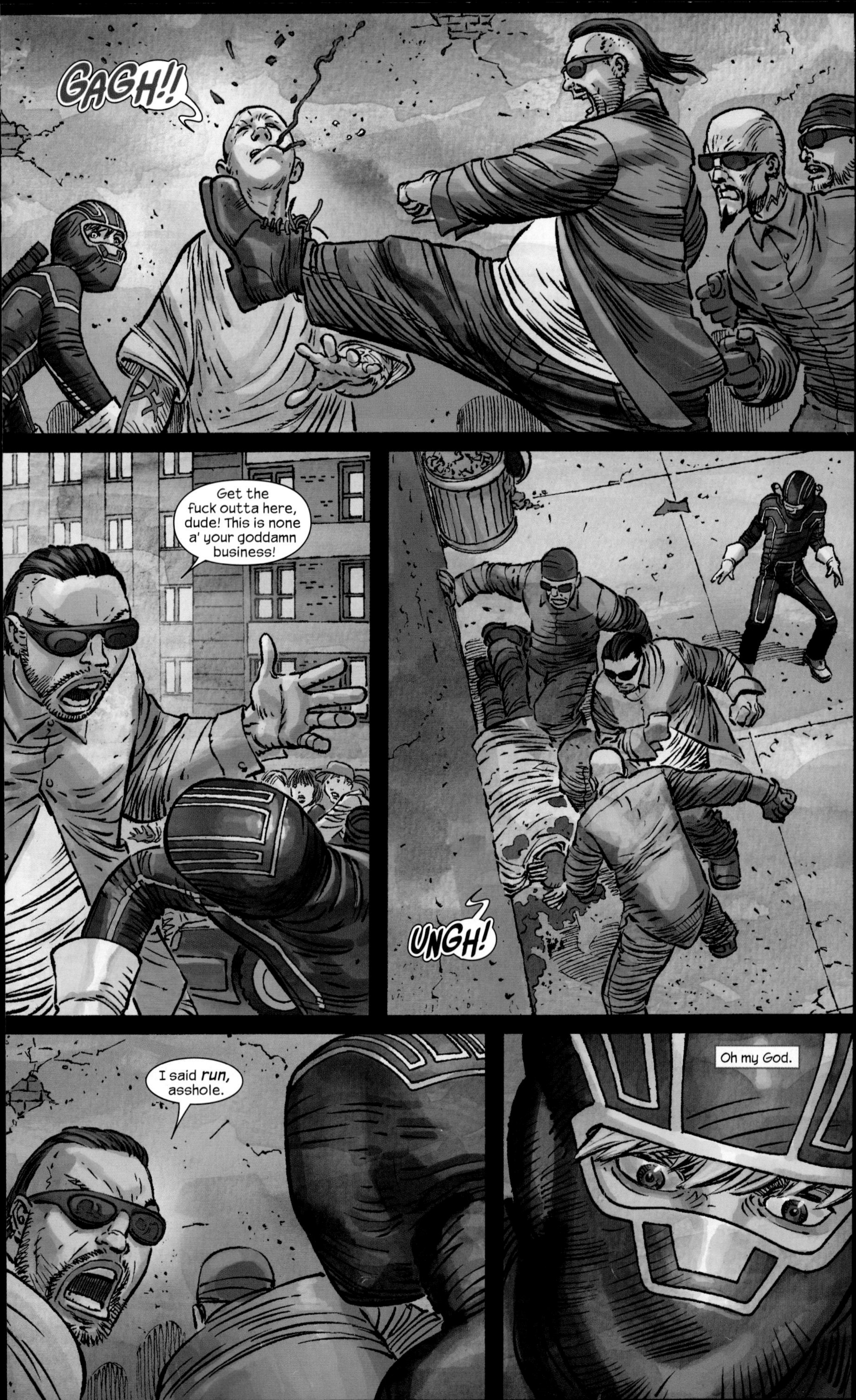
GAGH!!
Get the fuck outta here, dude! This is none a' your goddamn business!
UNGH!
I said run, asshole.
Oh my God.

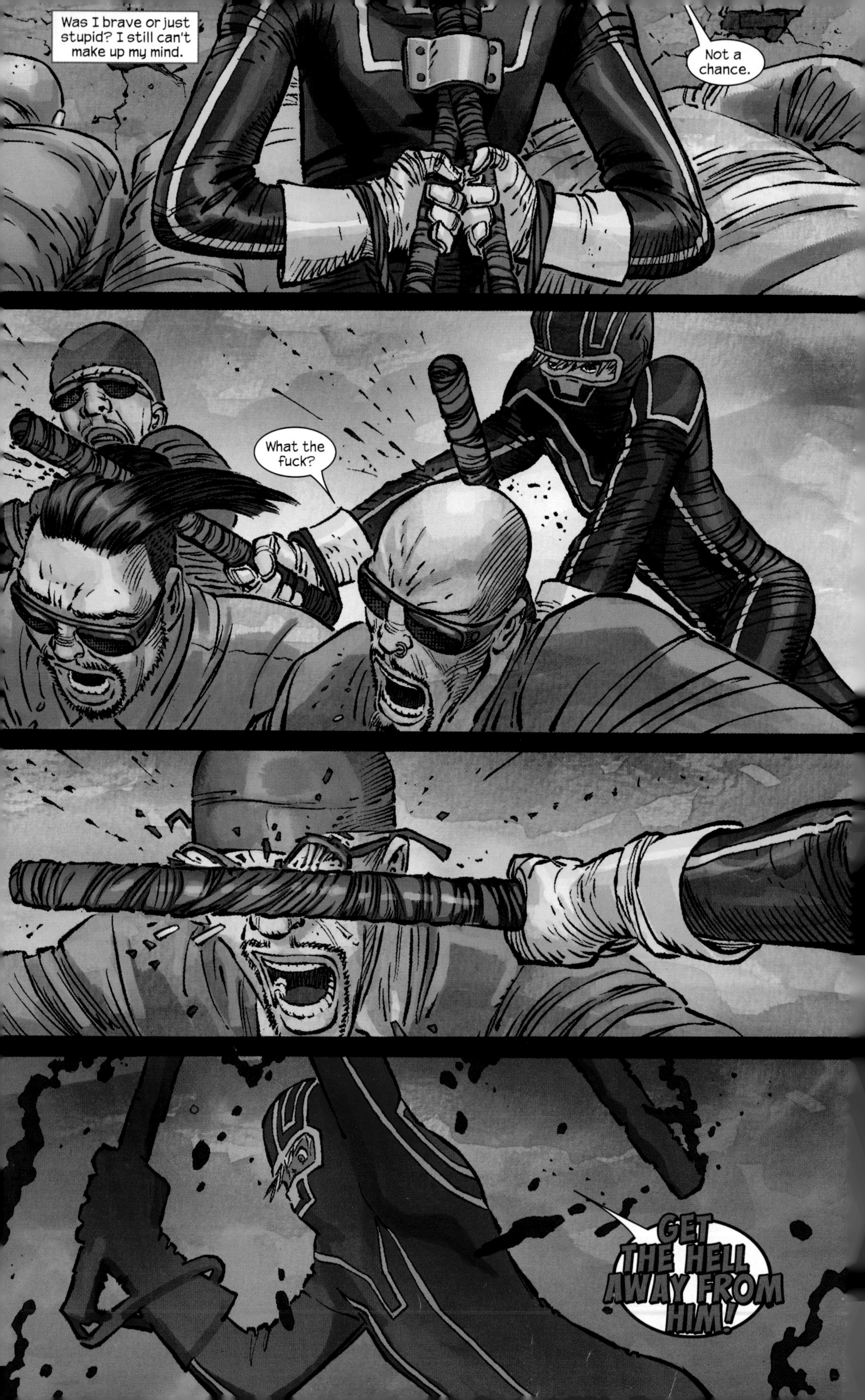
Was I brave or just stupid? I still can't make up my mind.
Not a chance.
What the fuck?
GET THE HELL AWAY FROM HIM!

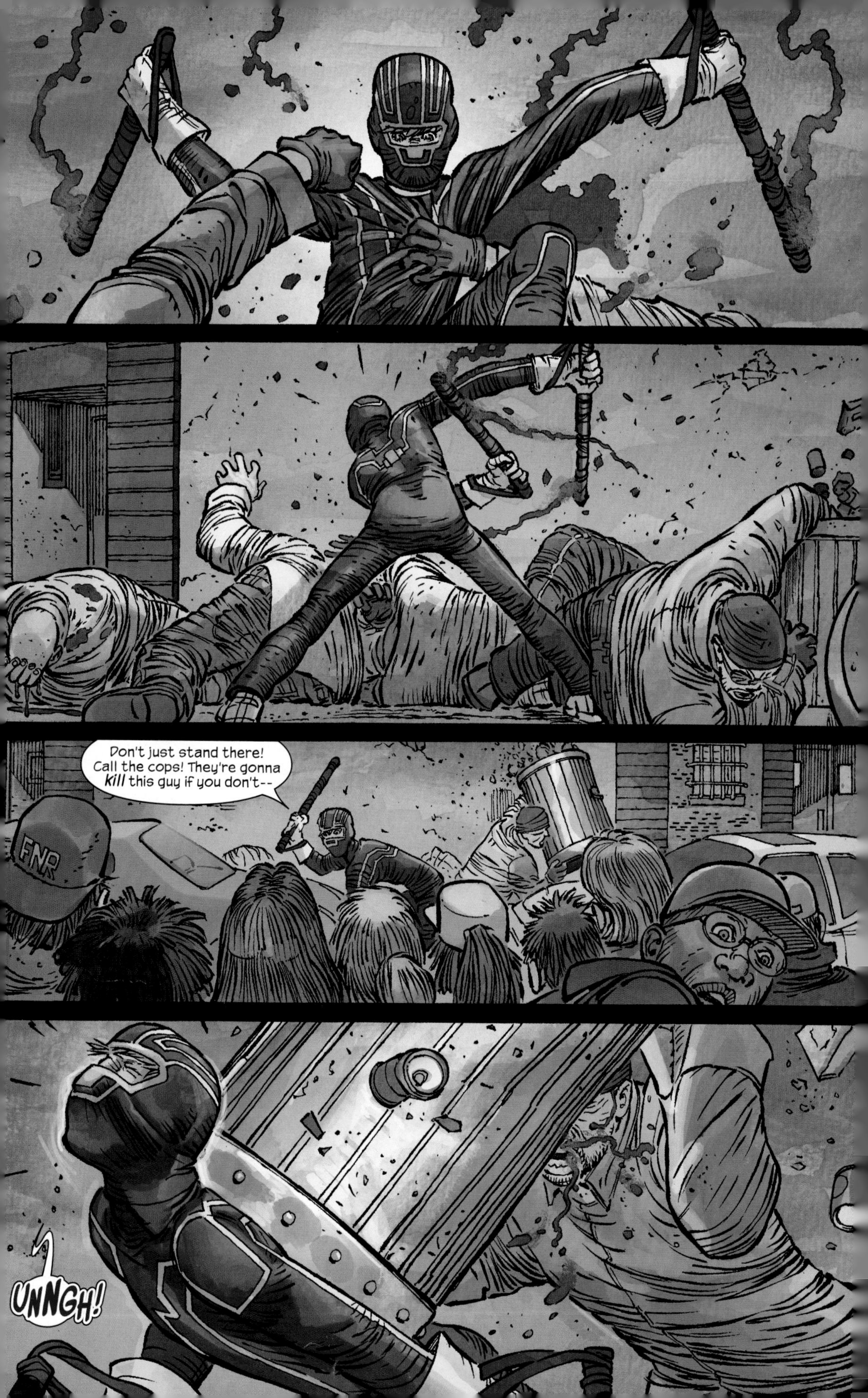
Don't just stand there! Call the cops! They're gonna *kill* this guy if you don't--
FNR
UNNGH!

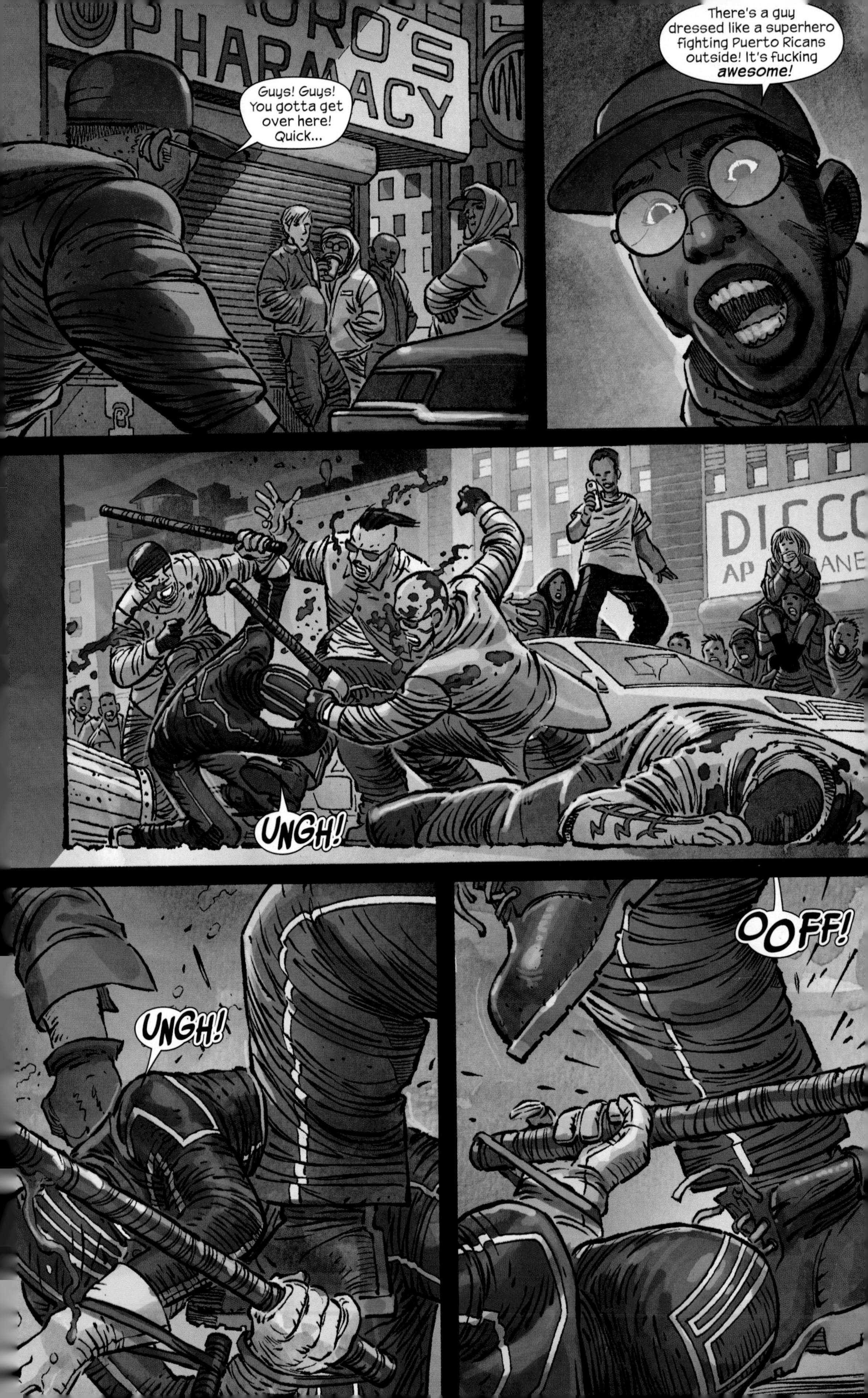

Guys! Guys! You gotta get over here! Quick...
There's a guy dressed like a superhero fighting Puerto Ricans outside! It's fucking *awesome!*
UNGH!
UNGH!
OOFF!

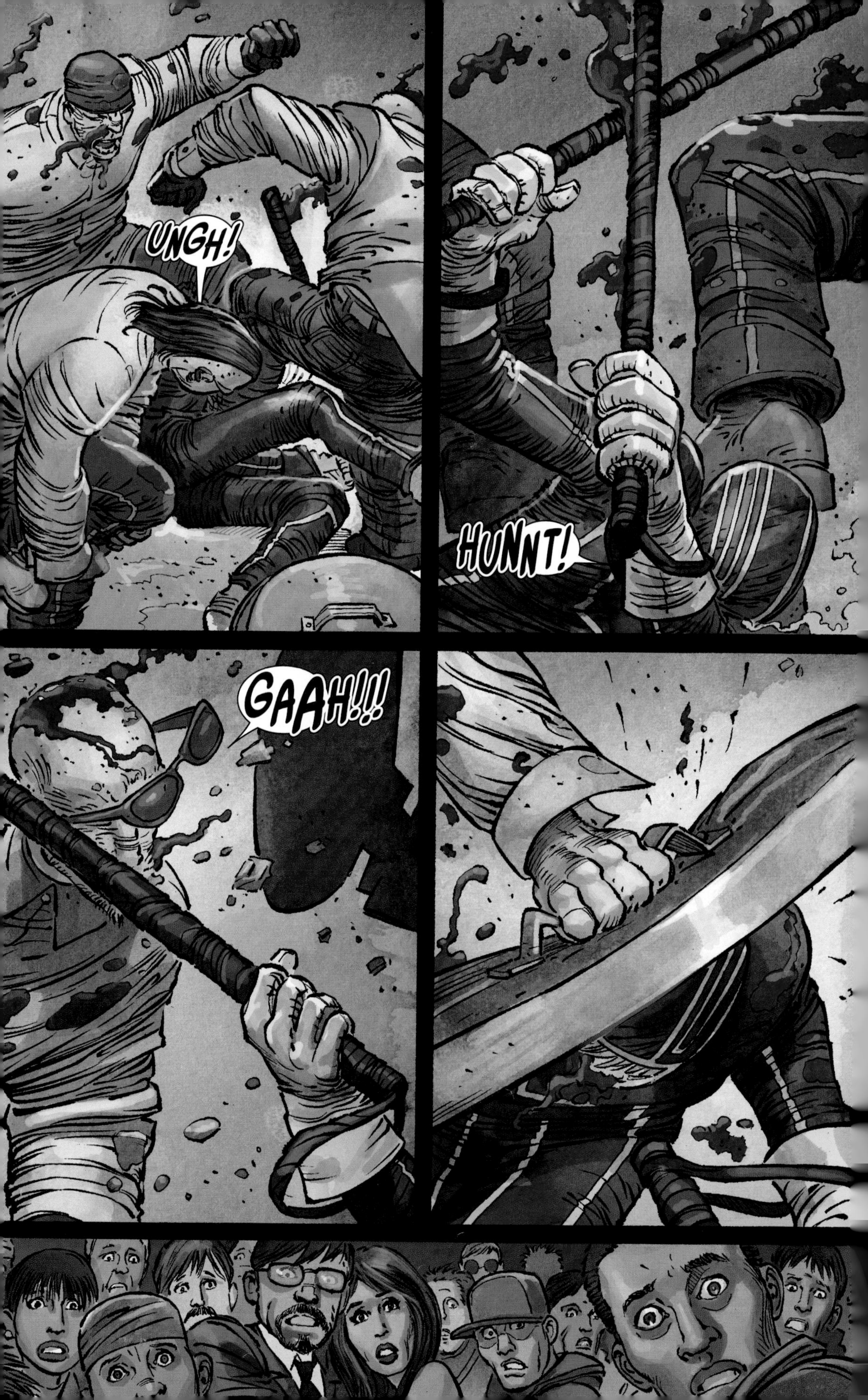
UNGH!
HUNNT!
GAAH!!!

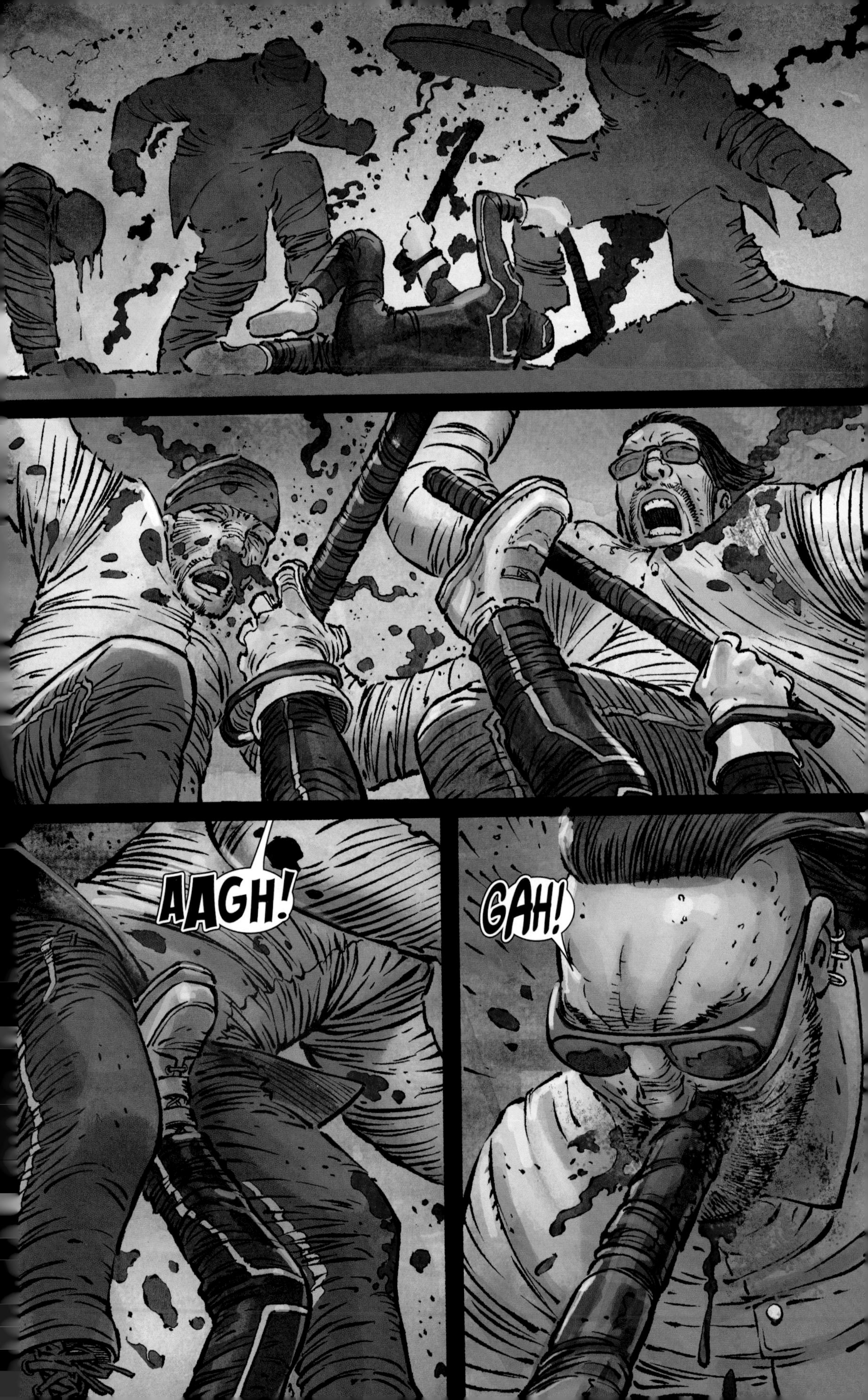
AAGH!
GAH!

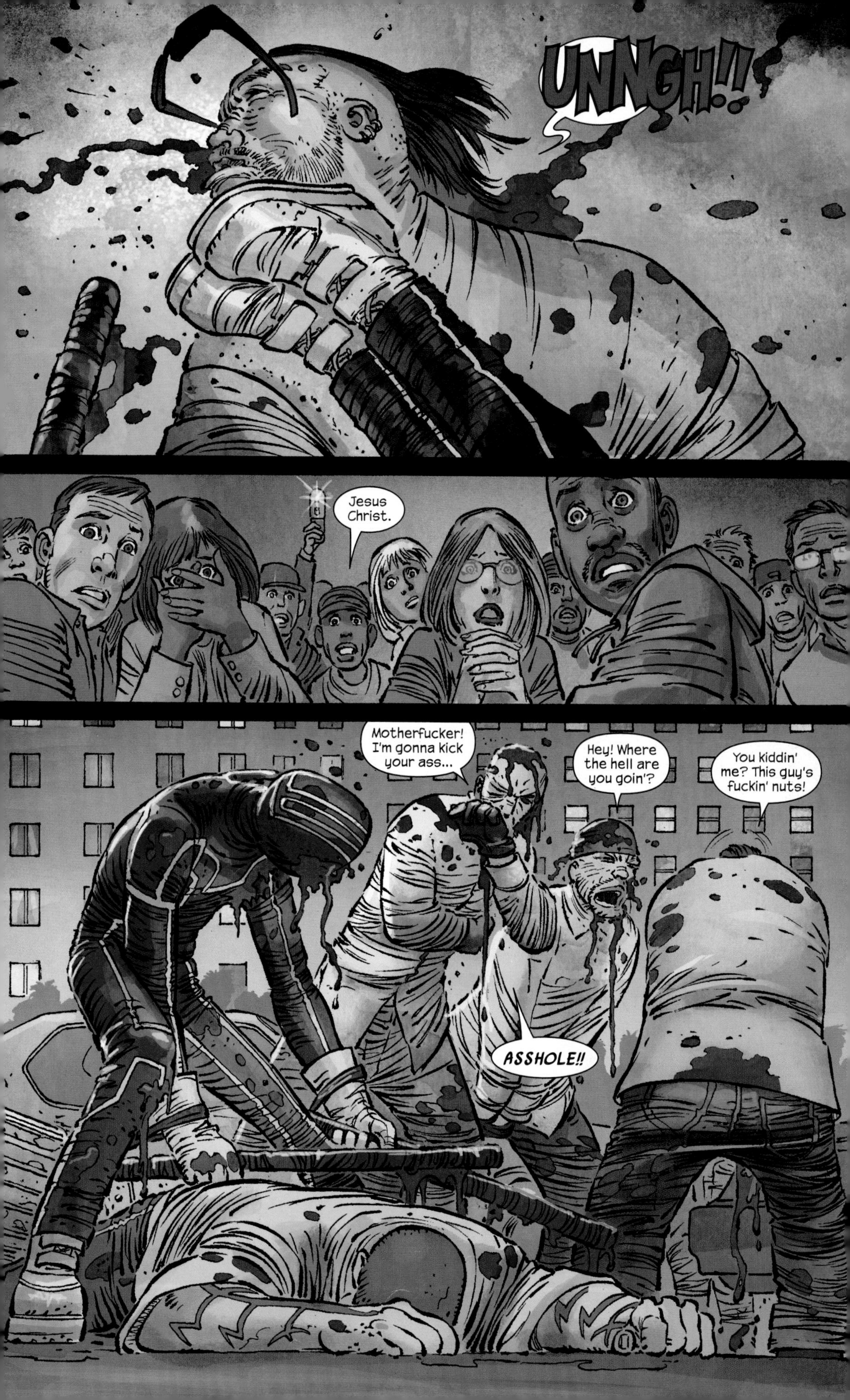
UNNGH!!
Jesus Christ.
Motherfucker! I'm gonna kick your ass...
Hey! Where the hell are you goin'?
You kiddin' me? This guy's fuckin' nuts!
ASSHOLE!!

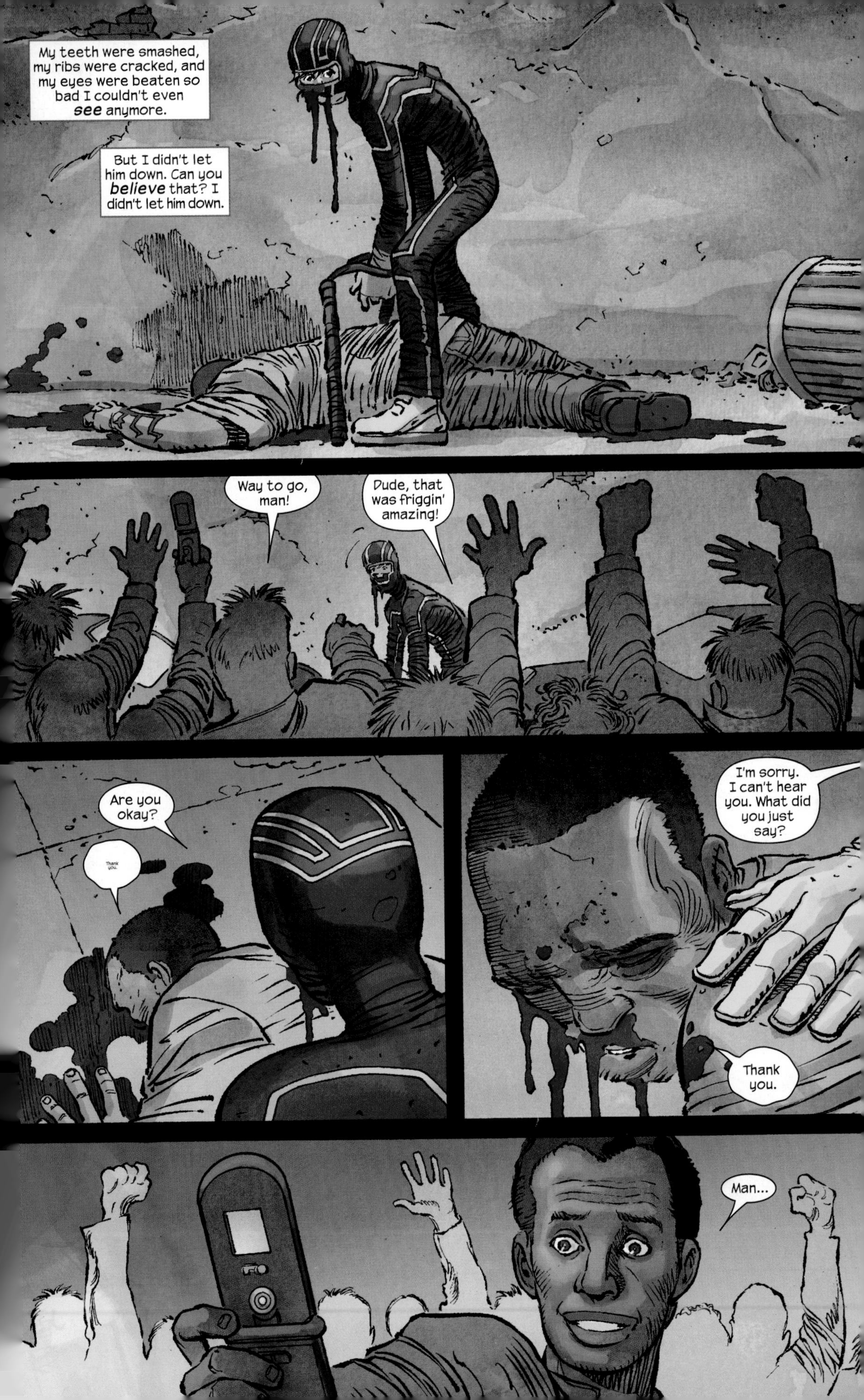

My teeth were smashed, my ribs were cracked, and my eyes were beaten so bad I couldn't even ***see*** anymore.
But I didn't let him down. Can you ***believe*** that? I didn't let him down.
Way to go, man!
Dude, that was friggin' amazing!
Are you okay?
I'm sorry. I can't hear you. What did you just say?
Thank you.
Man...

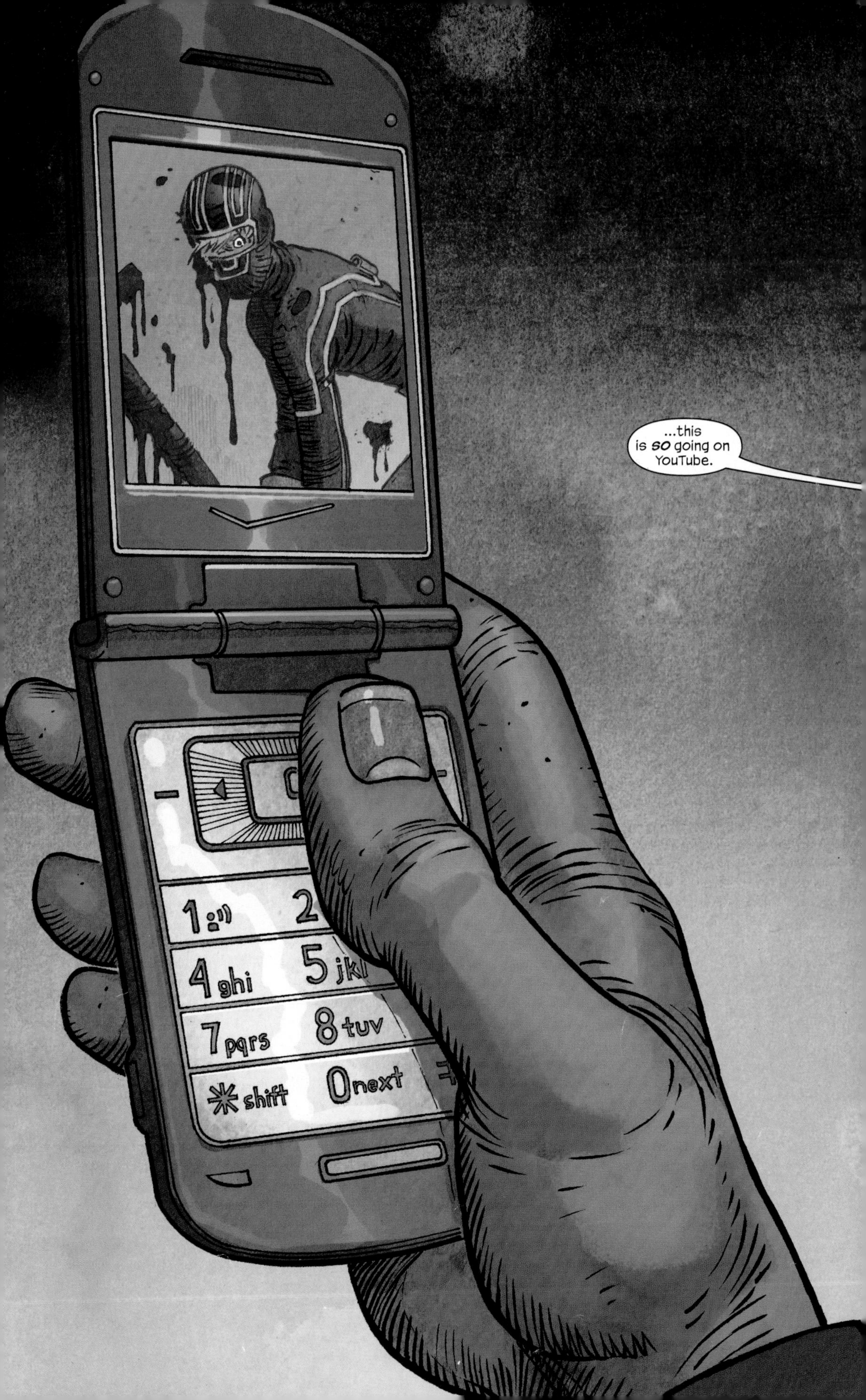
...this is *SO* going on YouTube.

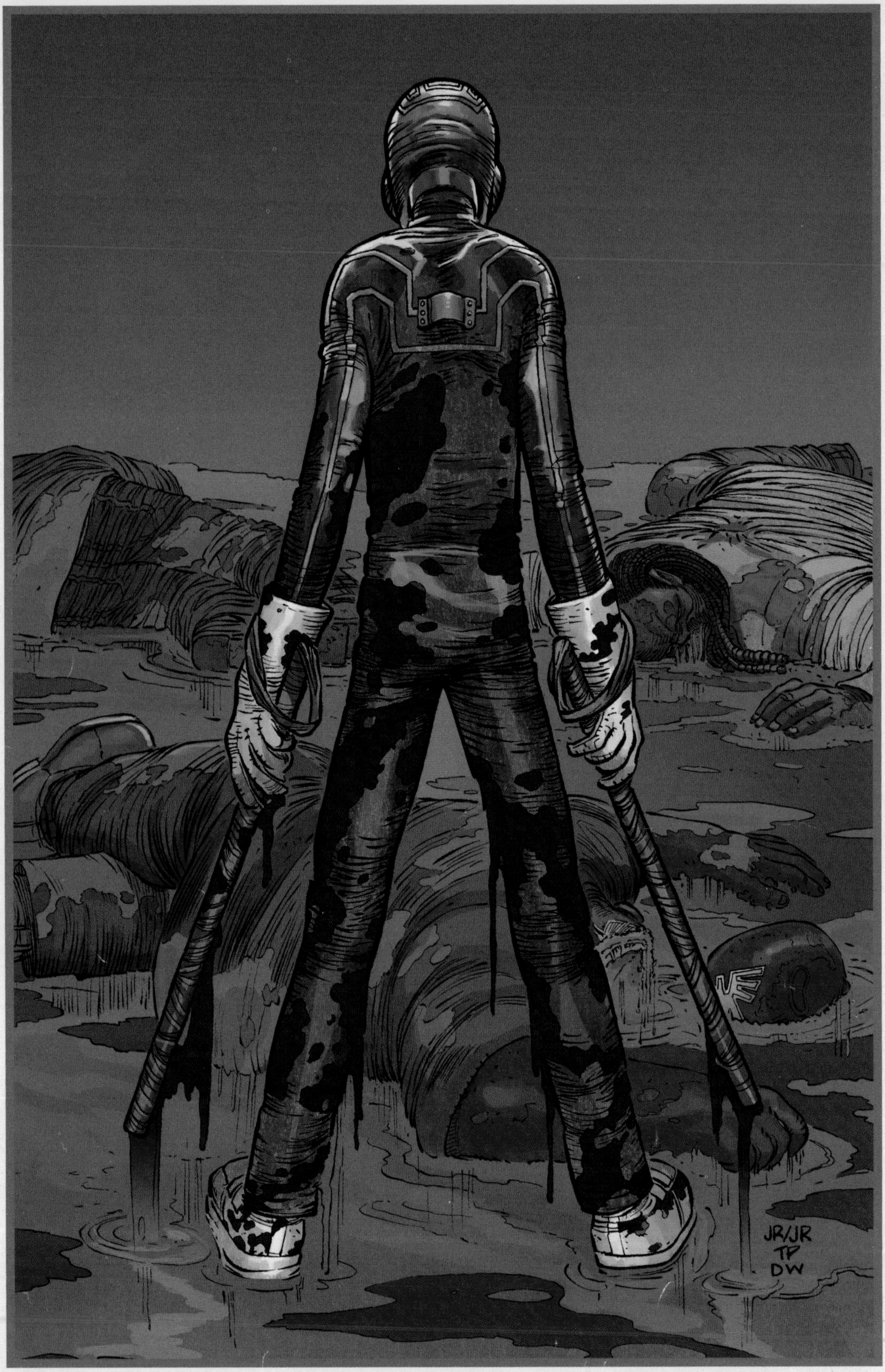
JR/JR
TP
DW

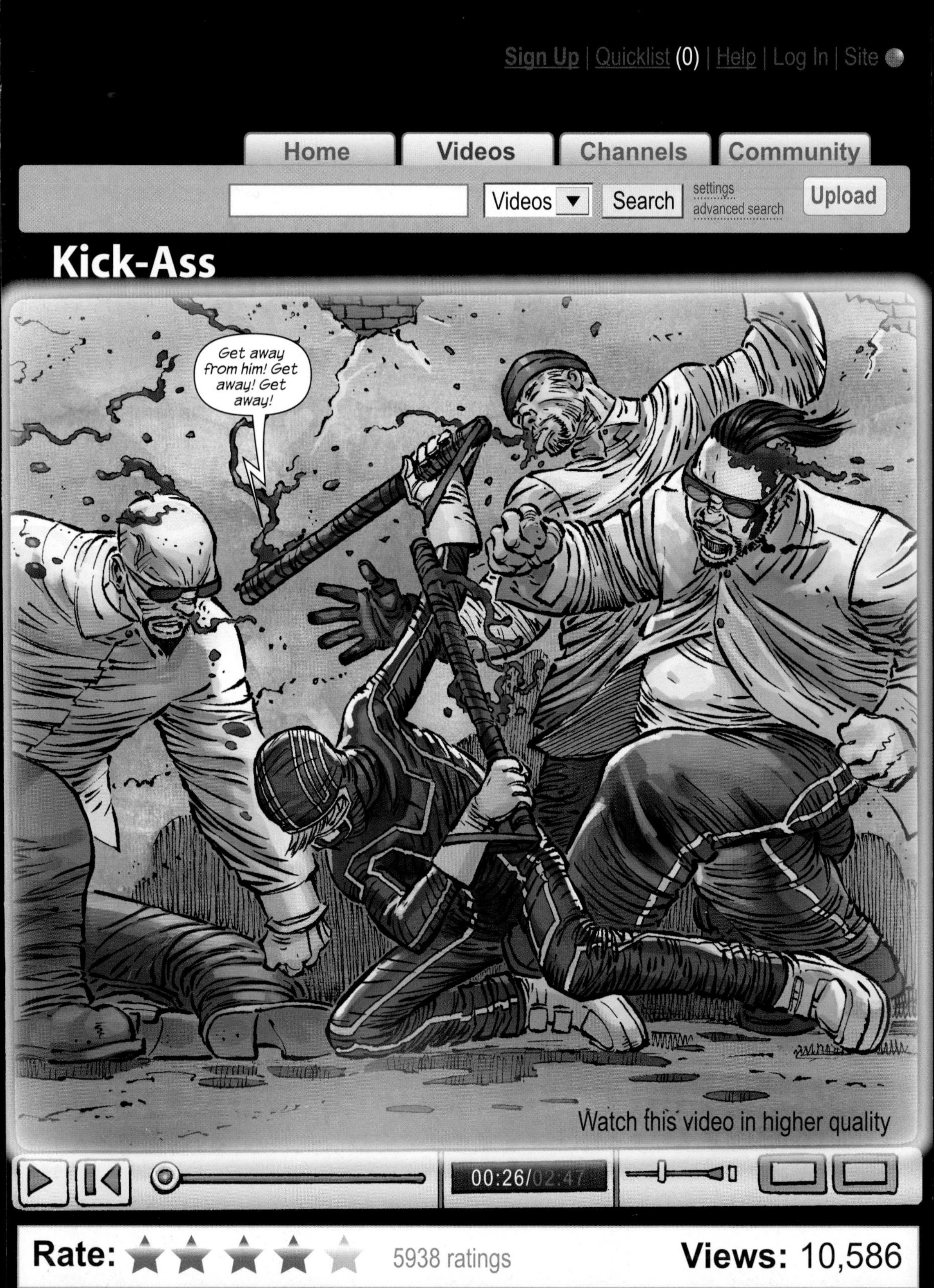
Sign Up | Quicklist (0) | Help | Log In | Site
Home
Videos
Channels
Community
Videos
Search
settings
advanced search
Upload
Kick-Ass
Get away from him! Get away! Get away!
Watch this video in higher quality
00:26/02:47
Rate:
5938 ratings
Views: 10,586

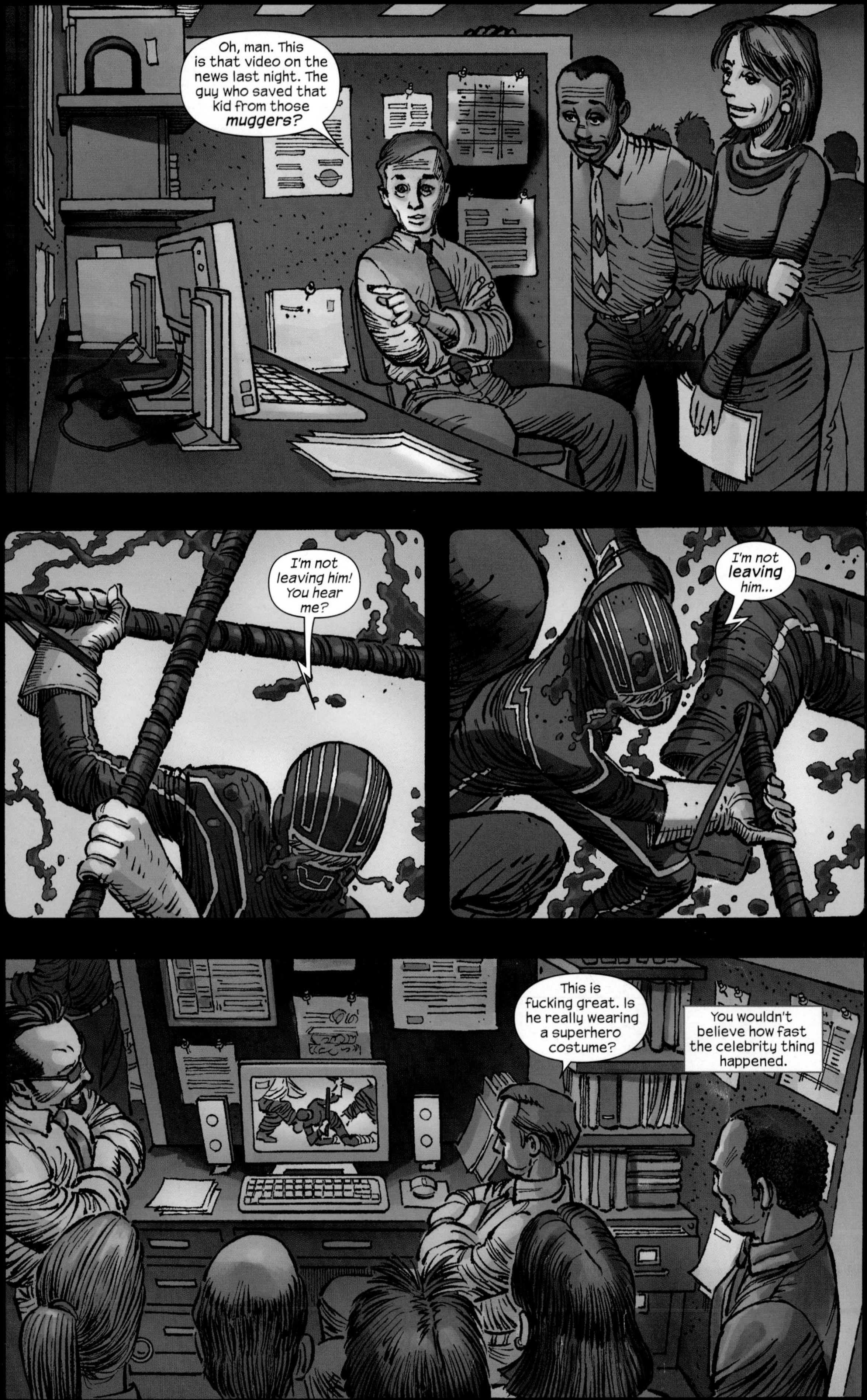
Oh, man. This is that video on the news last night. The guy who saved that kid from those *muggers?*
I'm not leaving him! You hear me?
I'm not ***leaving*** *him...*
This is fucking great. Is he really wearing a superhero costume?
You wouldn't believe how fast the celebrity thing happened.

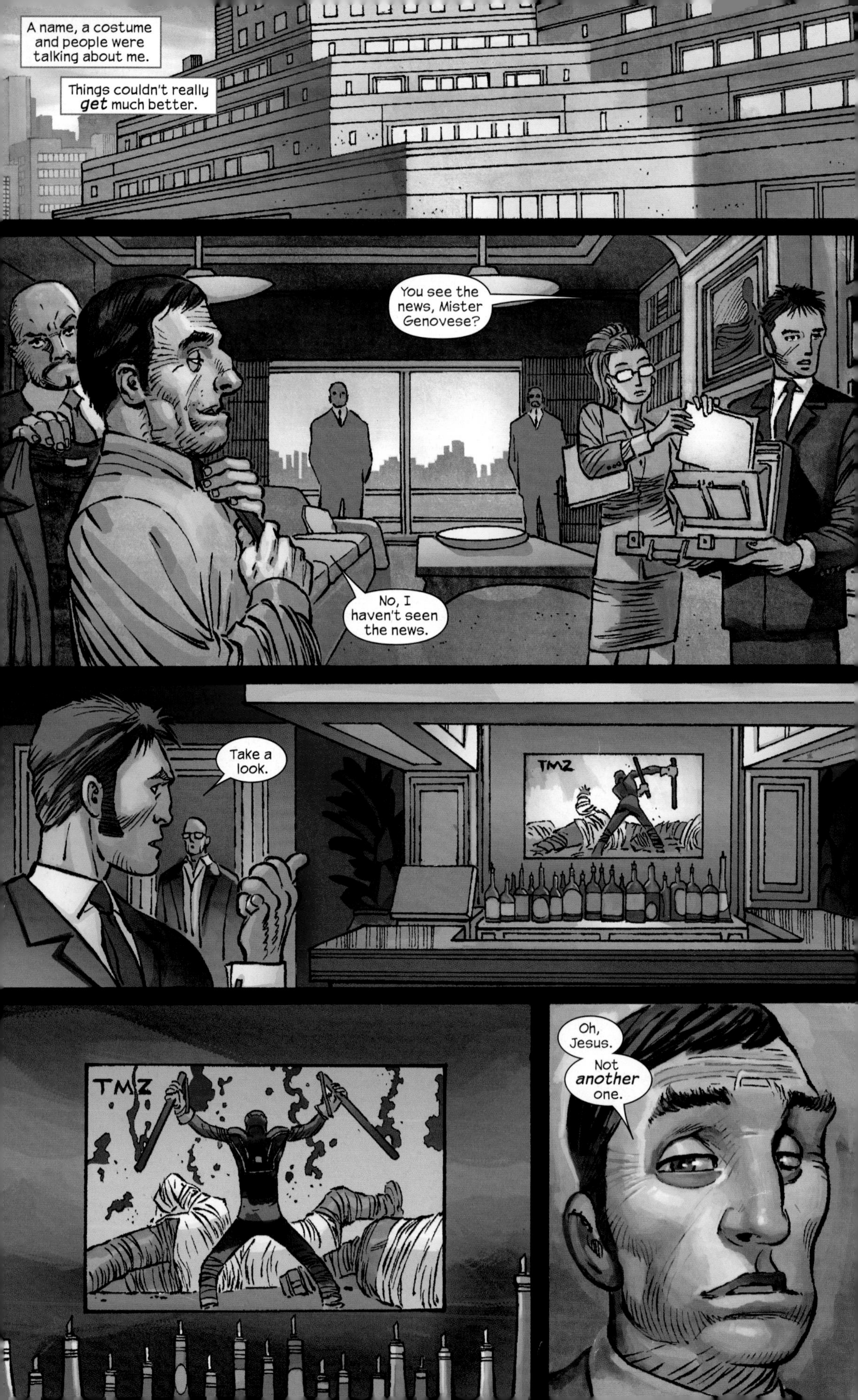
A name, a costume and people were talking about me.
Things couldn't really *get* much better.
You see the news, Mister Genovese?
No, I haven't seen the news.
Take a look.
TMZ
TMZ
Oh, Jesus.
Not *another* one.

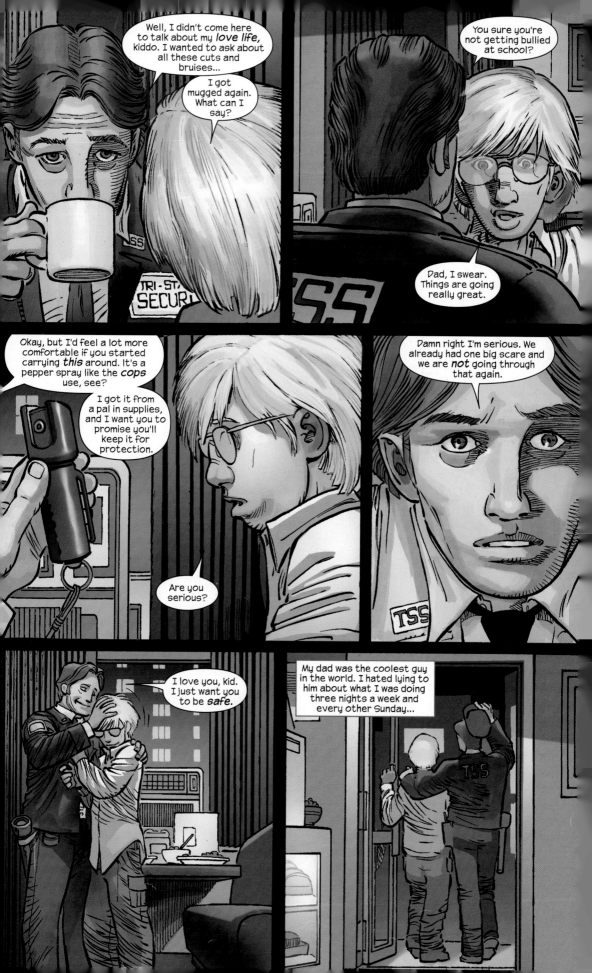

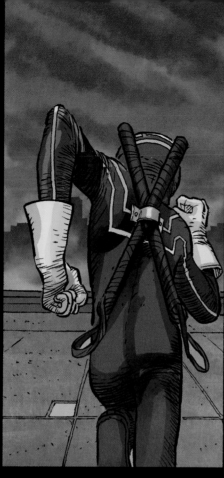

Okay. Time to do what superheroes do and finally jump some rooftops.

Shit.

Higher up than they look in the comic books too.

Fuck this. I'm walking.

ROOF

EXIT

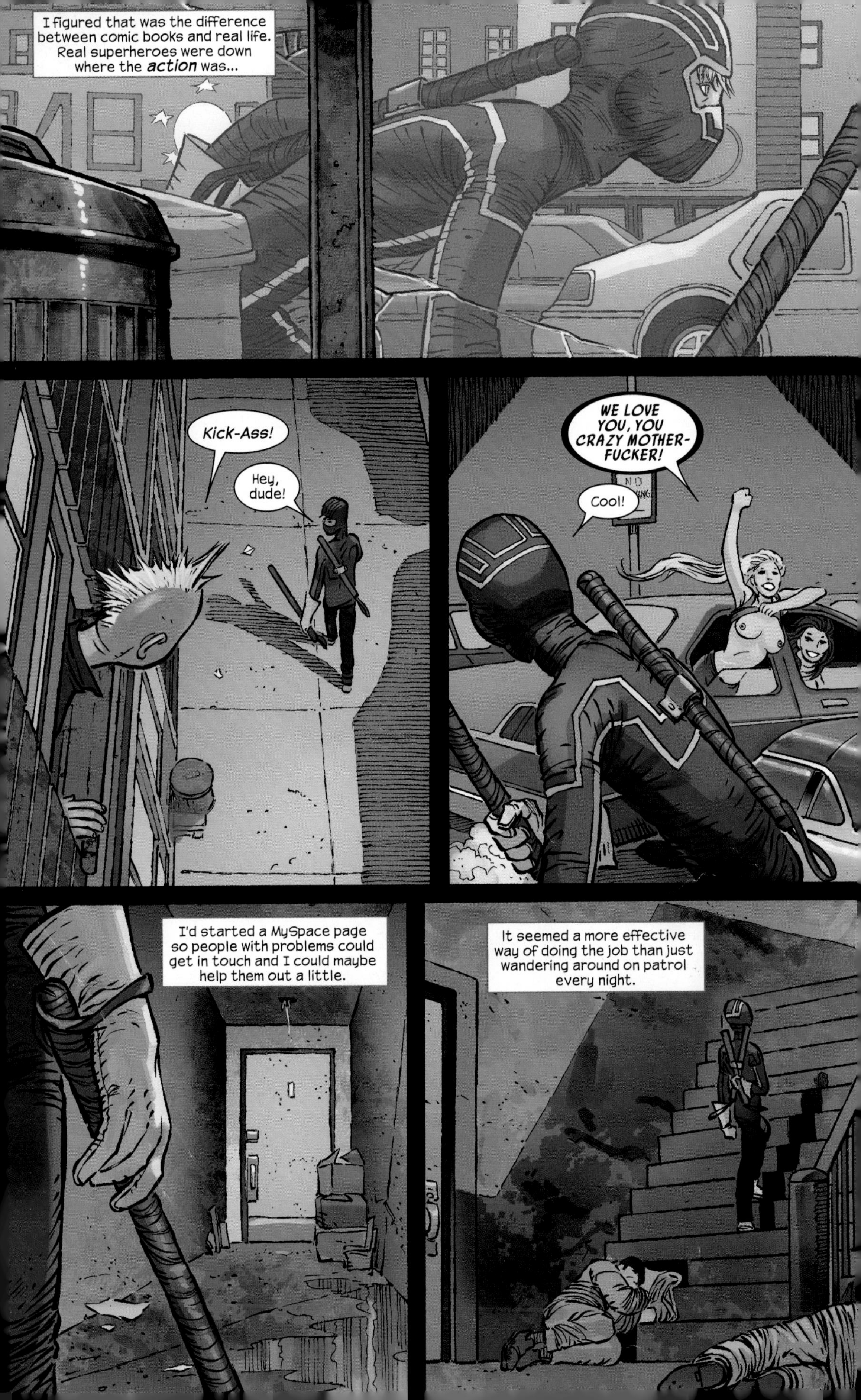
I figured that was the difference between comic books and real life. Real superheroes were down where the *action* was...
Kick-Ass!
Hey, dude!
WE LOVE YOU, YOU CRAZY MOTHER-FUCKER!
Cool!
I'd started a MySpace page so people with problems could get in touch and I could maybe help them out a little.
It seemed a more effective way of doing the job than just wandering around on patrol every night.

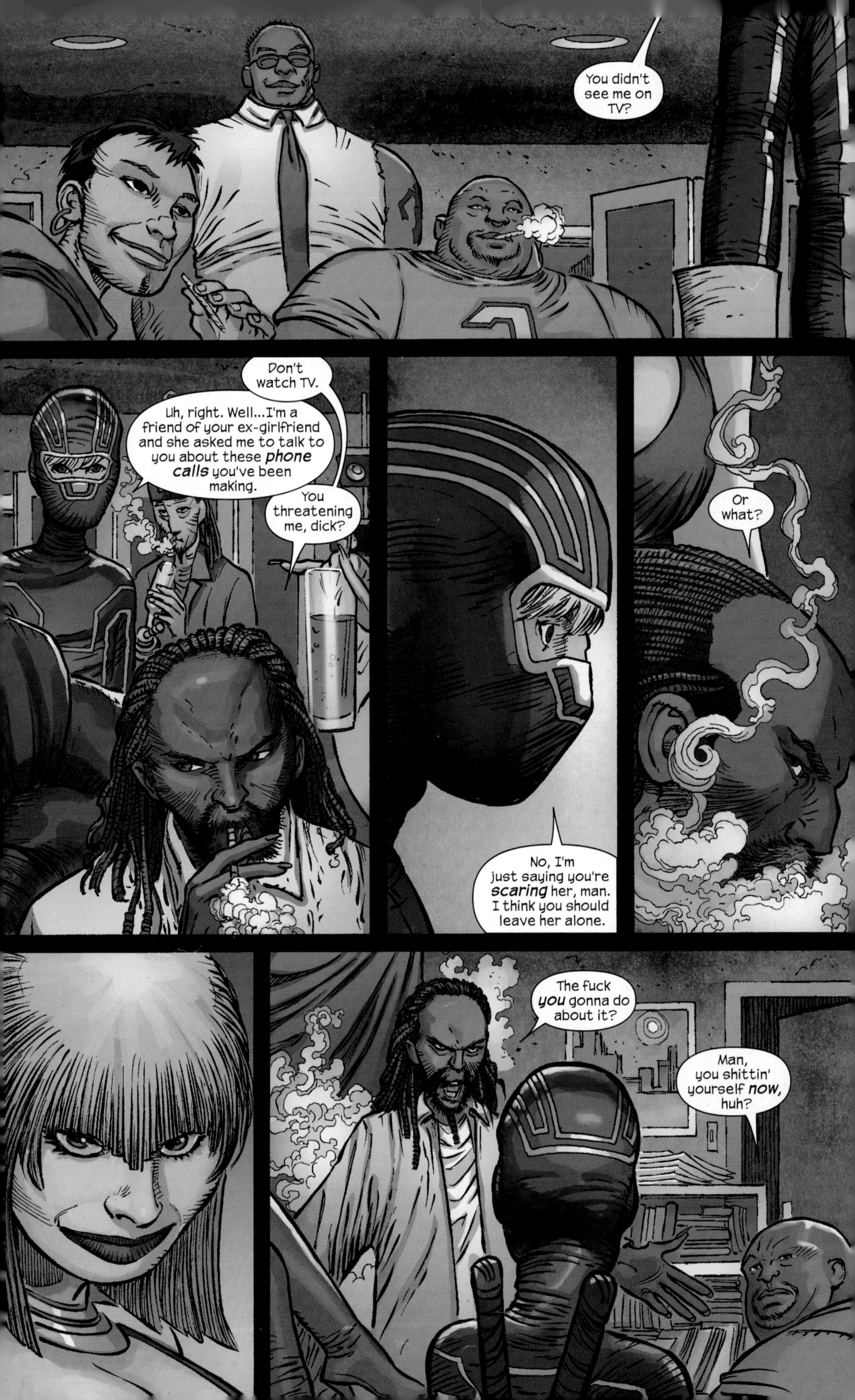
You didn't see me on TV?
Don't watch TV.
Uh, right. Well...I'm a friend of your ex-girlfriend and she asked me to talk to you about these *phone calls* you've been making.
You threatening me, dick?
No, I'm just saying you're *scaring* her, man. I think you should leave her alone.
Or what?
The fuck *you* gonna do about it?
Man, you shittin' yourself *now*, huh?

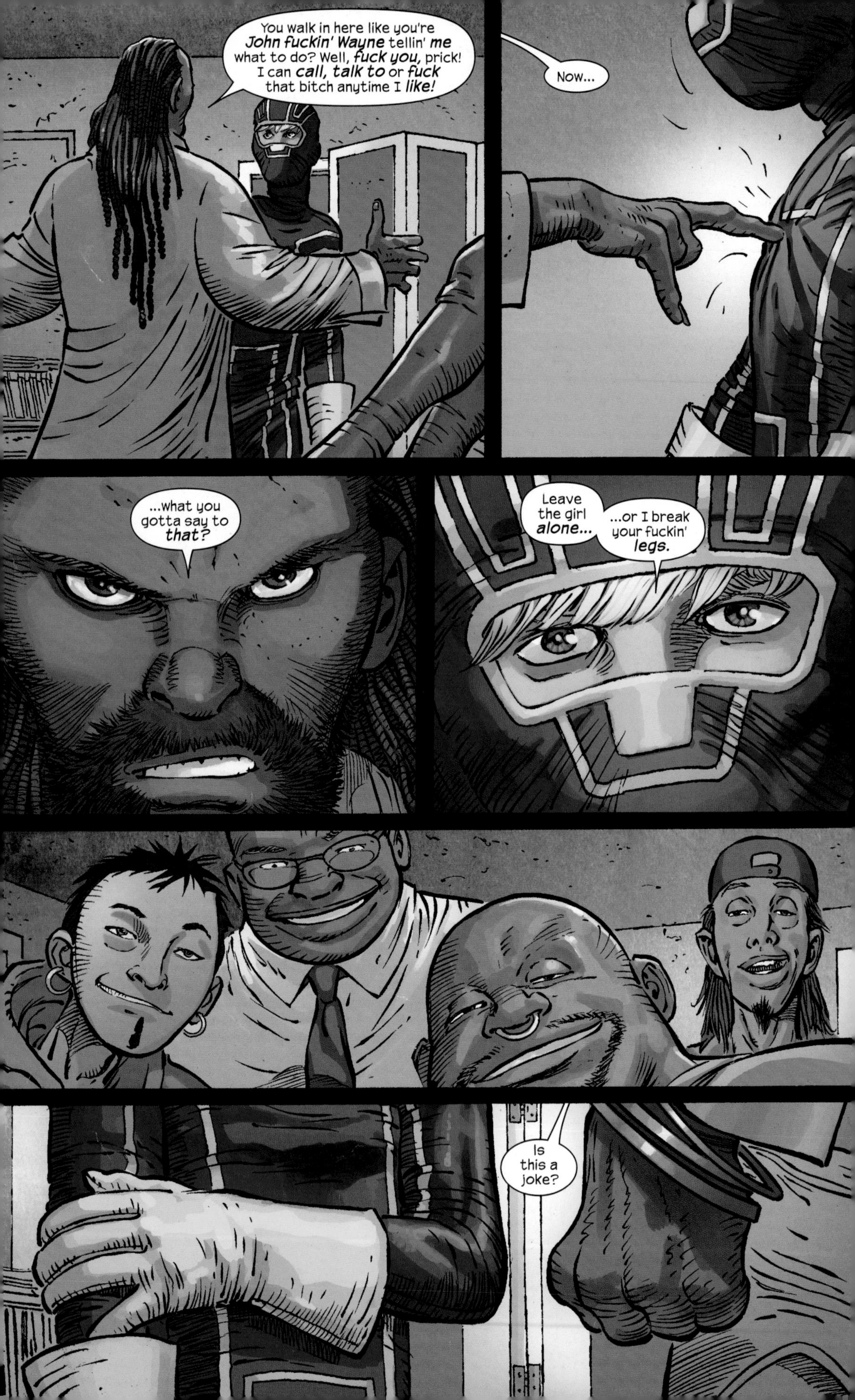
You walk in here like you're John fuckin' Wayne tellin' me what to do? Well, fuck you, prick! I can call, talk to or fuck that bitch anytime I like!
Now...
...what you gotta say to that?
Leave the girl alone...
...or I break your fuckin' legs.
Is this a joke?

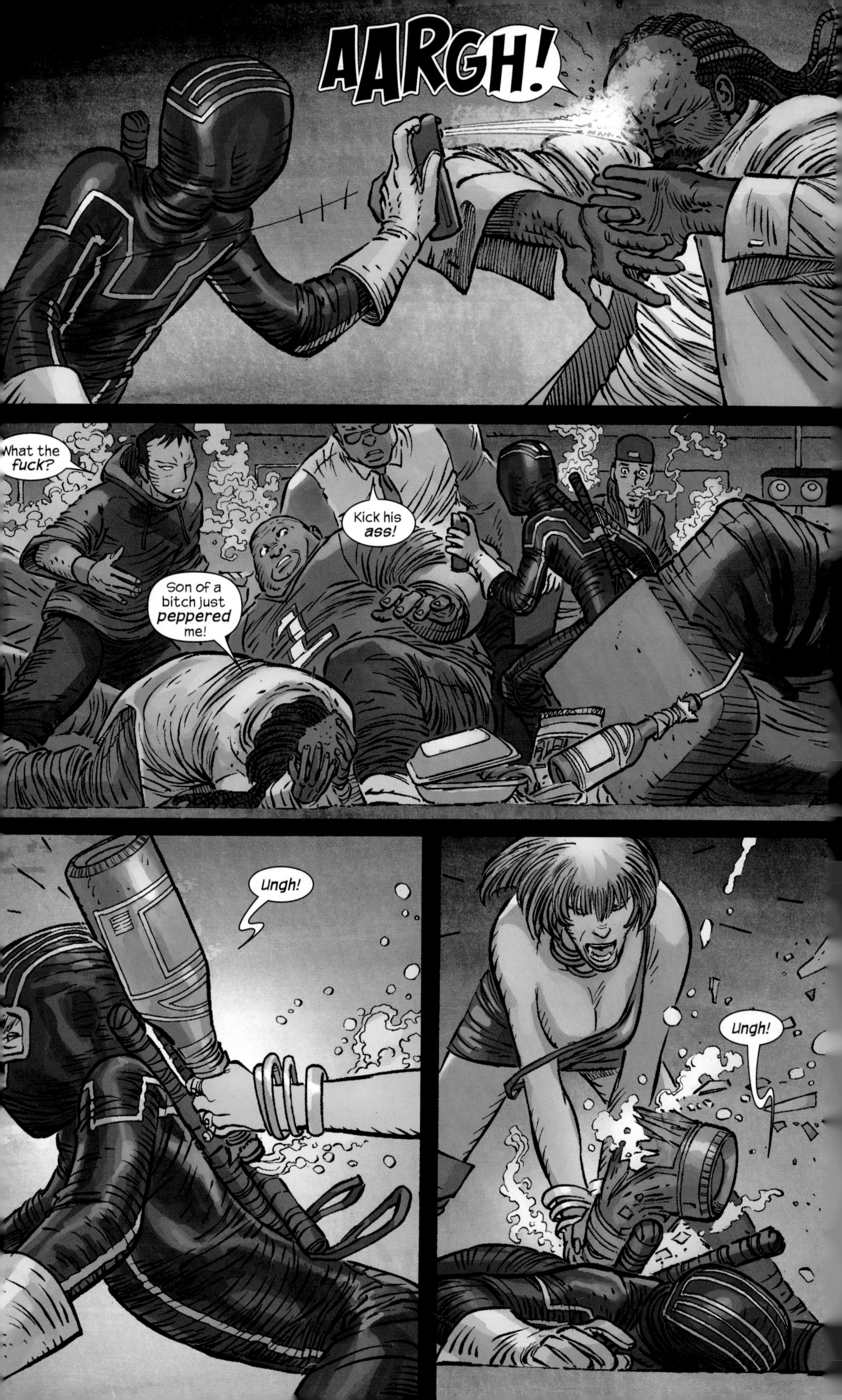
AARGH!
What the fuck?
Kick his ass!
Son of a bitch just peppered me!
Ungh!
Ungh!

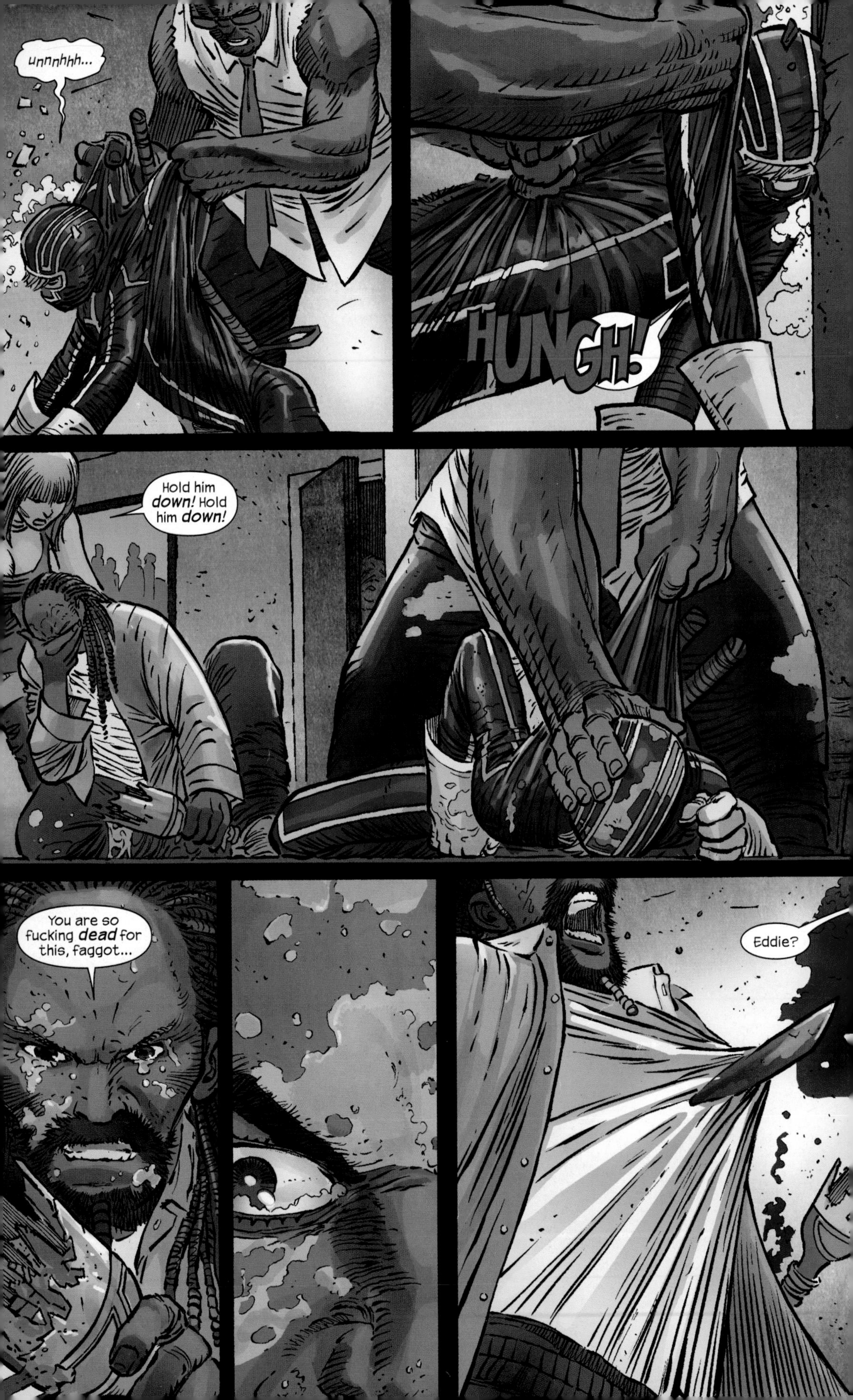
unnnhhh...
HUNGH!
Hold him down! Hold him down!
You are so fucking dead for this, faggot...
Eddie?

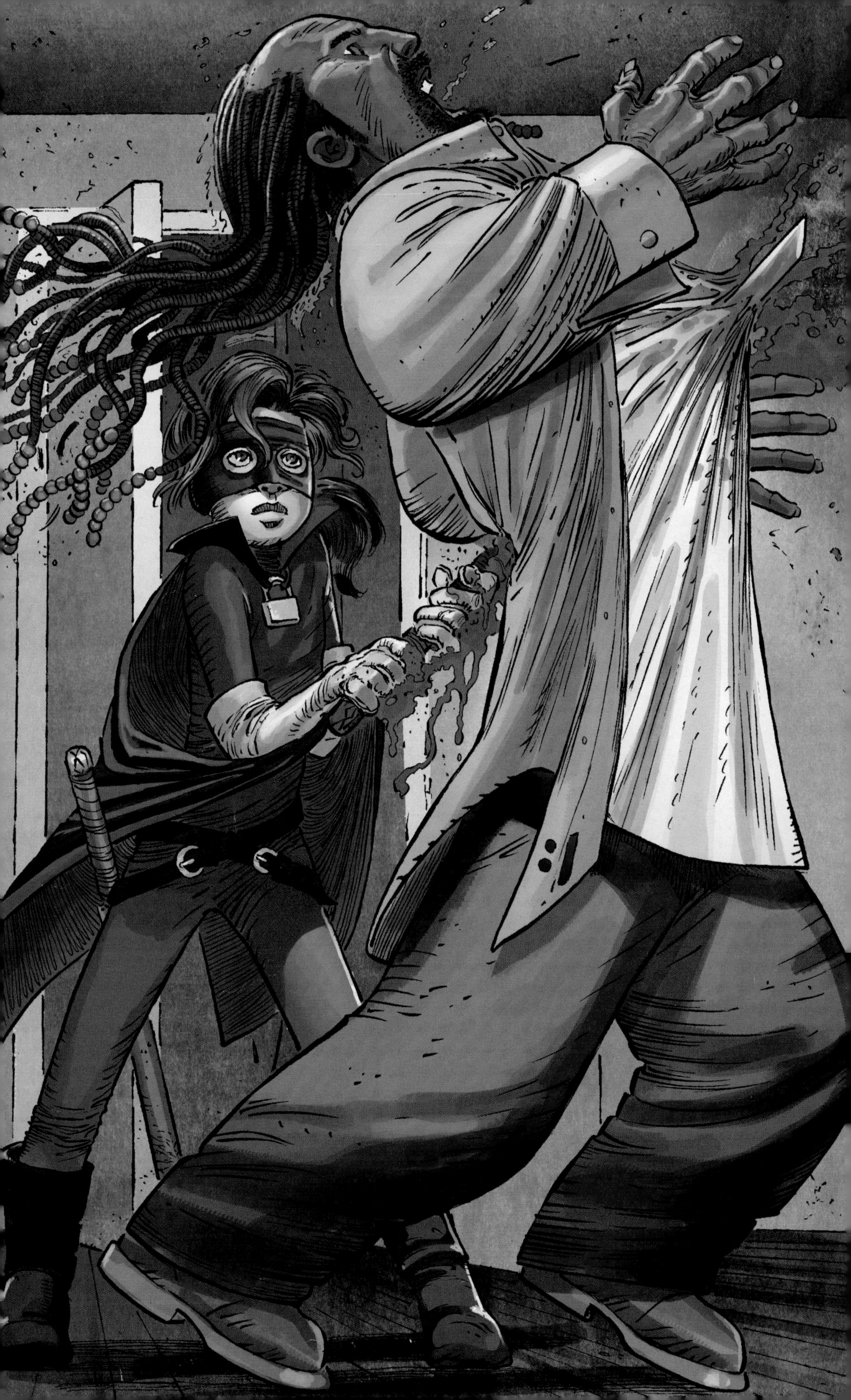

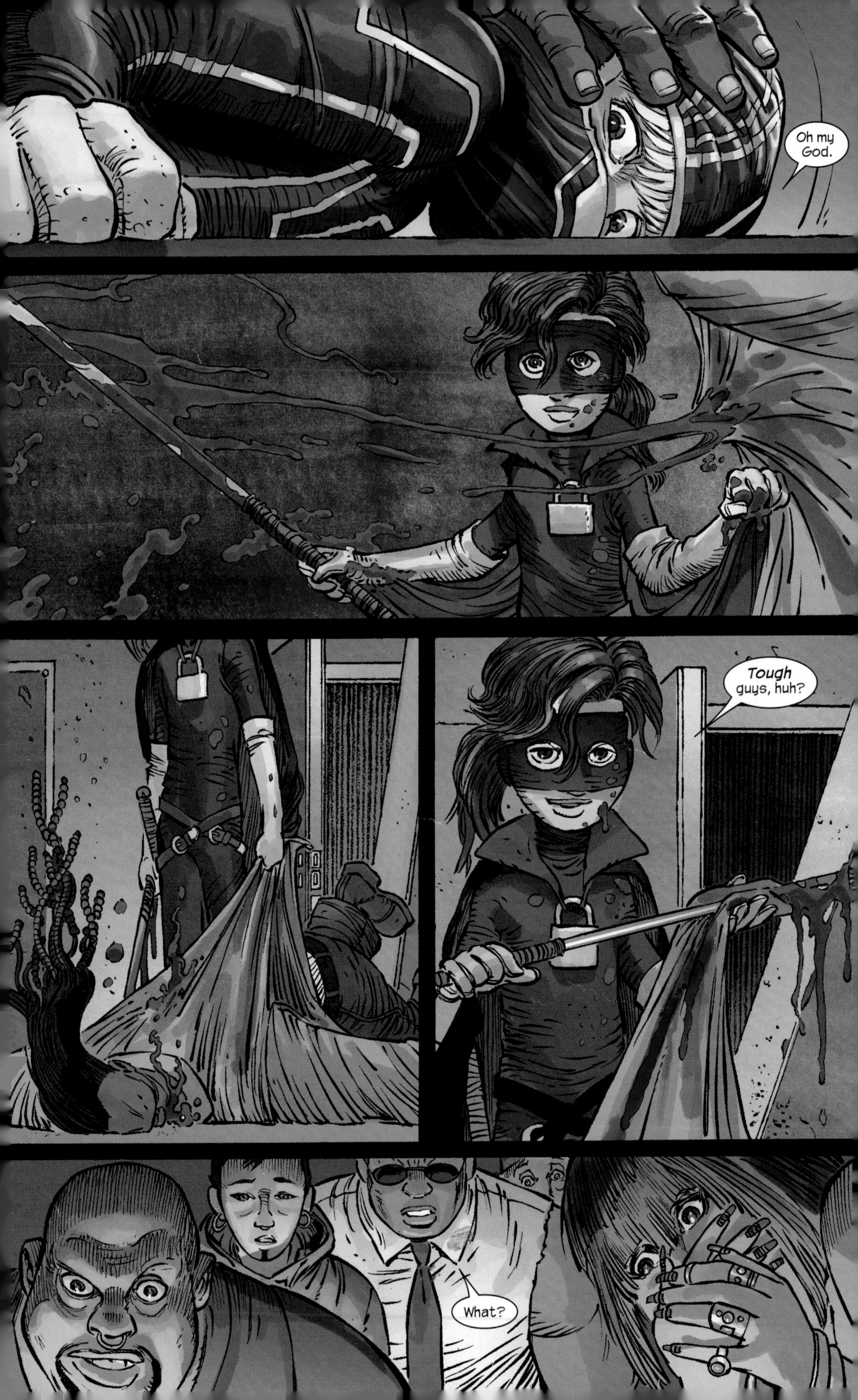

Oh my God.
Tough guys, huh?
What?

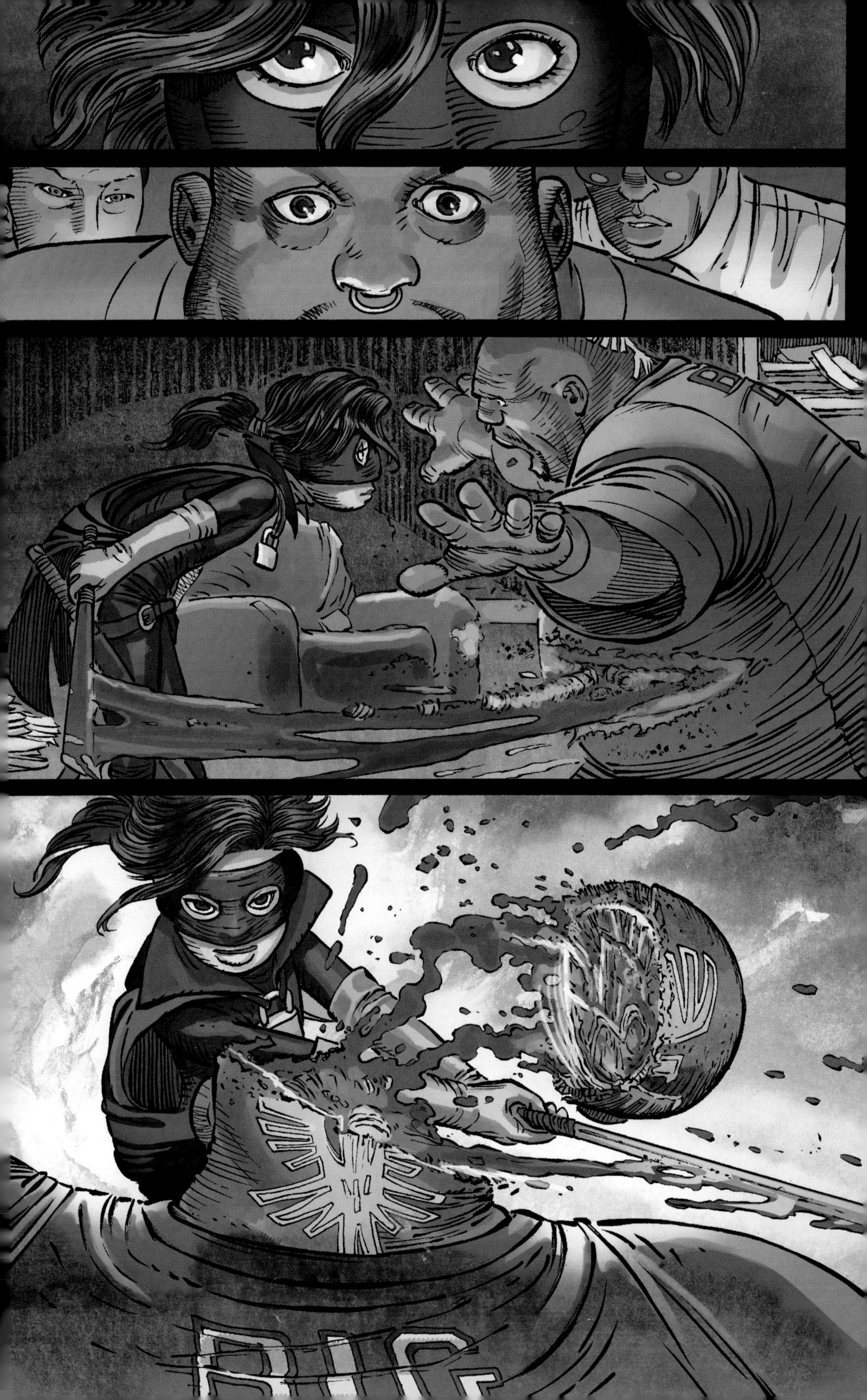

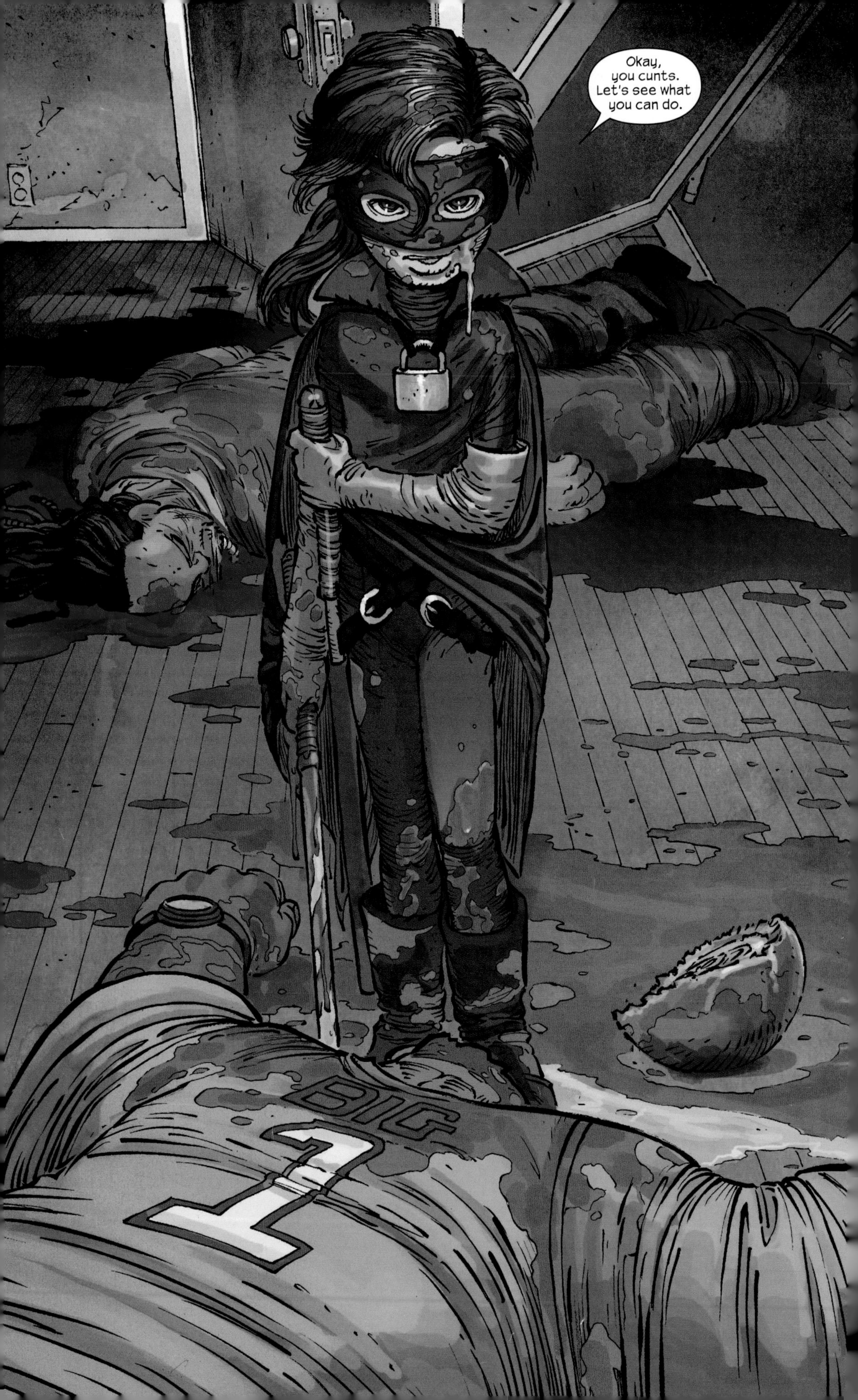
Okay, you cunts. Let's see what you can do.
BIG 1

FOUR

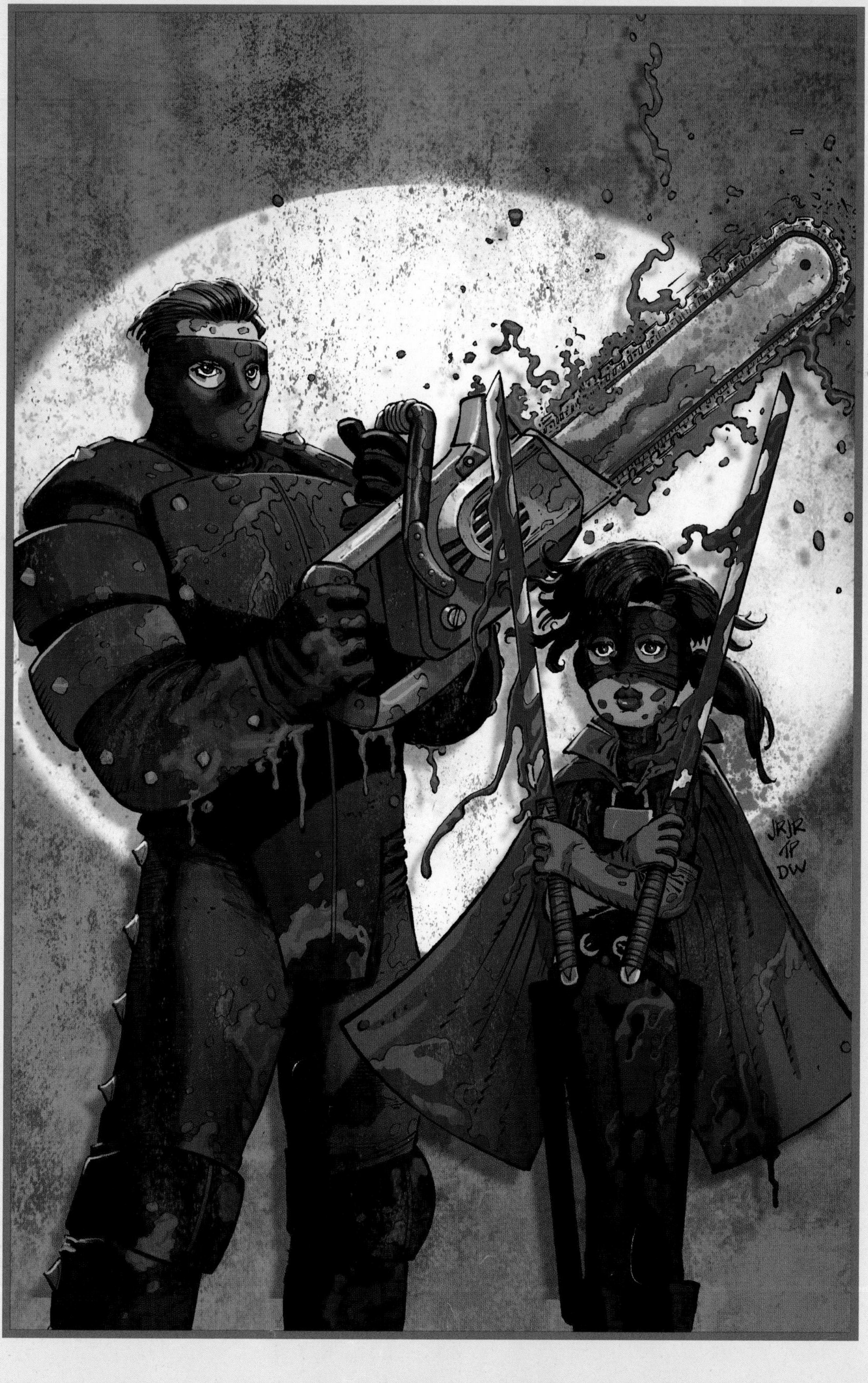
JRJR
TP
DW

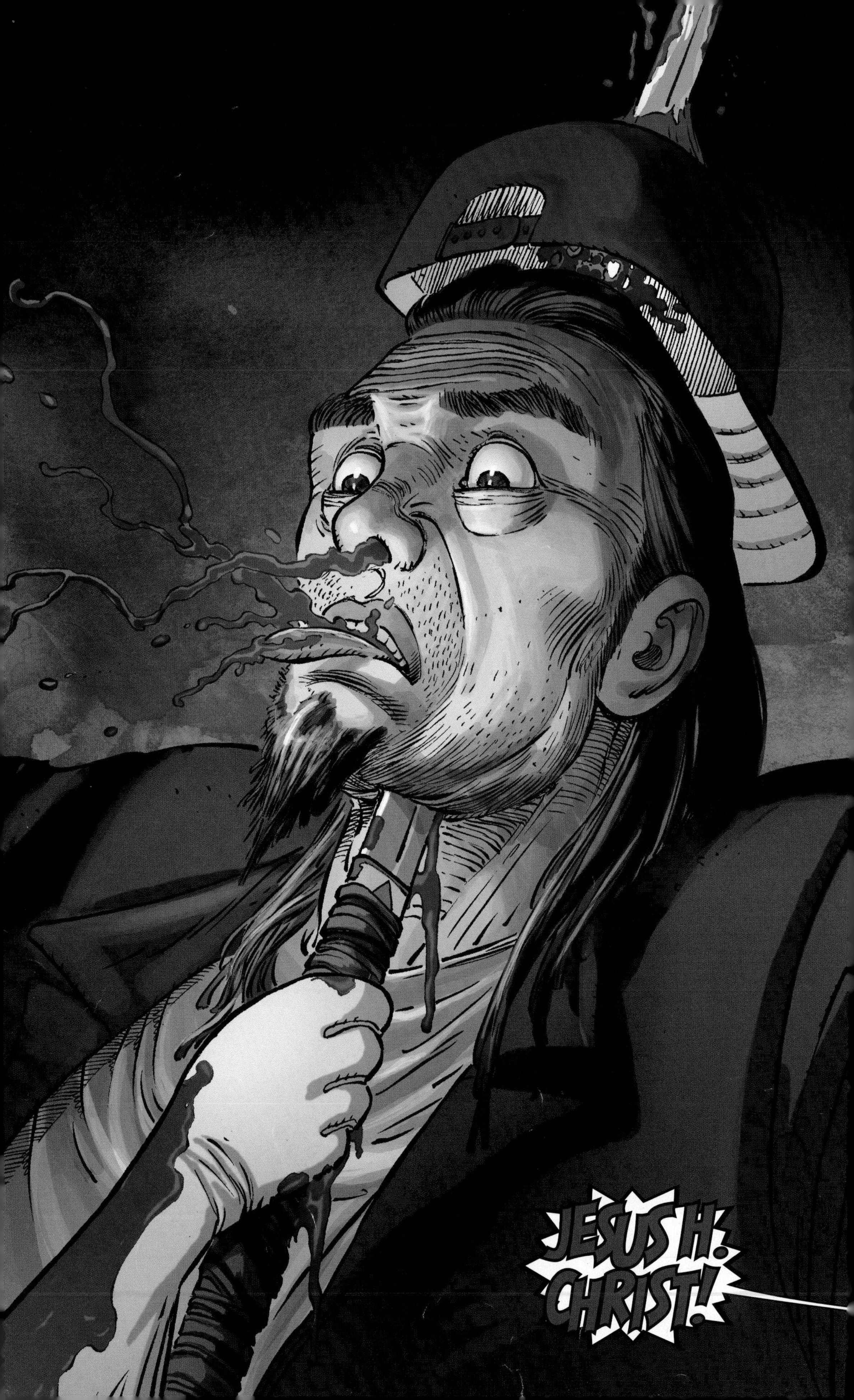
JESUS H. CHRIST!

She was like
John Rambo meets
Polly Pocket.

Dakota Fanning
crossed with
Death Wish 4.

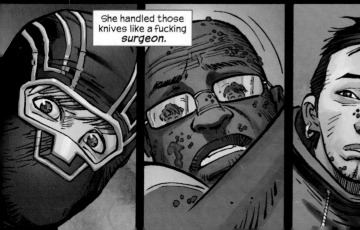

She handled those
knives like a fucking
surgeon.

I still can't
believe she was
only *ten...*

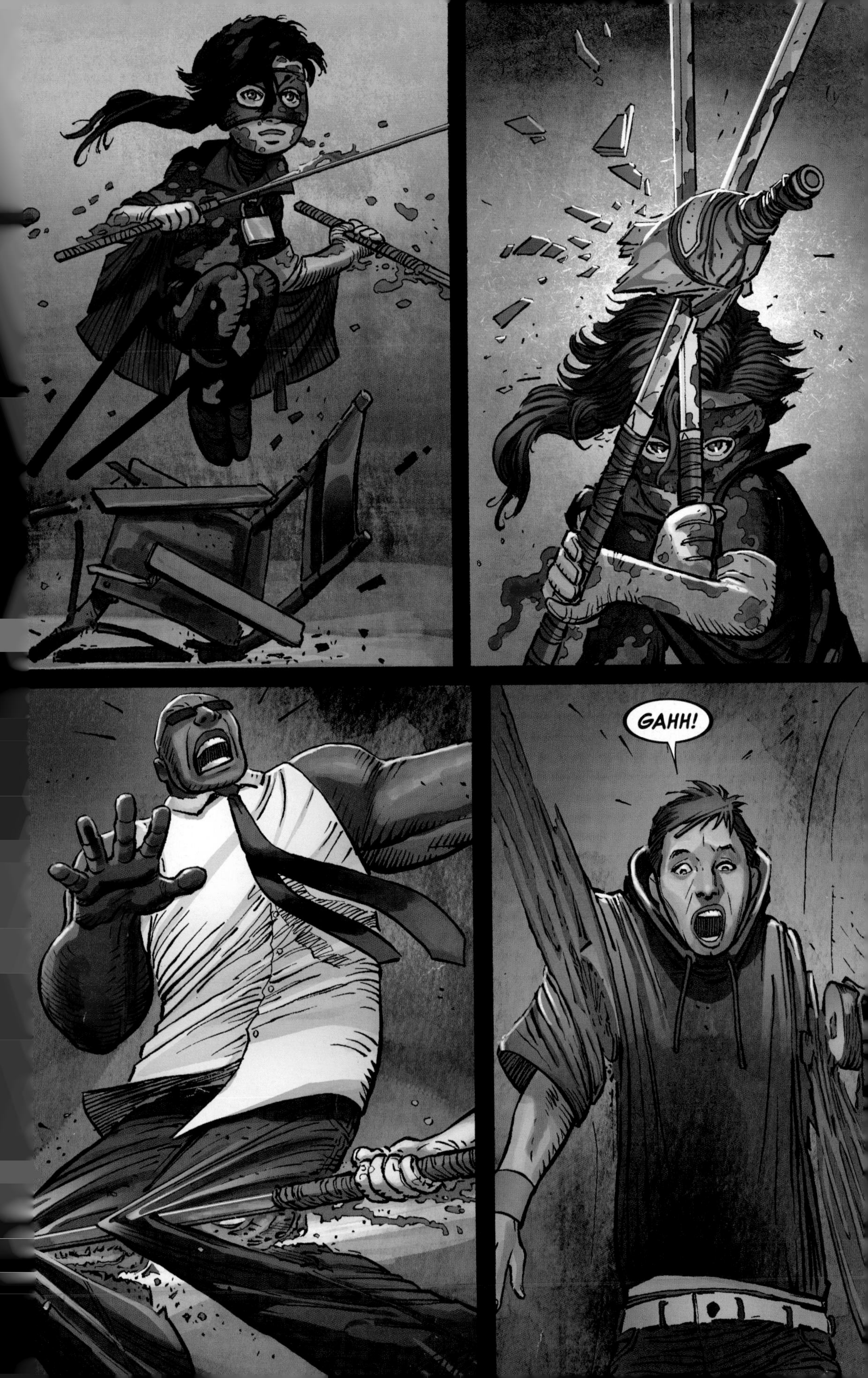
GAHH!

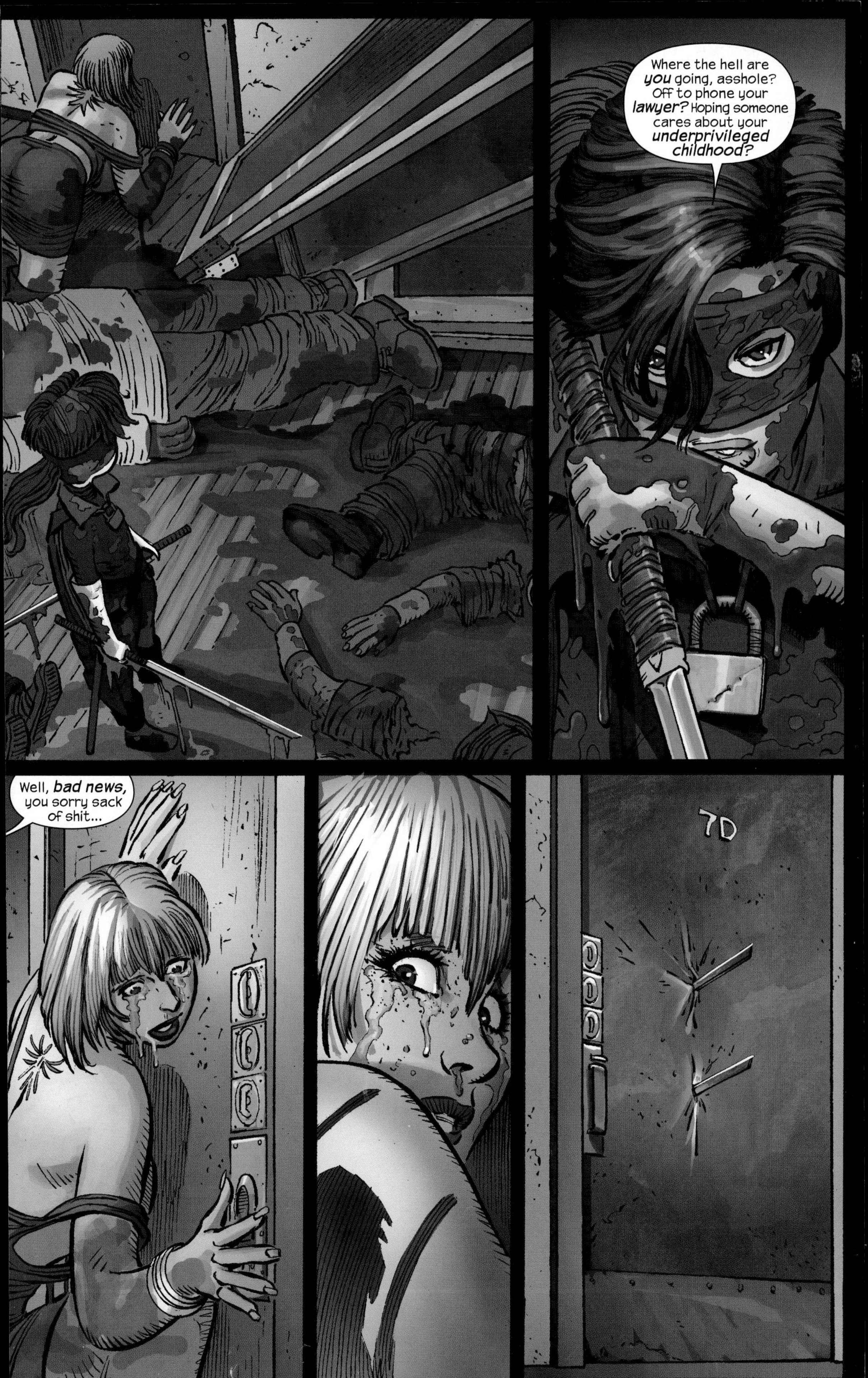
Where the hell are you going, asshole? Off to phone your lawyer? Hoping someone cares about your underprivileged childhood?
Well, bad news, you sorry sack of shit...
7D

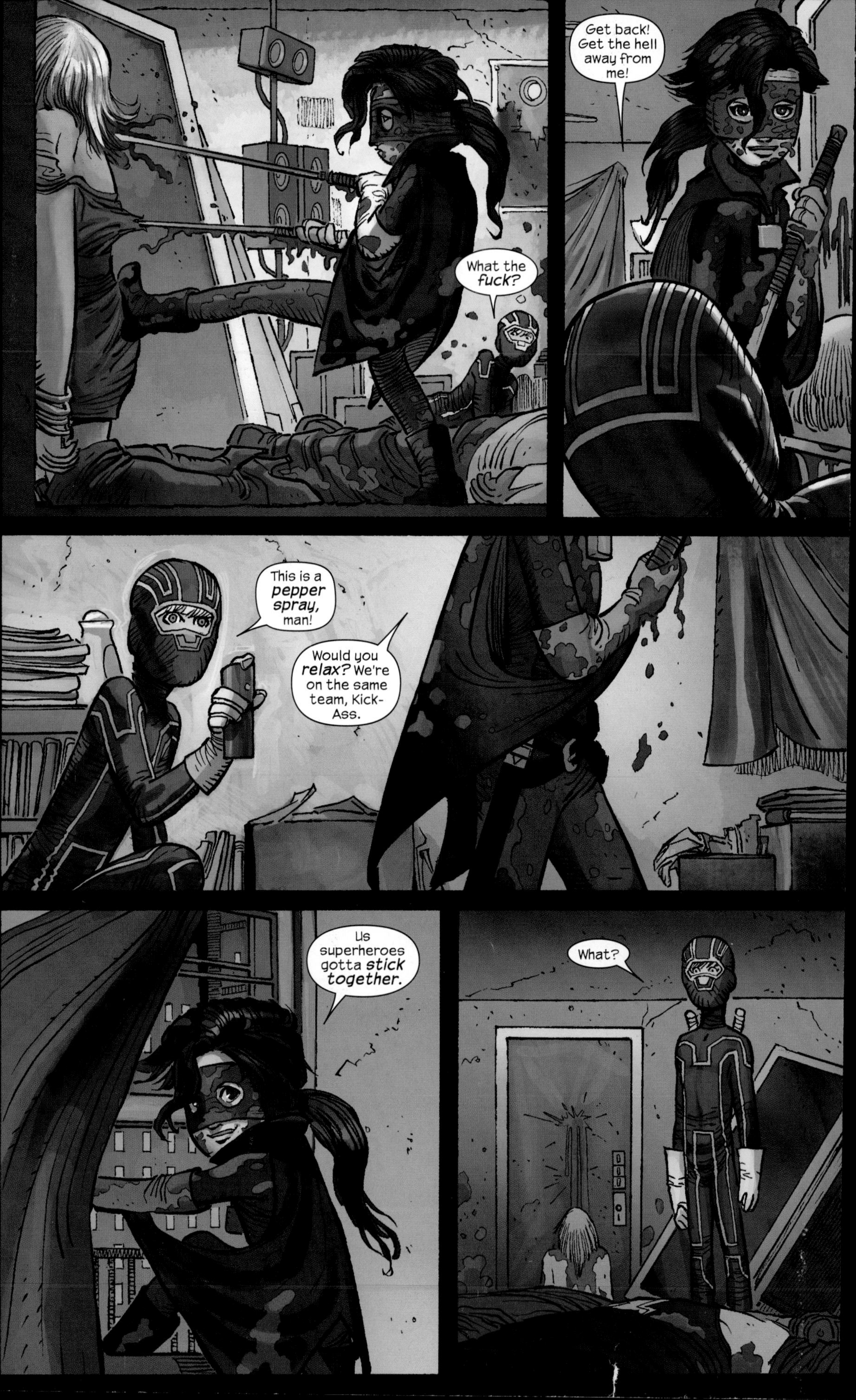

What the *fuck?*
Get back! Get the hell away from me!
This is a *pepper spray,* man!
Would you *relax?* We're on the same team, Kick-Ass.
Us superheroes gotta *stick together.*
What?

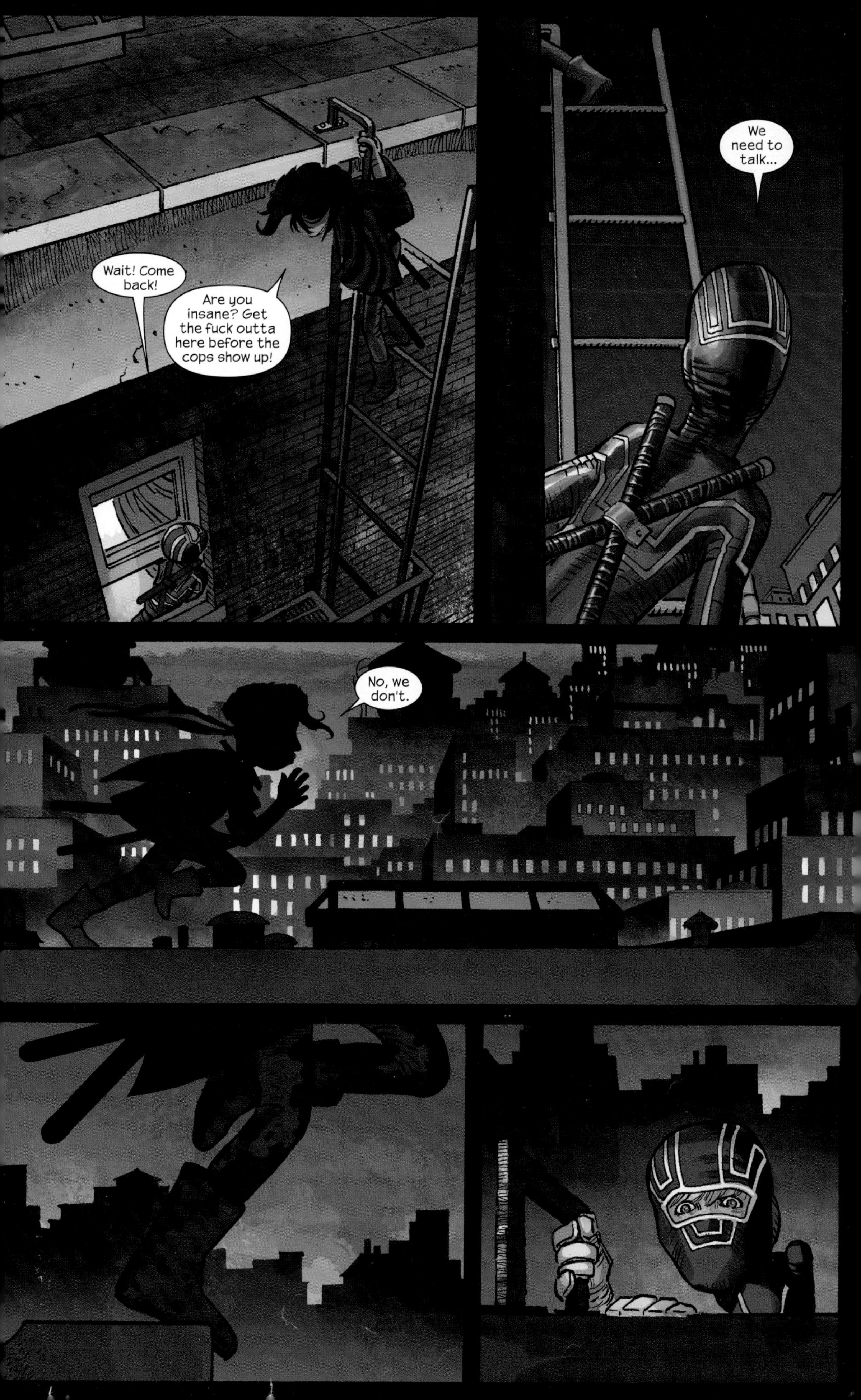
Wait! Come back!
Are you insane? Get the fuck outta here before the cops show up!
We need to talk...
No, we don't.

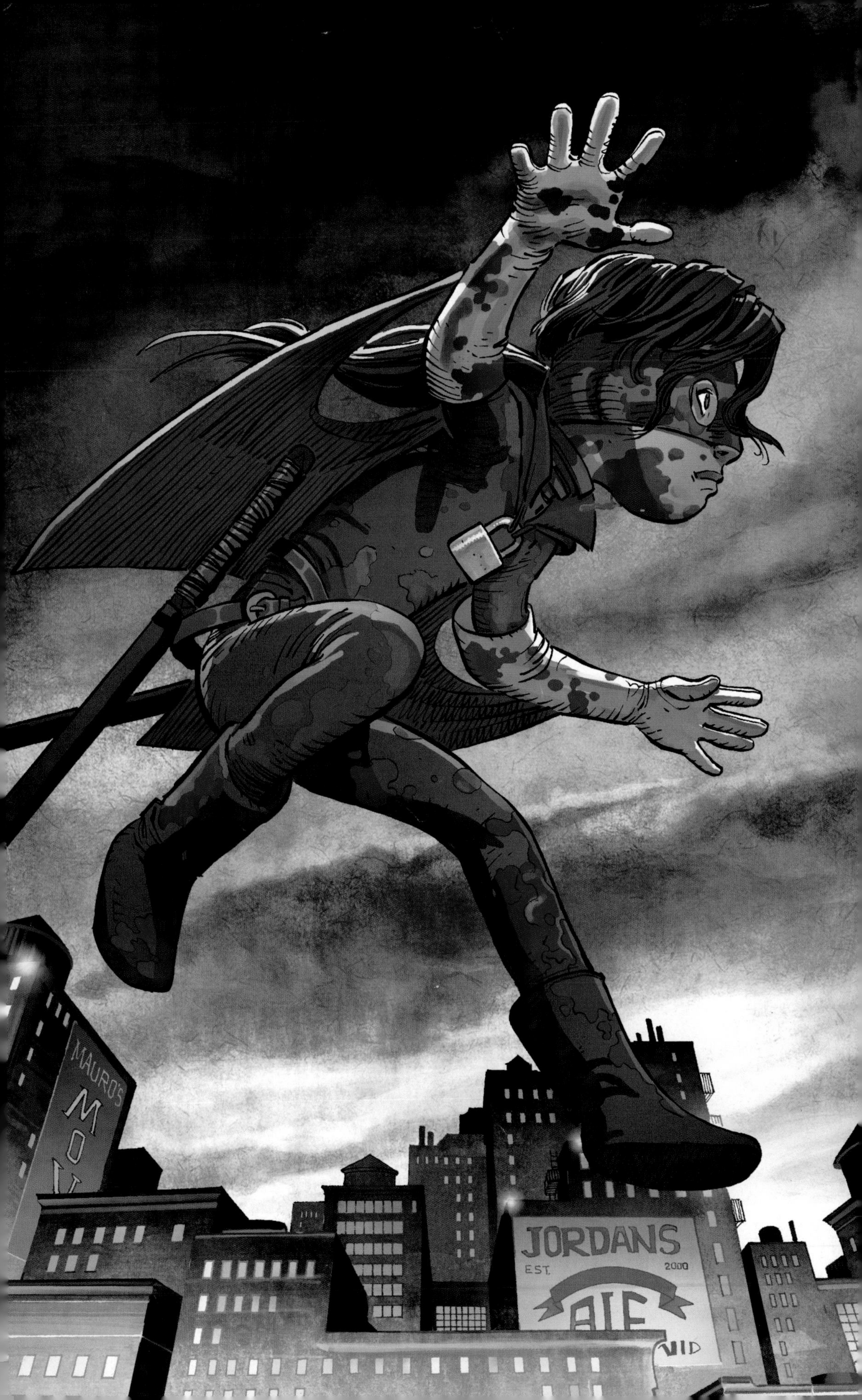
MAURO'S
JORDANS
EST. 2000

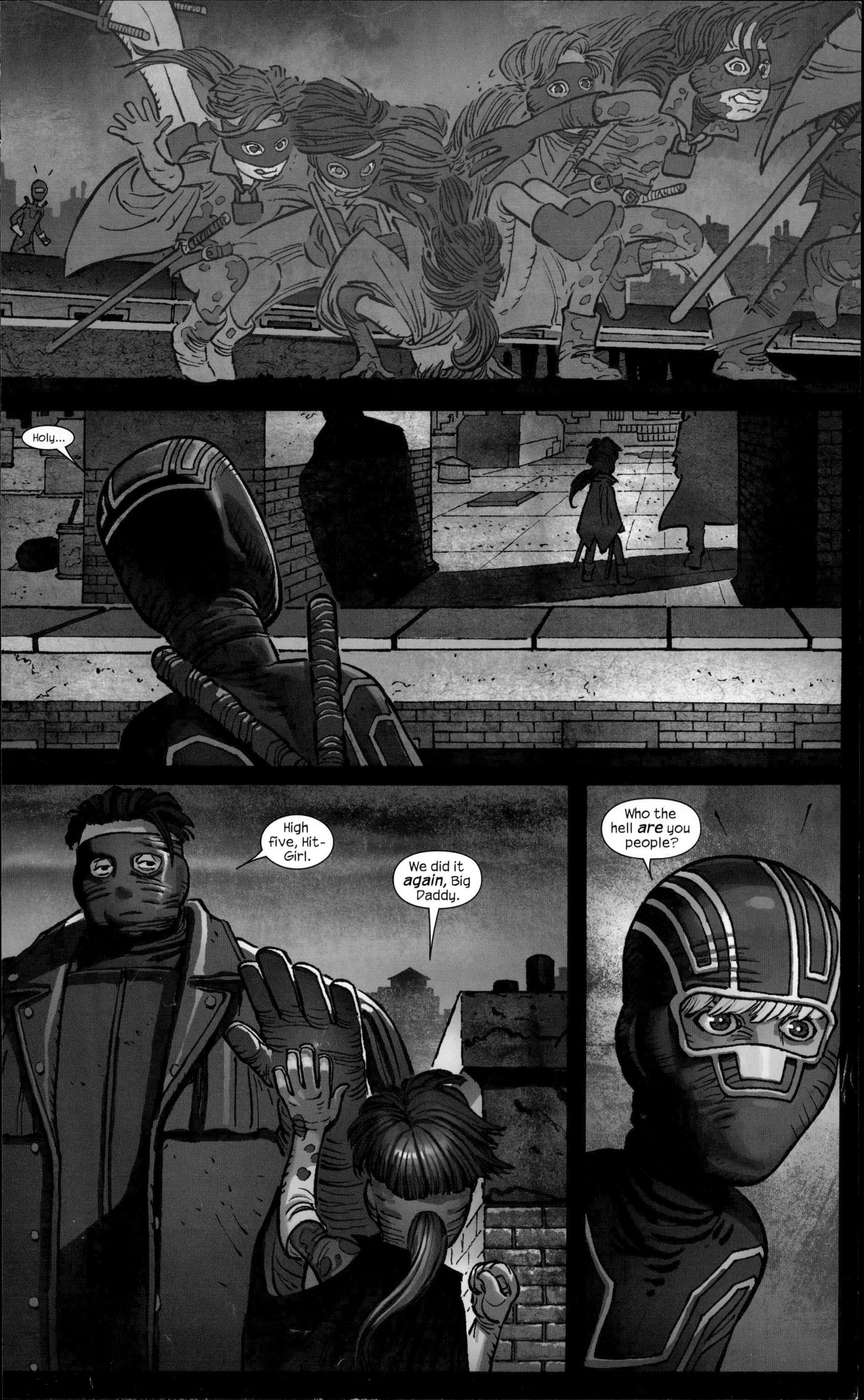
Holy...
High five, Hit-Girl.
We did it again, Big Daddy.
Who the hell are you people?

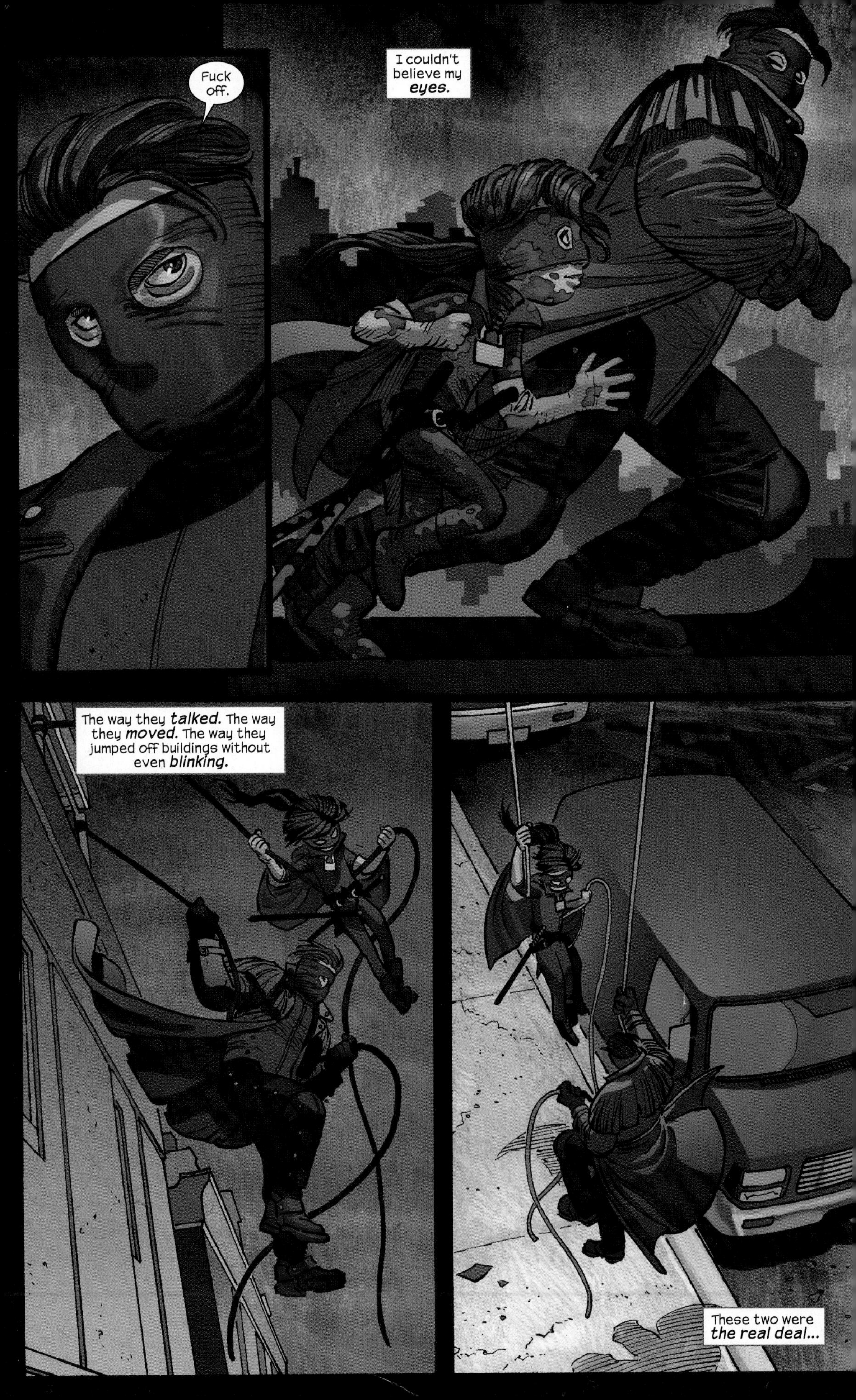

Fuck off.
I couldn't believe my *eyes.*
The way they *talked.* The way they *moved.* The way they jumped off buildings without even *blinking.*
These two were *the real deal...*

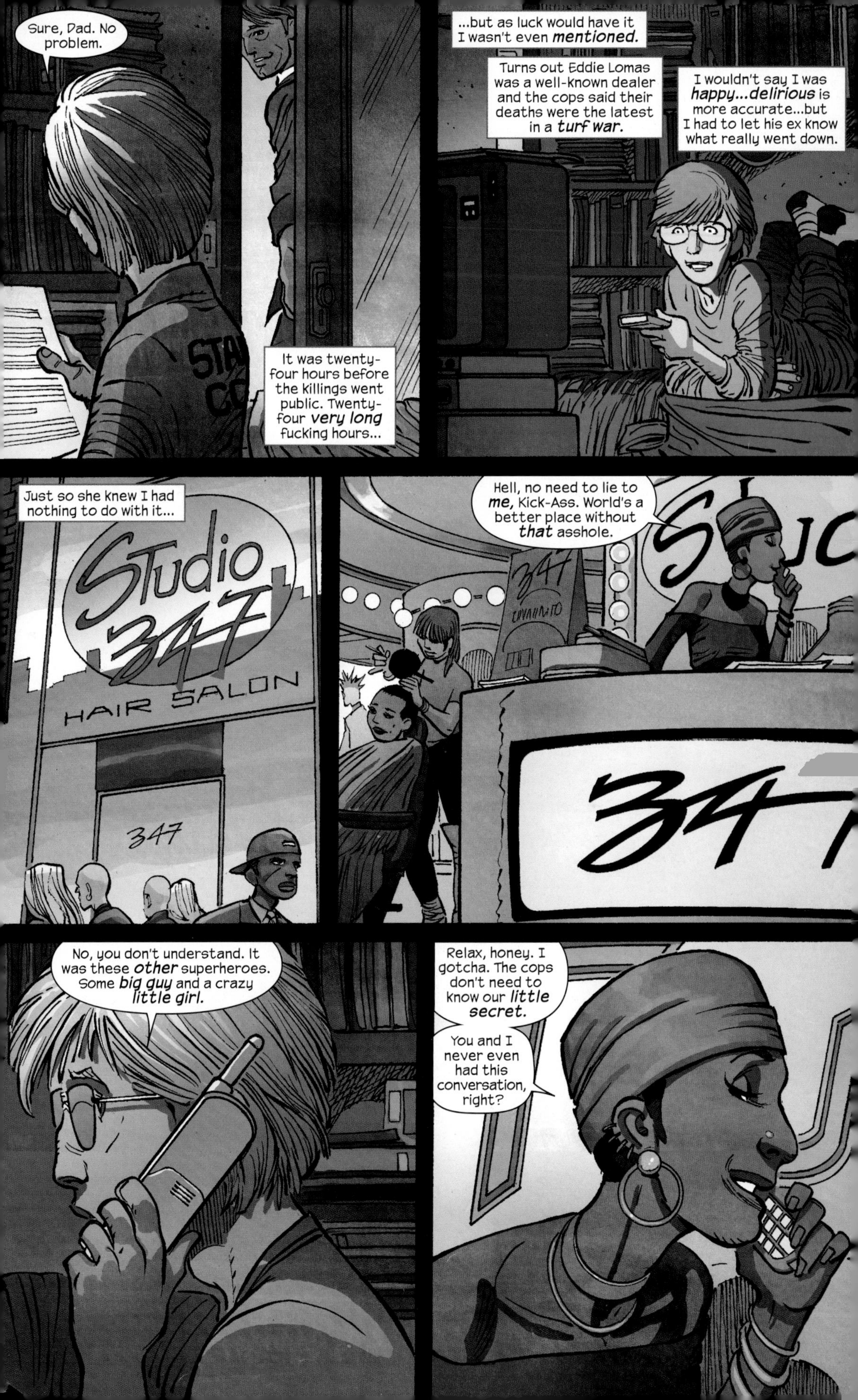
Sure, Dad. No problem.
It was twenty-four hours before the killings went public. Twenty-four very long fucking hours...
...but as luck would have it I wasn't even mentioned.
Turns out Eddie Lomas was a well-known dealer and the cops said their deaths were the latest in a turf war.
I wouldn't say I was happy...delirious is more accurate...but I had to let his ex know what really went down.
Just so she knew I had nothing to do with it...
Studio 347
HAIR SALON
347
Hell, no need to lie to me, Kick-Ass. World's a better place without that asshole.
No, you don't understand. It was these other superheroes. Some big guy and a crazy little girl.
Relax, honey. I gotcha. The cops don't need to know our little secret.
You and I never even had this conversation, right?

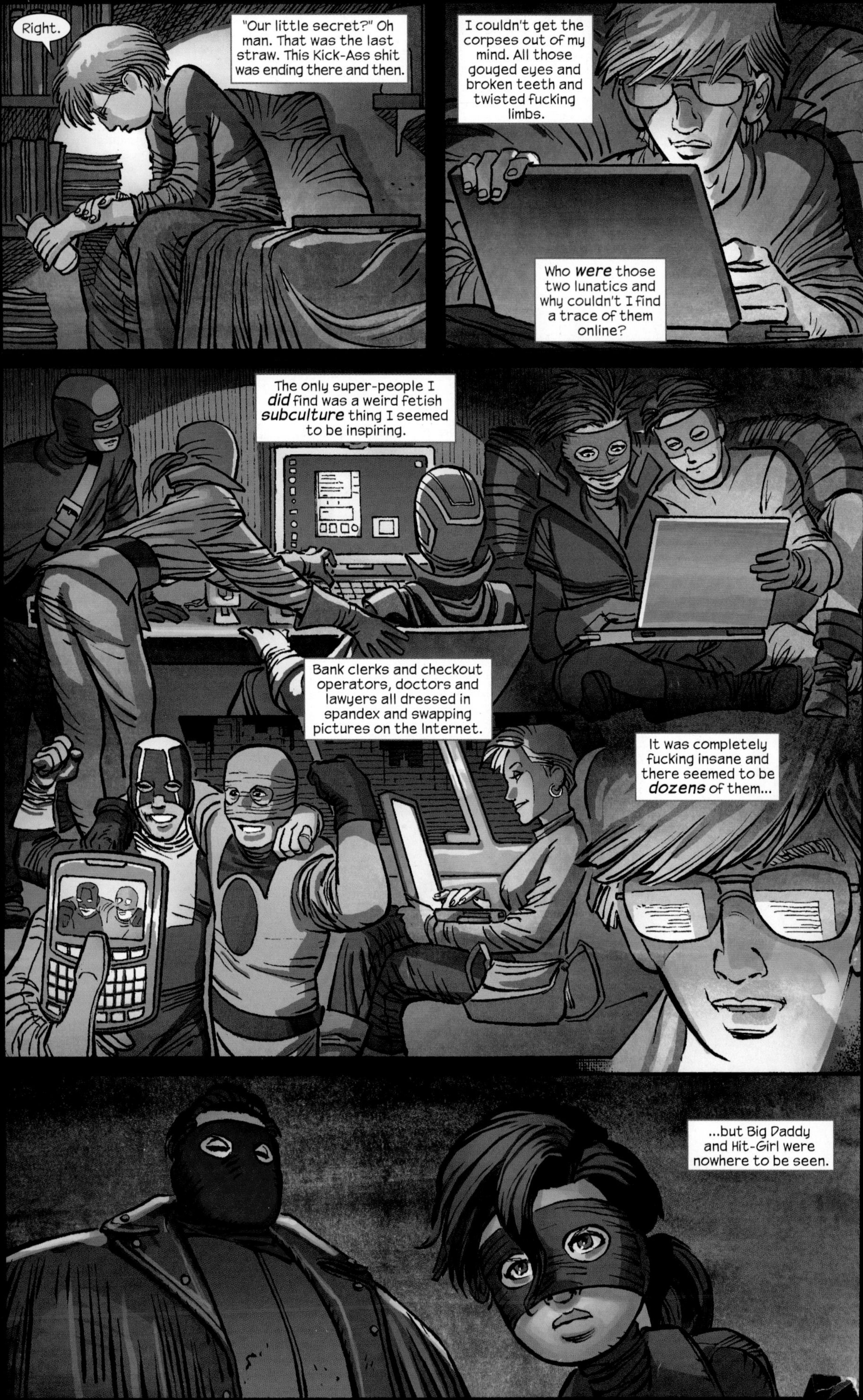
Right.
"Our little secret?" Oh man. That was the last straw. This Kick-Ass shit was ending there and then.
I couldn't get the corpses out of my mind. All those gouged eyes and broken teeth and twisted fucking limbs.
Who *were* those two lunatics and why couldn't I find a trace of them online?
The only super-people I *did* find was a weird fetish *subculture* thing I seemed to be inspiring.
Bank clerks and checkout operators, doctors and lawyers all dressed in spandex and swapping pictures on the Internet.
It was completely fucking insane and there seemed to be *dozens* of them...
...but Big Daddy and Hit-Girl were nowhere to be seen.

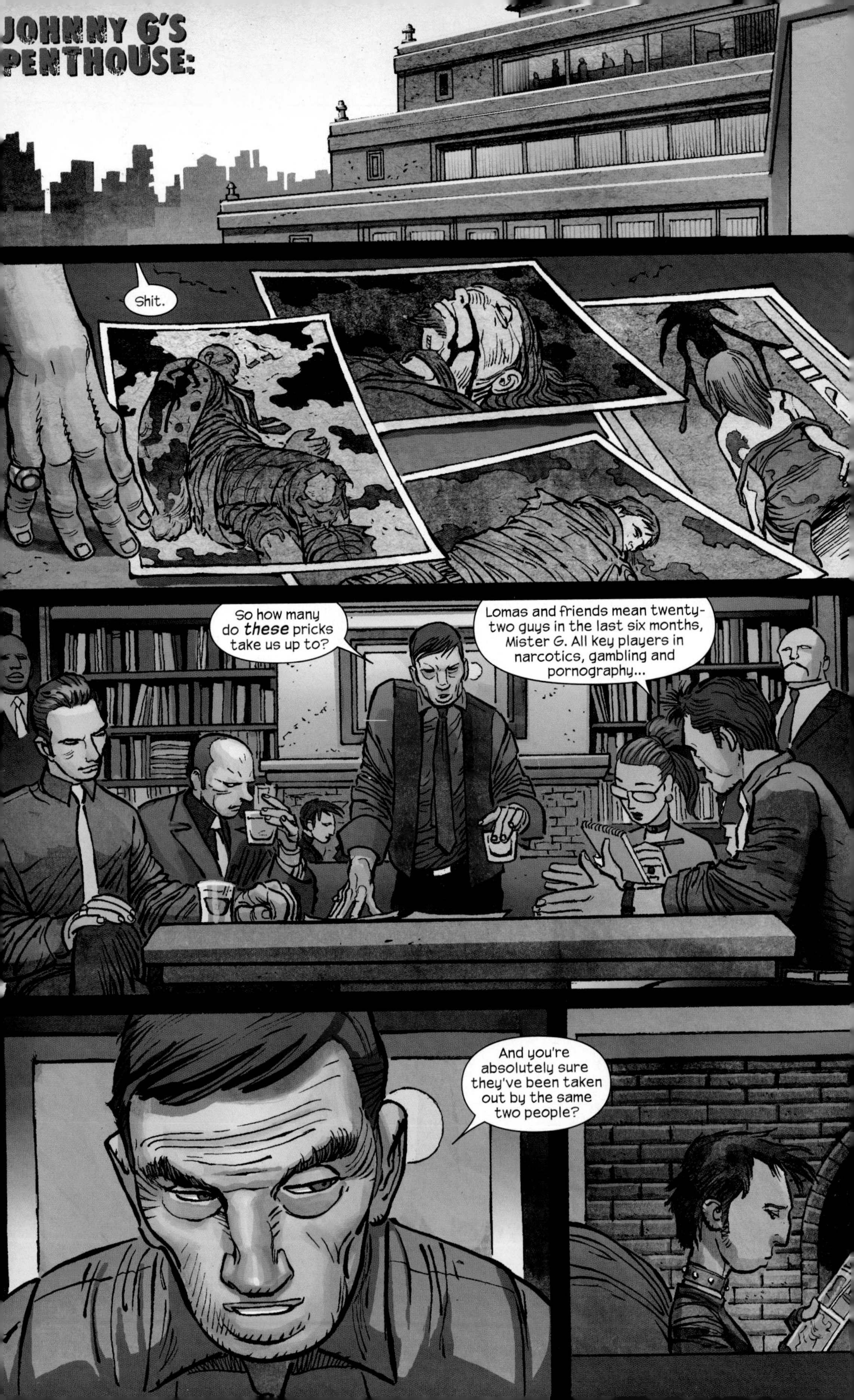
JOHNNY G'S PENTHOUSE:
Shit.
So how many do *these* pricks take us up to?
Lomas and friends mean twenty-two guys in the last six months, Mister G. All key players in narcotics, gambling and pornography...
And you're absolutely sure they've been taken out by the same two people?

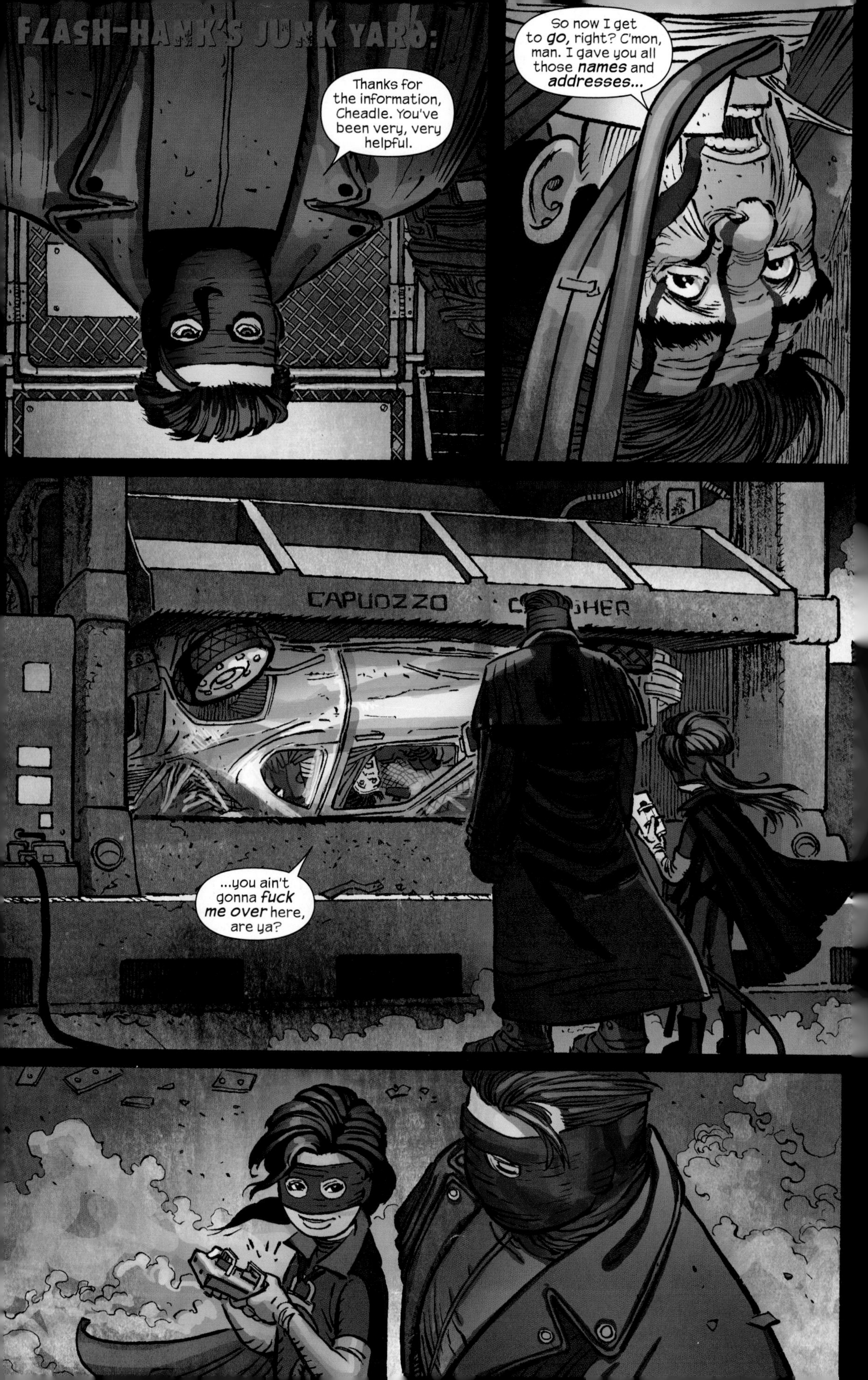
FLASH-HANK'S JUNK YARD:
Thanks for the information, Cheadle. You've been very, very helpful.
So now I get to *go,* right? C'mon, man. I gave you all those *names* and *addresses...*
CAPUOZZO
...you ain't gonna *fuck me over* here, are ya?

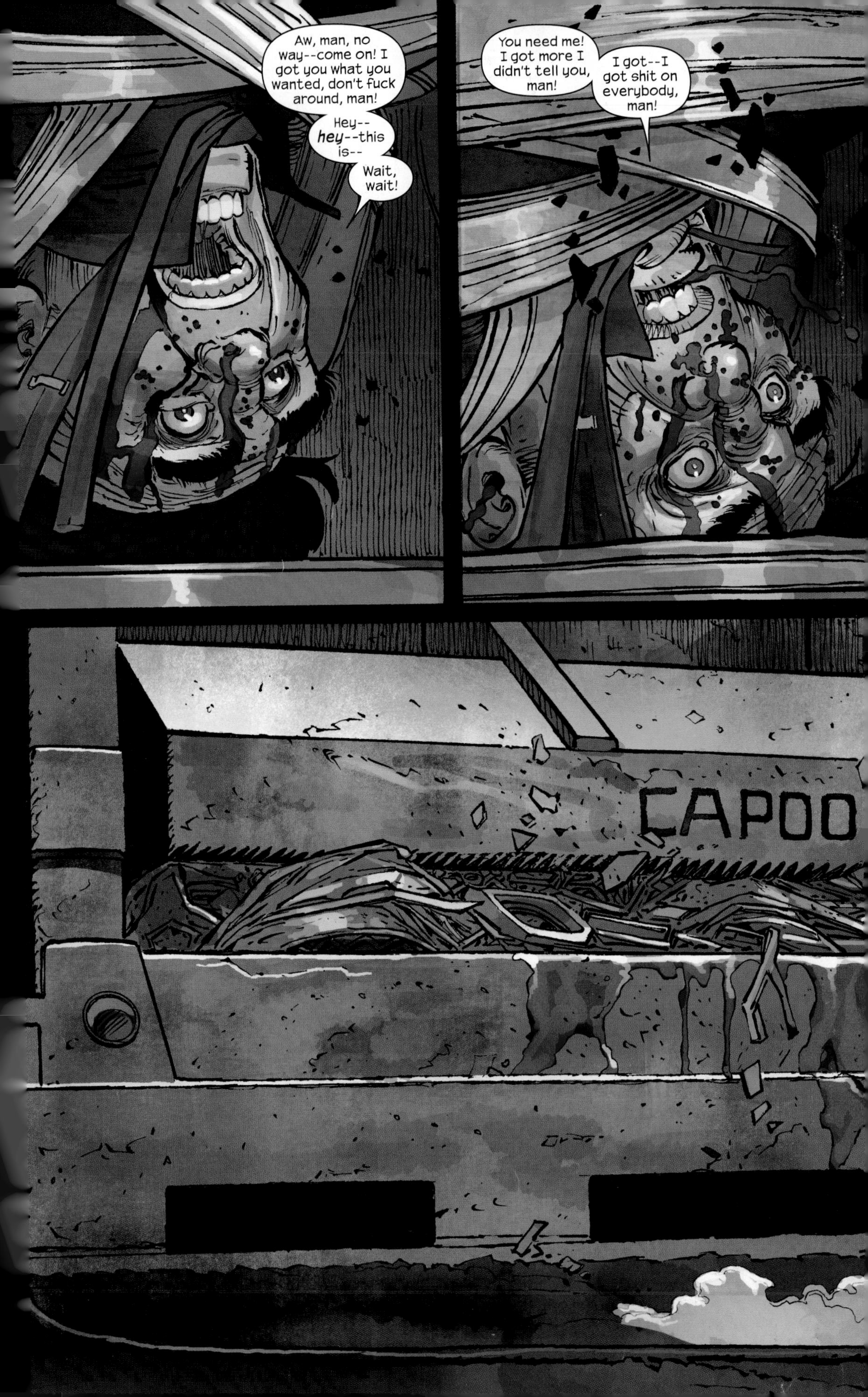
Aw, man, no way--come on! I got you what you wanted, don't fuck around, man!
Hey-- *hey*--this is--
Wait, wait!
You need me! I got more I didn't tell you, man!
I got--I got shit on everybody, man!
CAPOO

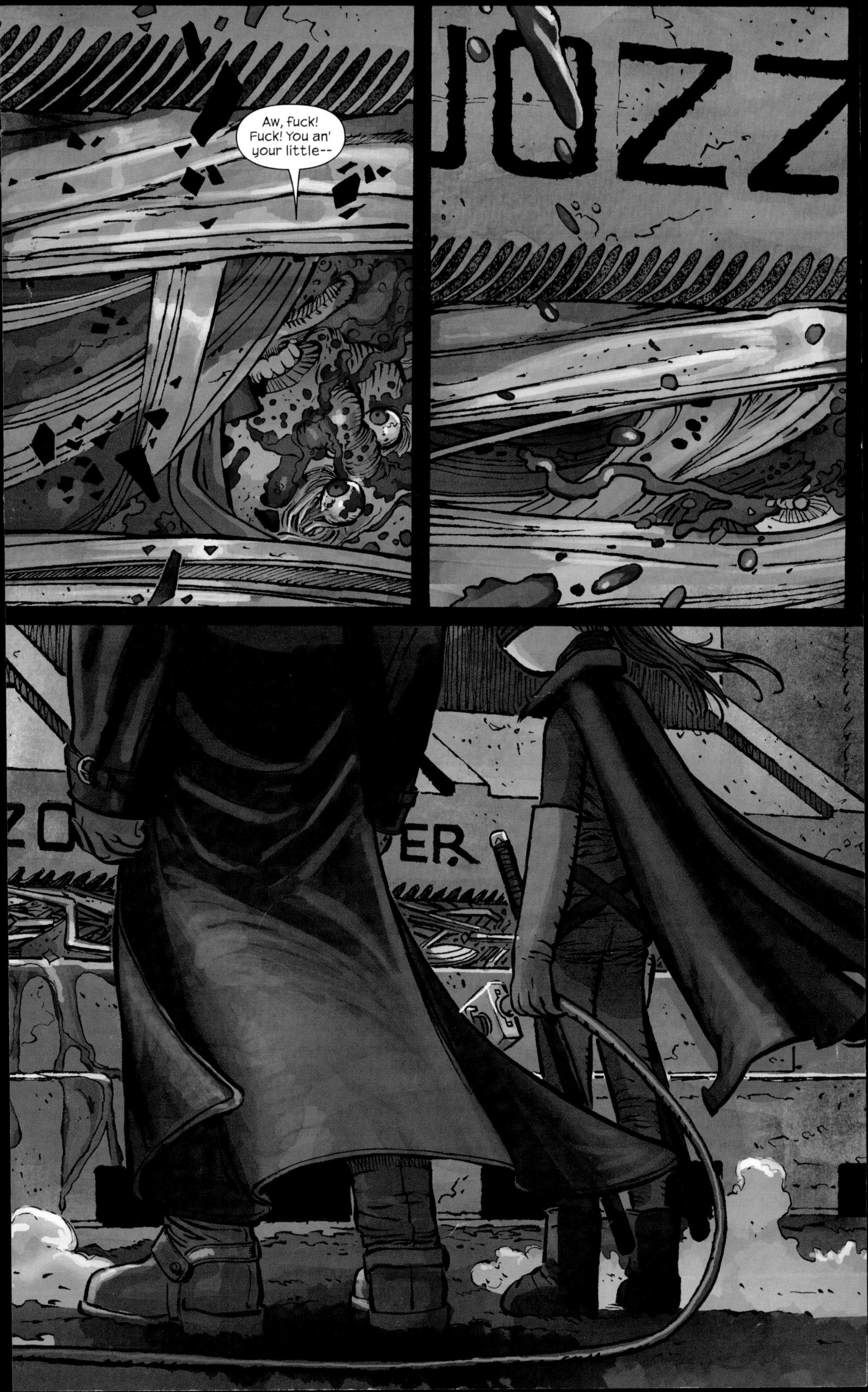
Aw, fuck! Fuck! You an' your little--
JOZZ
ZO
ER

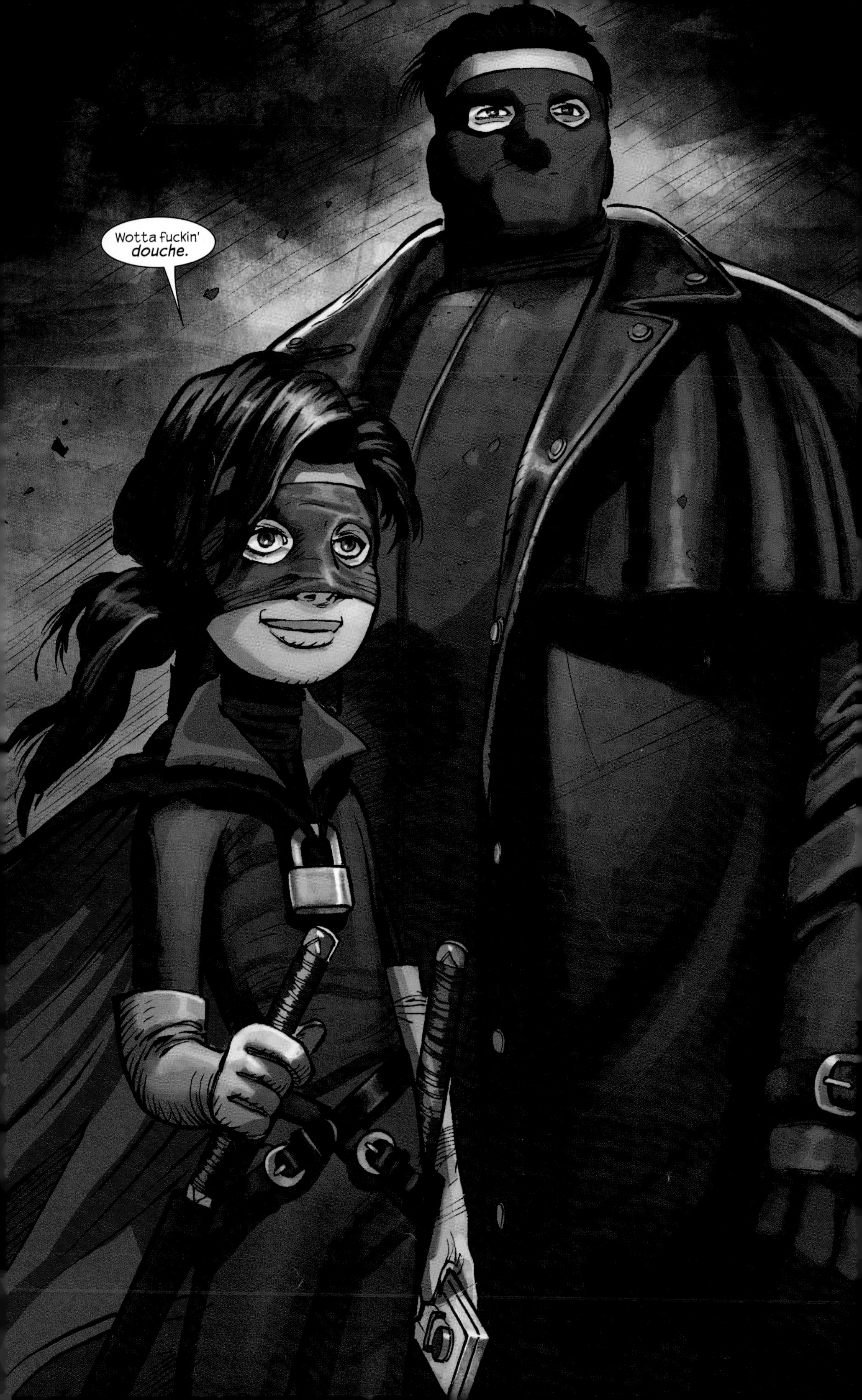
Wotta fuckin' *douche.*

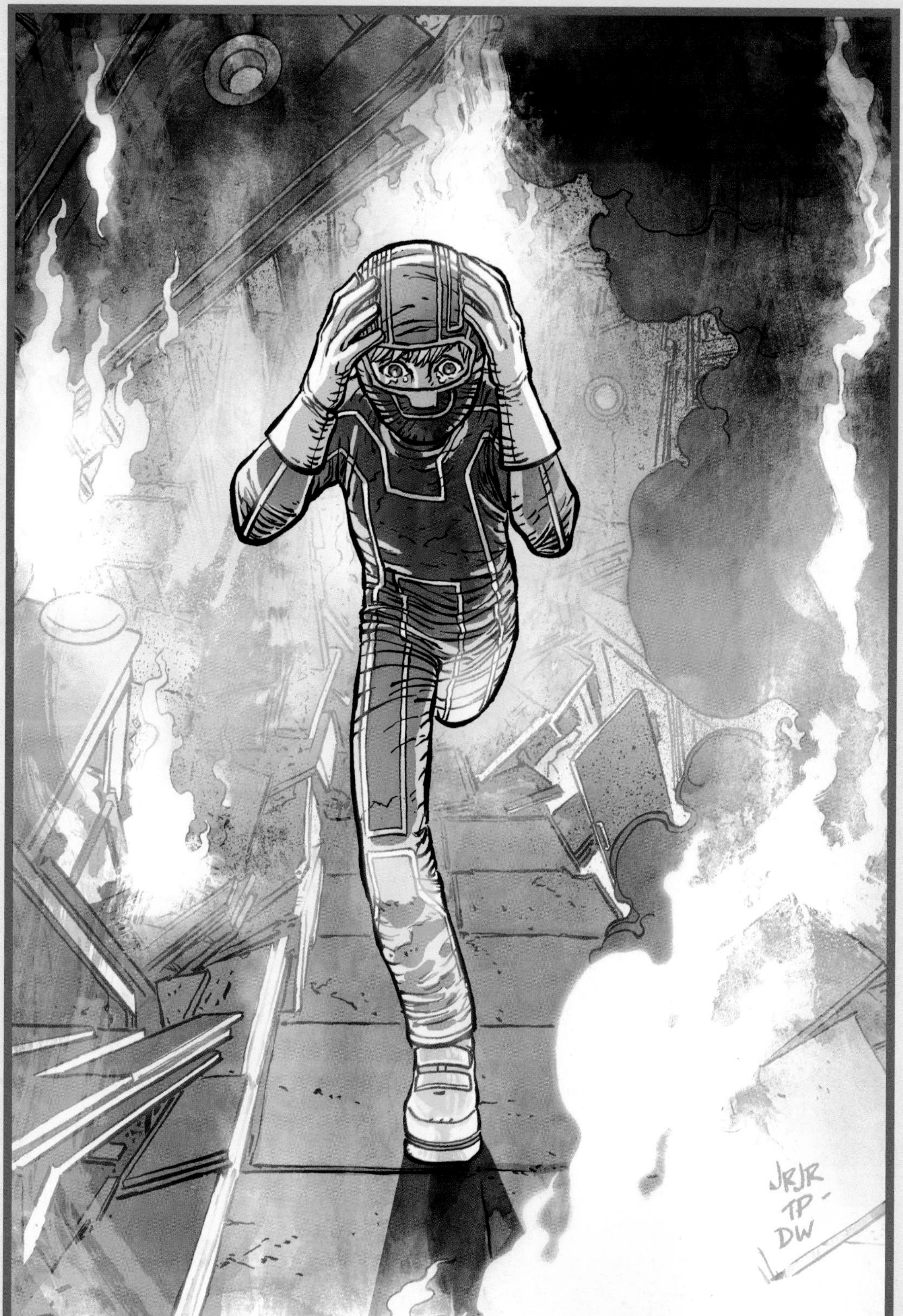
JRJR
TP -
DW

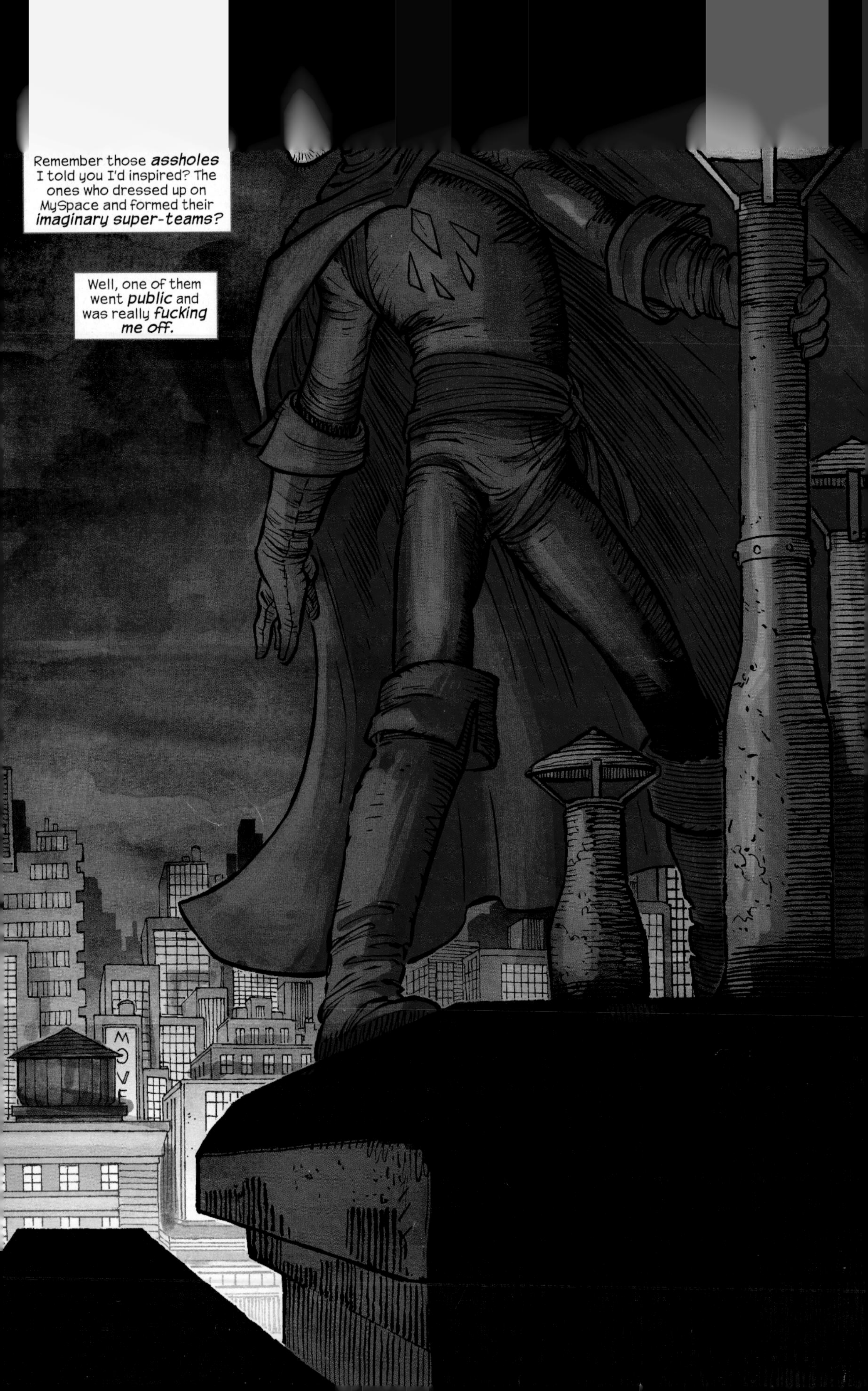
Remember those assholes I told you I'd inspired? The ones who dressed up on MySpace and formed their imaginary super-teams?
Well, one of them went public and was really fucking me off.
MOVE

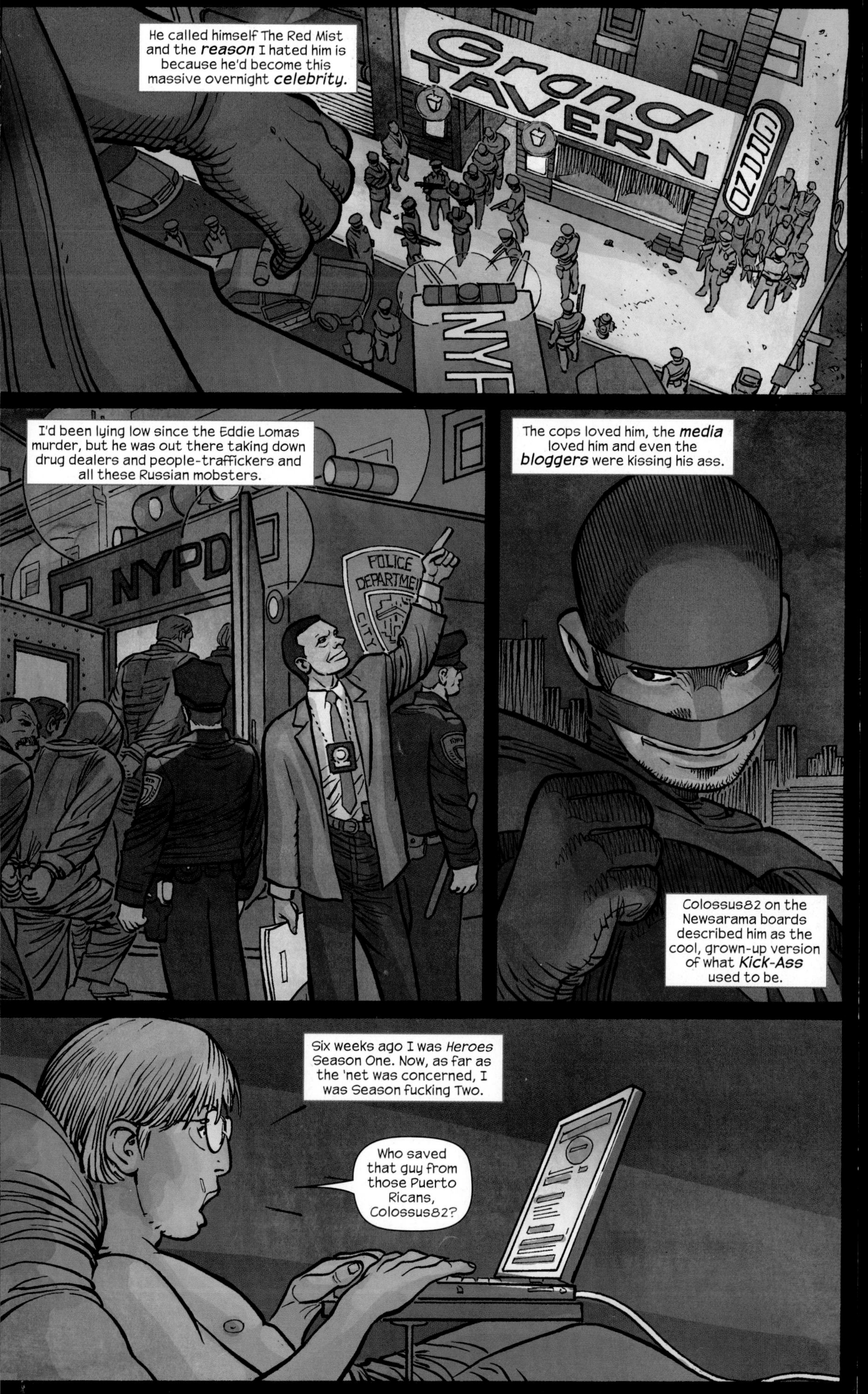
He called himself The Red Mist and the *reason* I hated him is because he'd become this massive overnight *celebrity*.
Grand TAVERN
GRAND
NYPD
I'd been lying low since the Eddie Lomas murder, but he was out there taking down drug dealers and people-traffickers and all these Russian mobsters.
NYPD
POLICE DEPARTMENT CITY
The cops loved him, the *media* loved him and even the *bloggers* were kissing his ass.
Colossus82 on the Newsarama boards described him as the cool, grown-up version of what *Kick-Ass* used to be.
Six weeks ago I was *Heroes* Season One. Now, as far as the 'net was concerned, I was Season fucking Two.
Who saved that guy from those Puerto Ricans, Colossus82?

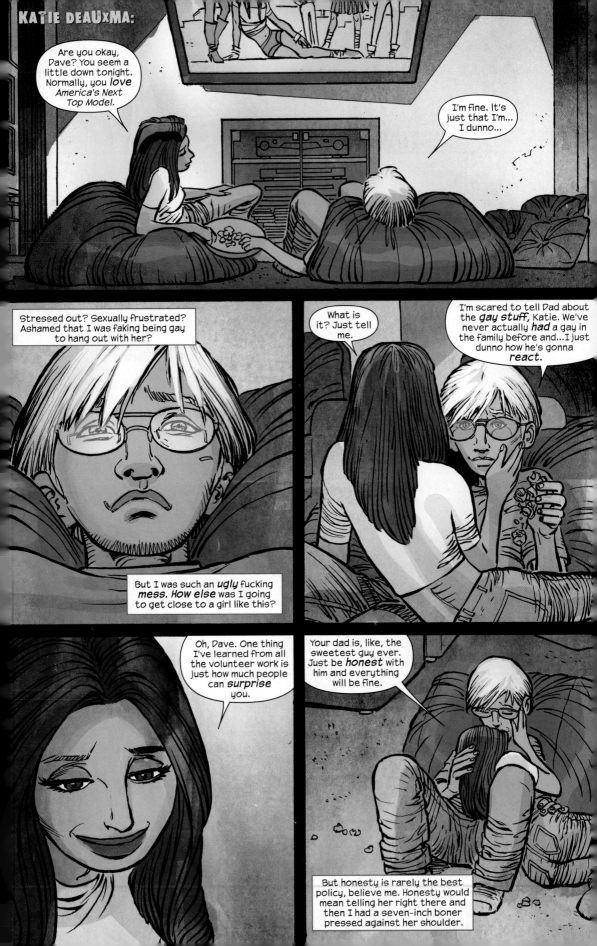

KATIE DEAUxMA:

Are you okay, Dave? You seem a little down tonight. Normally, you *love* America's Next Top Model.

I'm fine. It's just that I'm... I dunno...

Stressed out? Sexually frustrated? Ashamed that I was faking being gay to hang out with her?

But I was such an *ugly* fucking *mess*. *How else* was I going to get close to a girl like this?

What is it? Just tell me.

I'm scared to tell Dad about the *gay stuff*, Katie. We've never actually *had* a gay in the family before and...I just dunno how he's gonna *react*.

Oh, Dave. One thing I've learned from all the volunteer work is just how much people can *surprise* you.

Your dad is, like, the sweetest guy ever. Just be *honest* with him and everything will be fine.

But honesty is rarely the best policy, believe me. Honesty would mean telling her right there and then I had a seven-inch boner pressed against her shoulder.

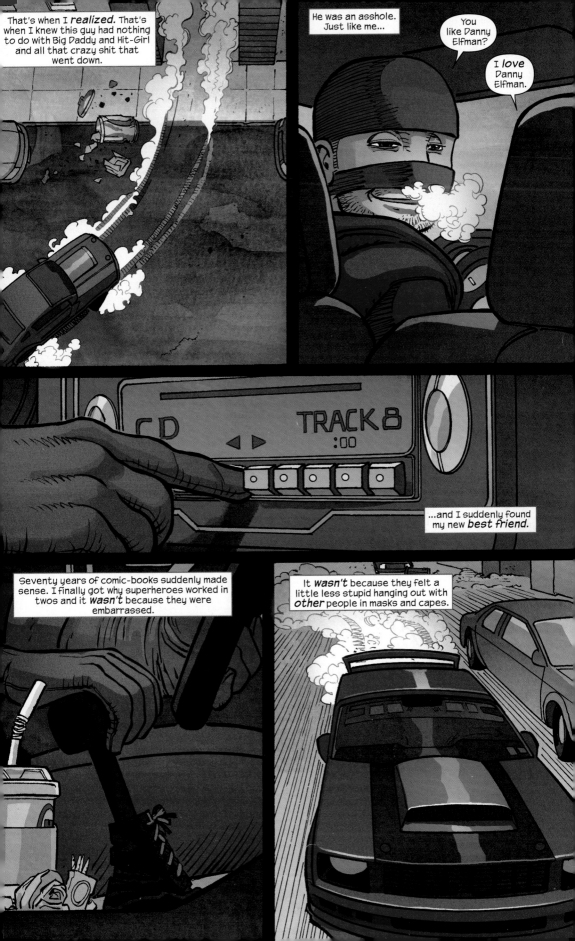

That's when I *realized.* That's when I knew this guy had nothing to do with Big Daddy and Hit-Girl and all that crazy shit that went down.

He was an asshole. Just like me...

You like Danny Elfman?

I *love* Danny Elfman.

CD   TRACK 8 :00

...and I suddenly found my new *best friend.*

Seventy years of comic-books suddenly made sense. I finally got why superheroes worked in twos and it *wasn't* because they were embarrassed.

It *wasn't* because they felt a little less stupid hanging out with *other* people in masks and capes.

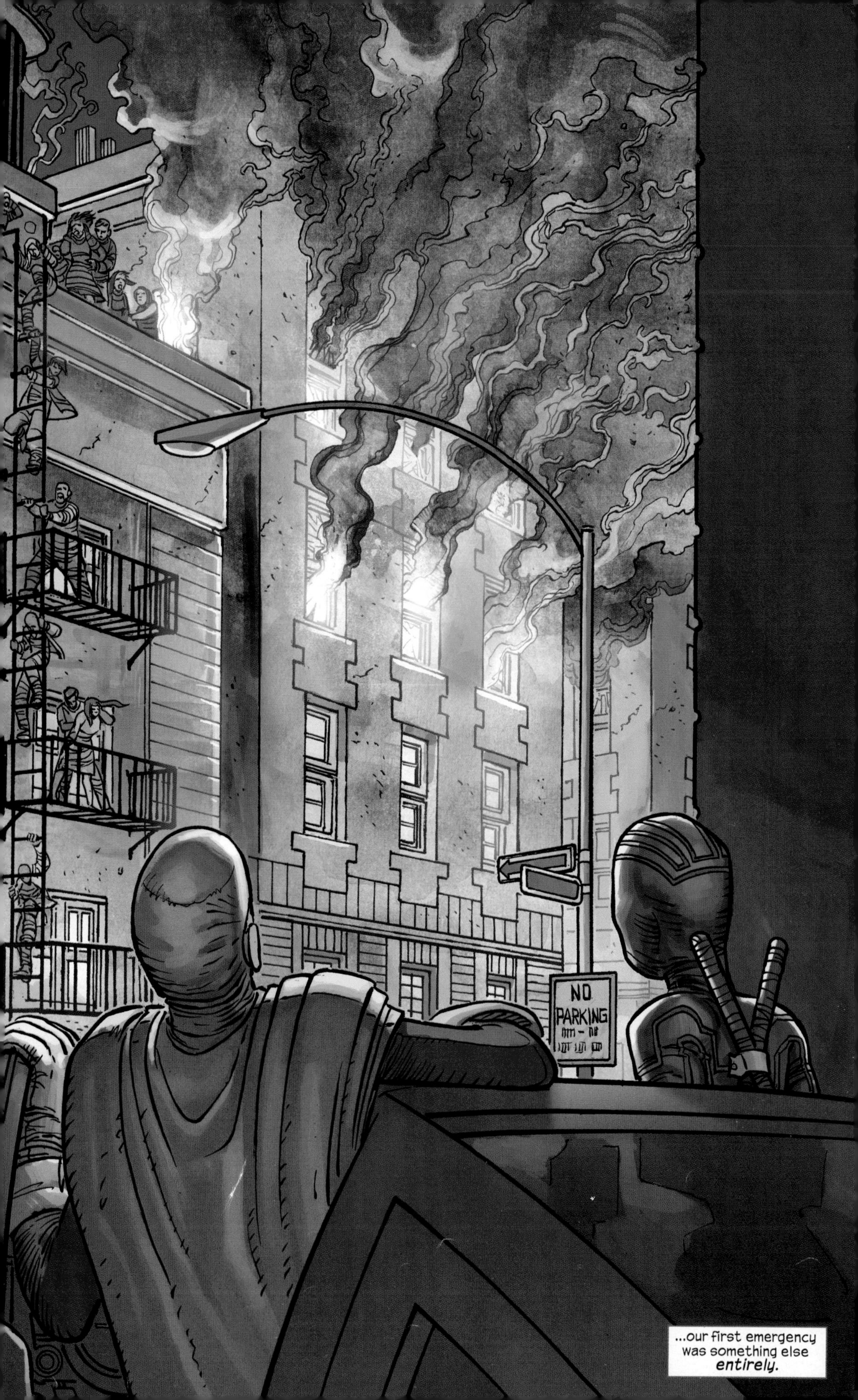

NO PARKING
...our first emergency was something else *entirely*.

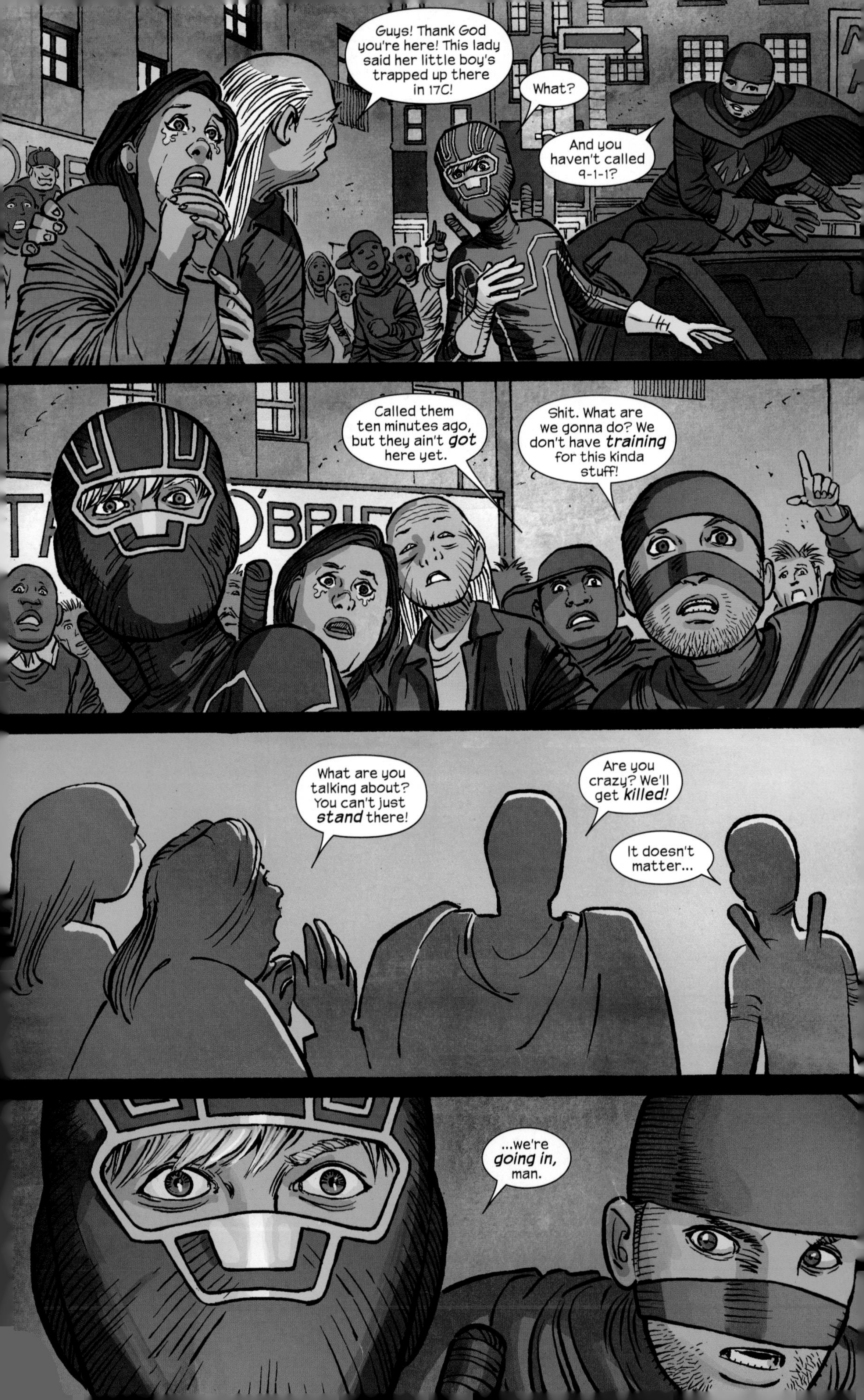
Guys! Thank God you're here! This lady said her little boy's trapped up there in 17C!
What?
And you haven't called 9-1-1?
Called them ten minutes ago, but they ain't *got* here yet.
Shit. What are we gonna do? We don't have *training* for this kinda stuff!
What are you talking about? You can't just *stand* there!
Are you crazy? We'll get *killed!*
It doesn't matter...
...we're *going in,* man.

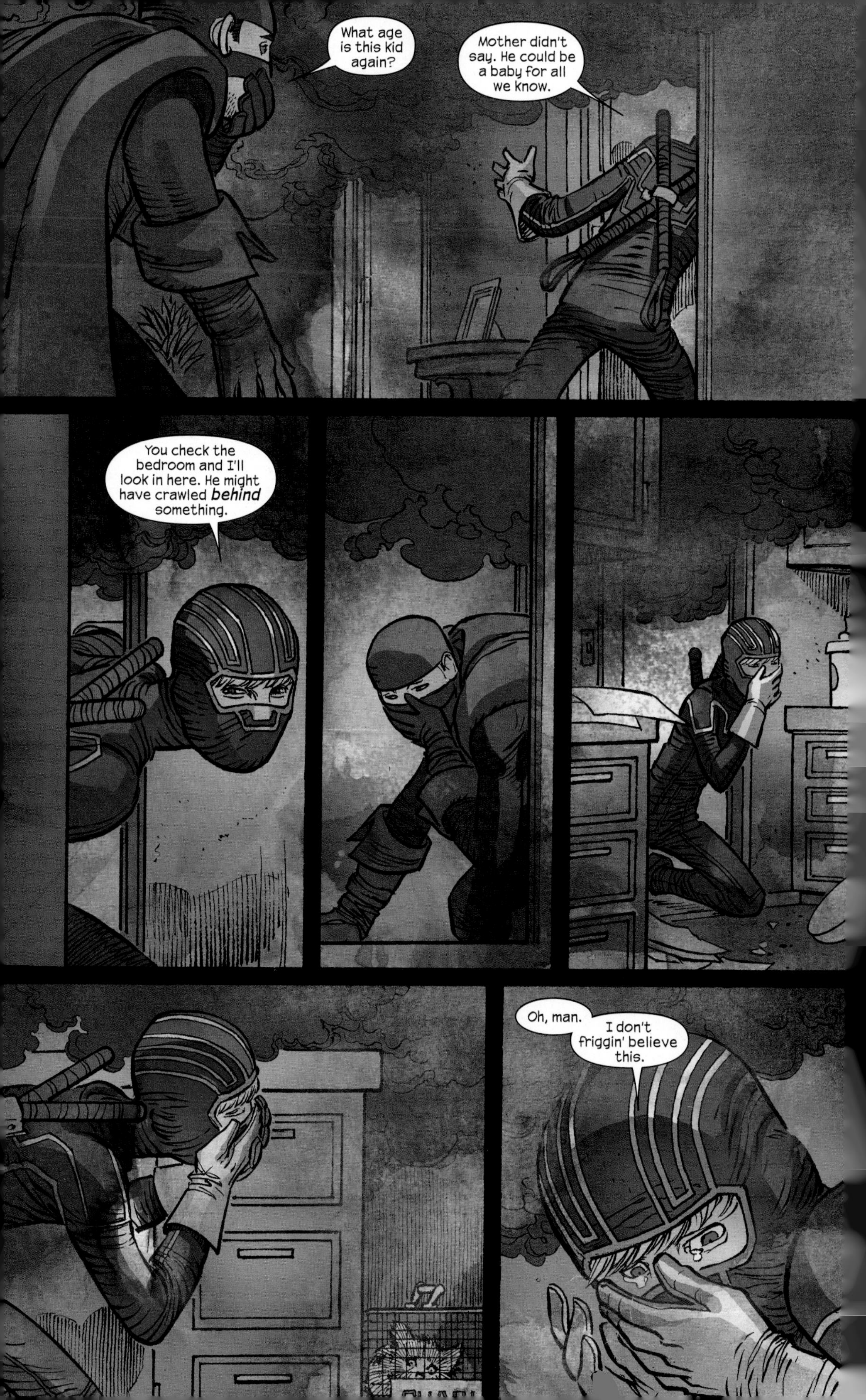
What age is this kid again?
Mother didn't say. He could be a baby for all we know.
You check the bedroom and I'll look in here. He might have crawled *behind* something.
Oh, man.
I don't friggin' believe this.

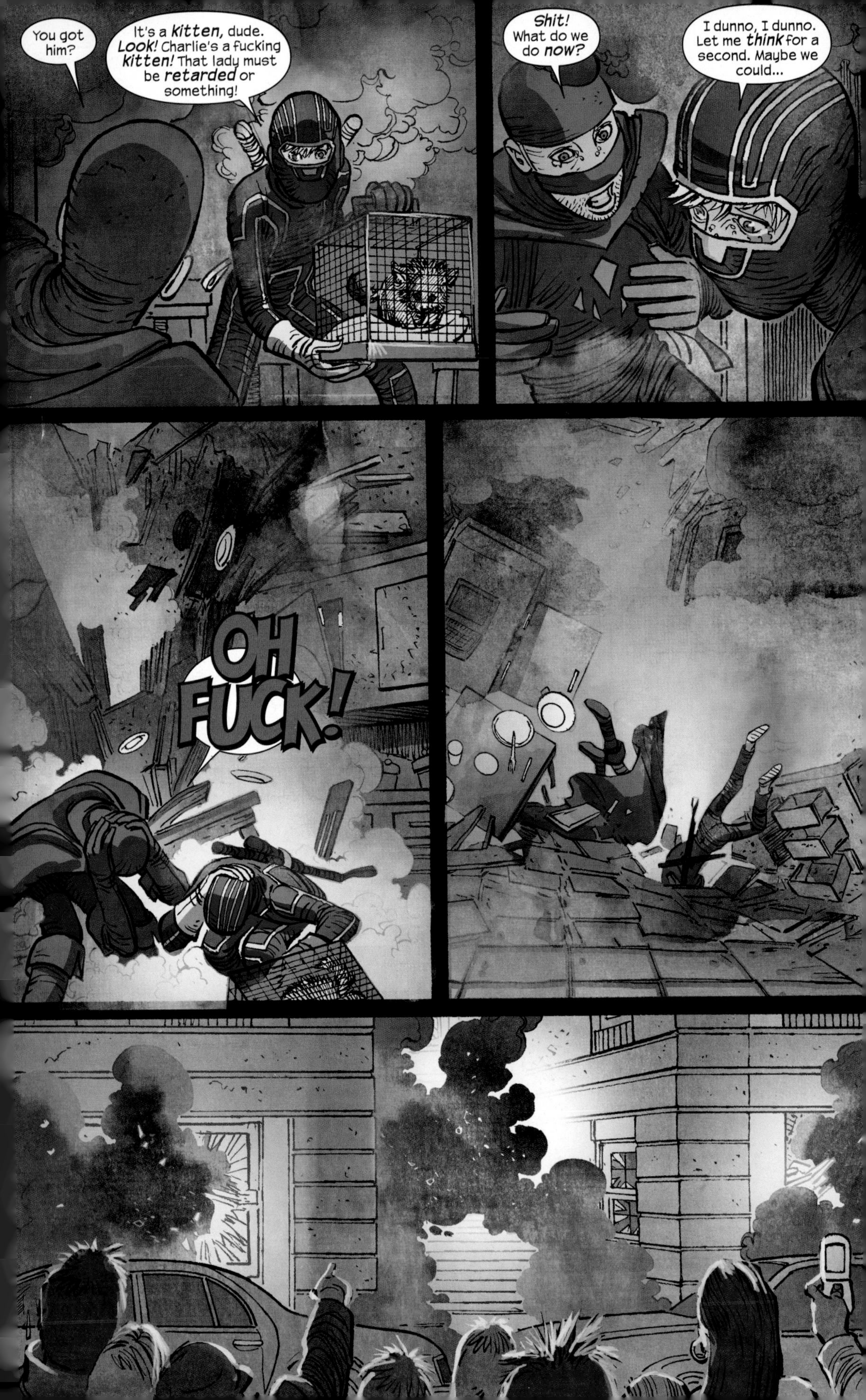
You got him?
It's a kitten, dude. Look! Charlie's a fucking kitten! That lady must be retarded or something!
Shit! What do we do now?
I dunno, I dunno. Let me think for a second. Maybe we could...
OH FUCK!

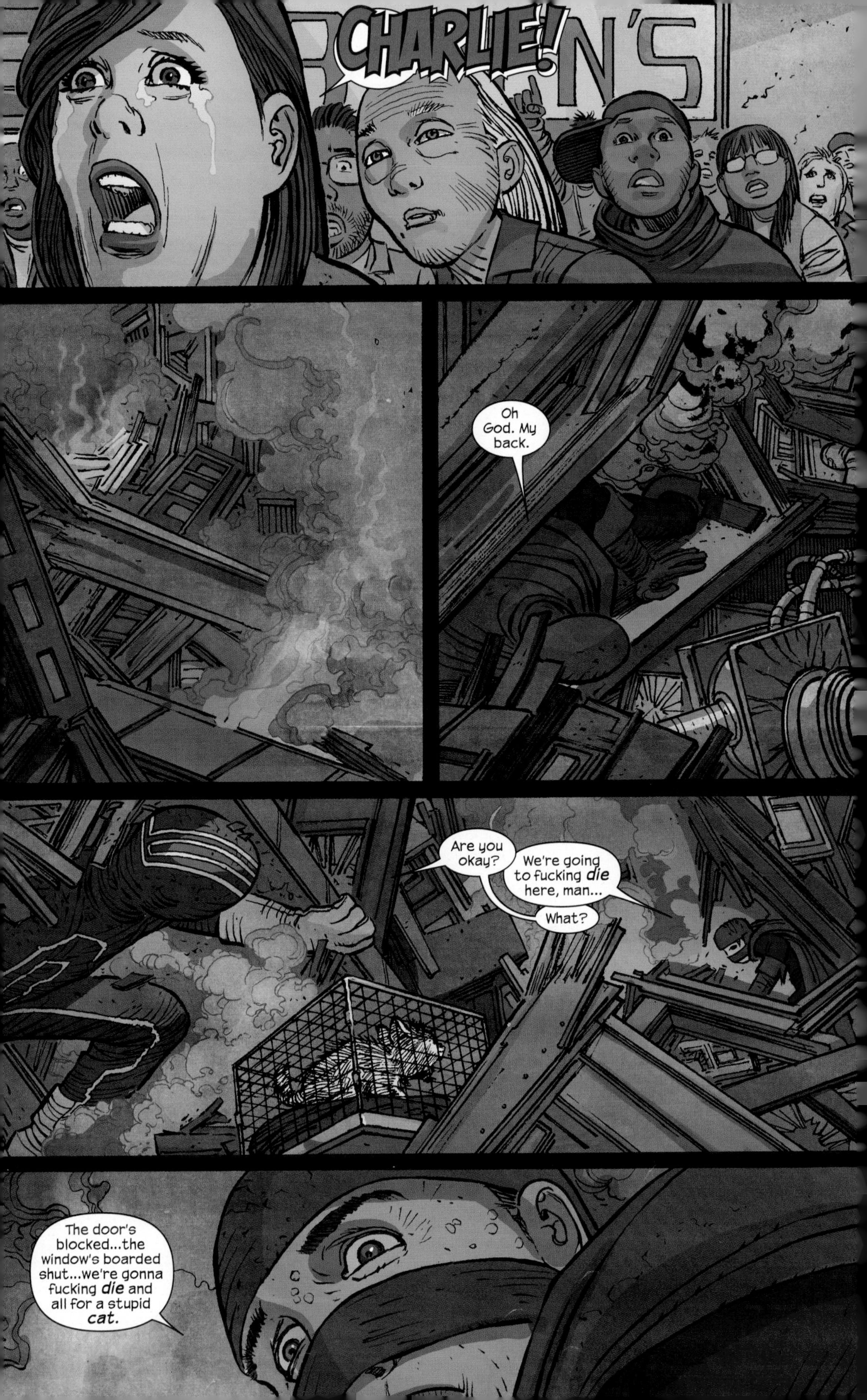
CHARLIE!
N'S
Oh God. My back.
Are you okay?
We're going to fucking *die* here, man...
What?
The door's blocked...the window's boarded shut...we're gonna fucking *die* and all for a stupid *cat*.

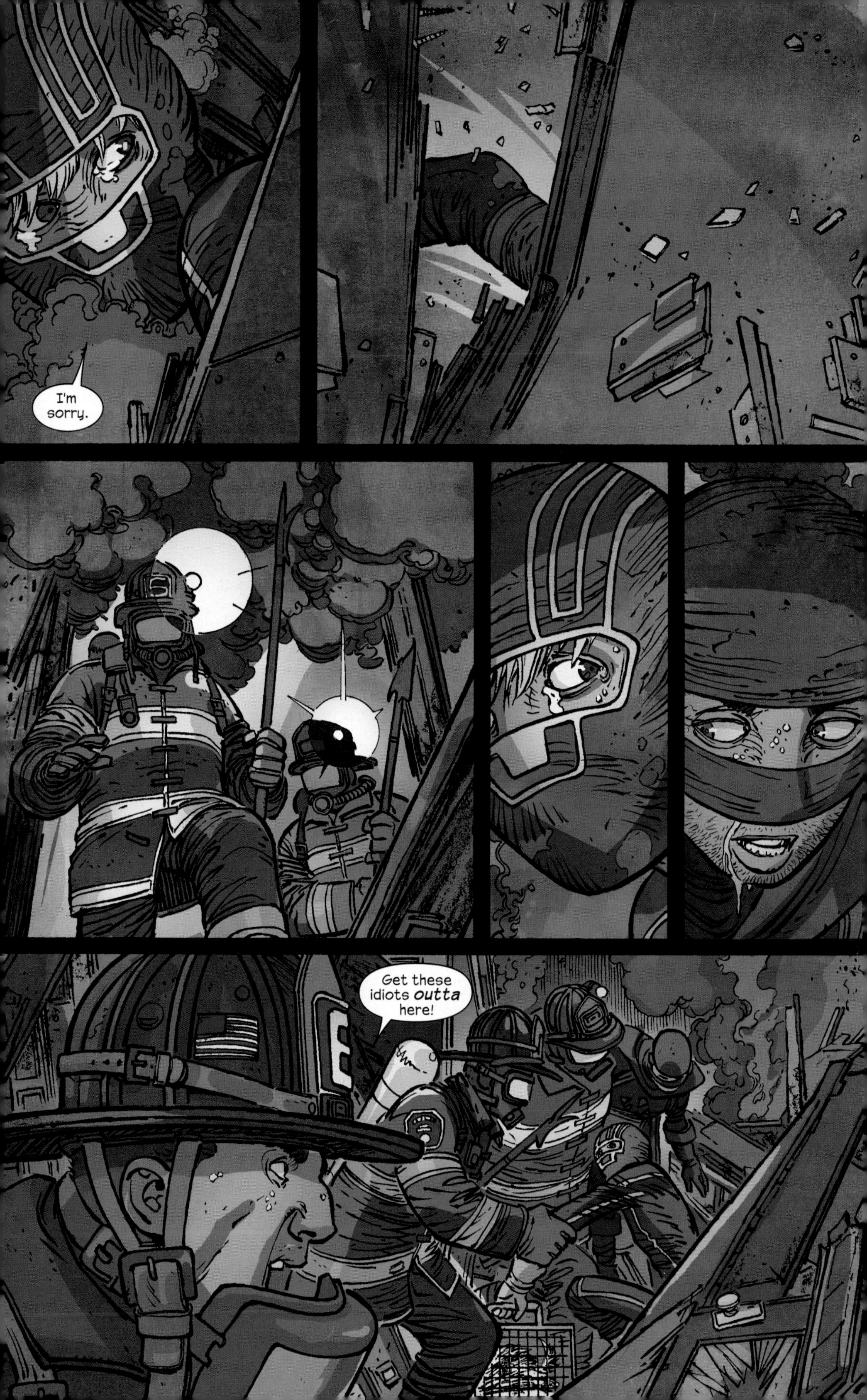
I'm sorry.
Get these idiots *outta* here!

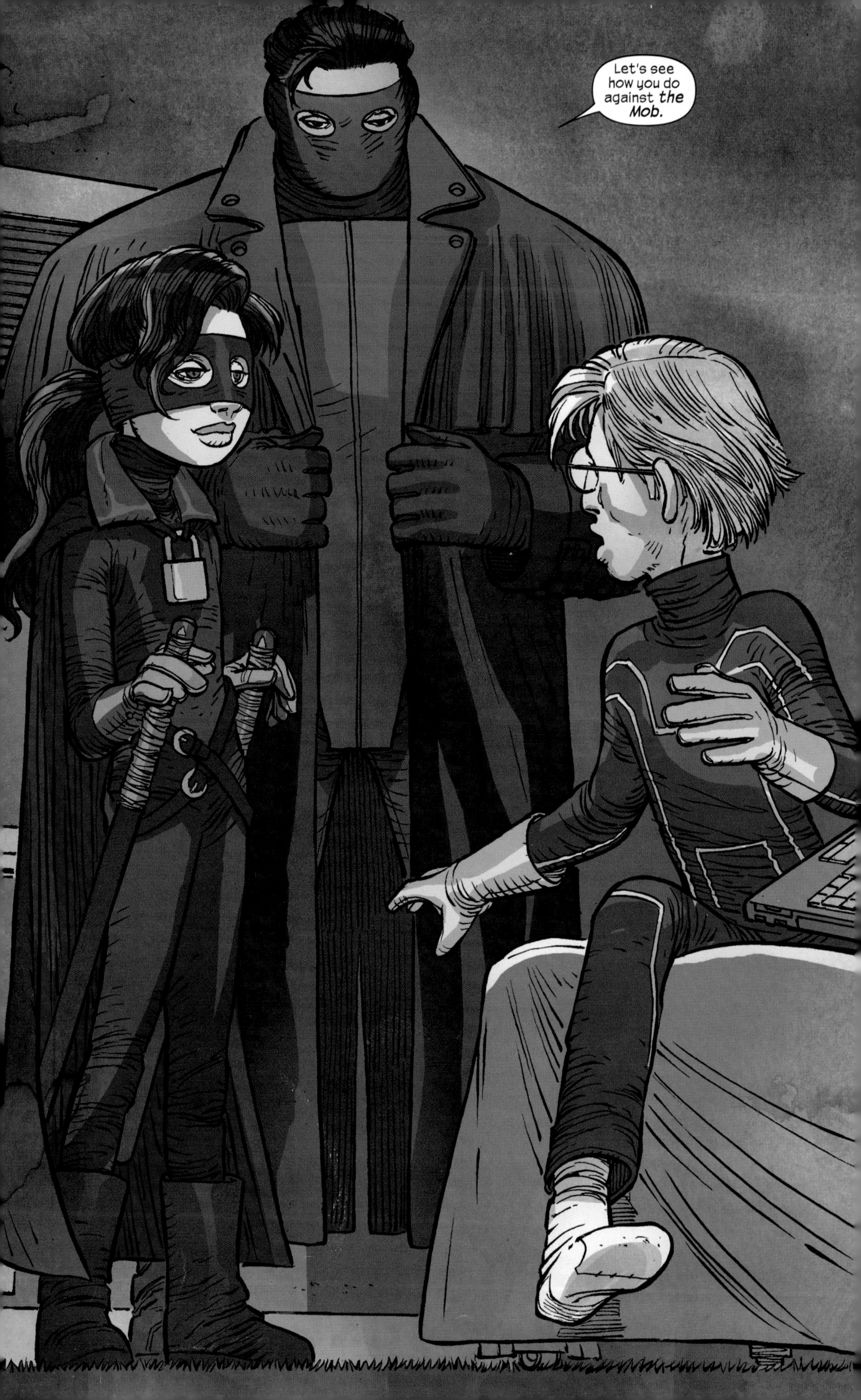
Let's see how you do against *the Mob.*

SIX

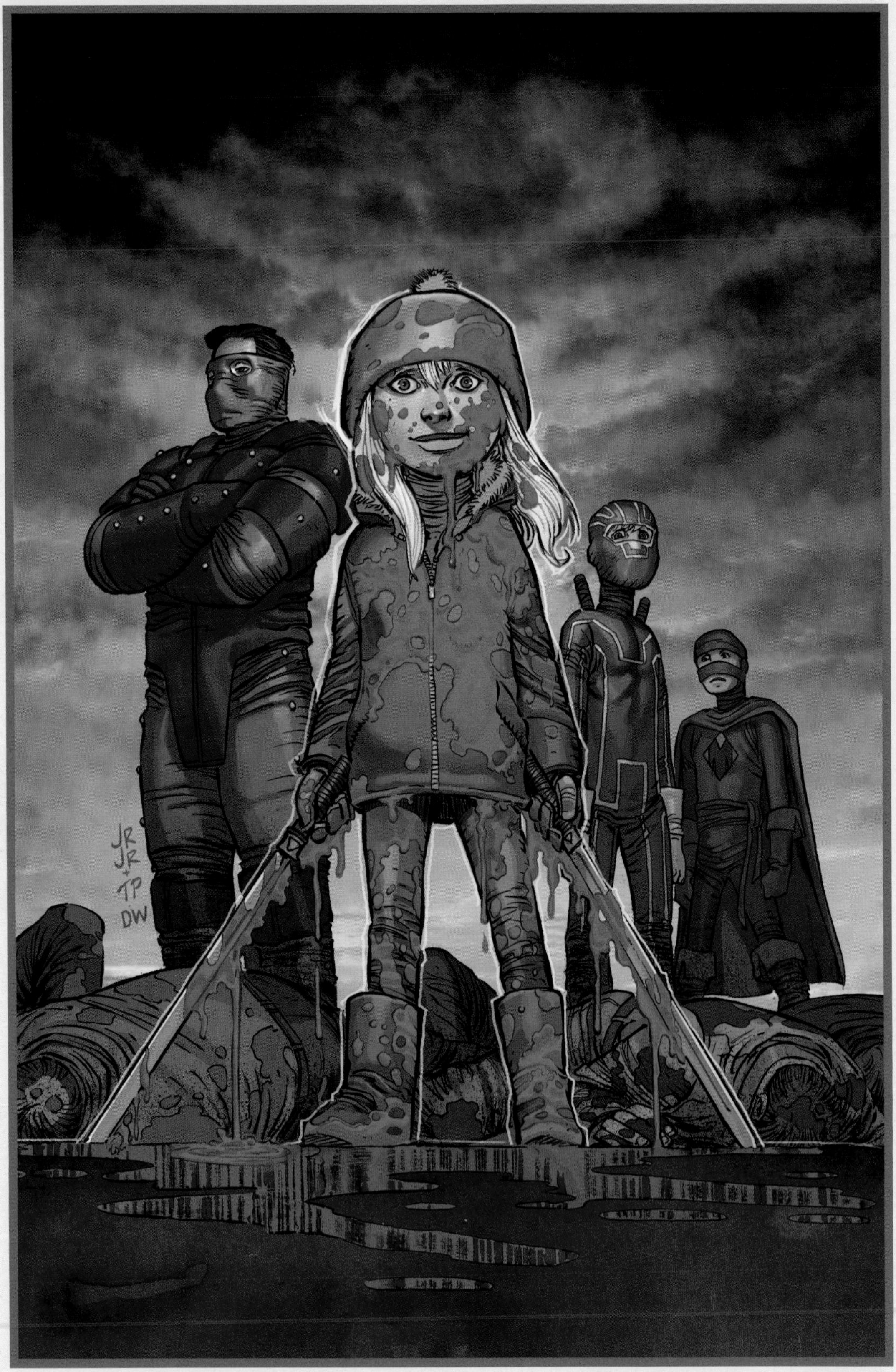
JR
JR
+
TP
DW

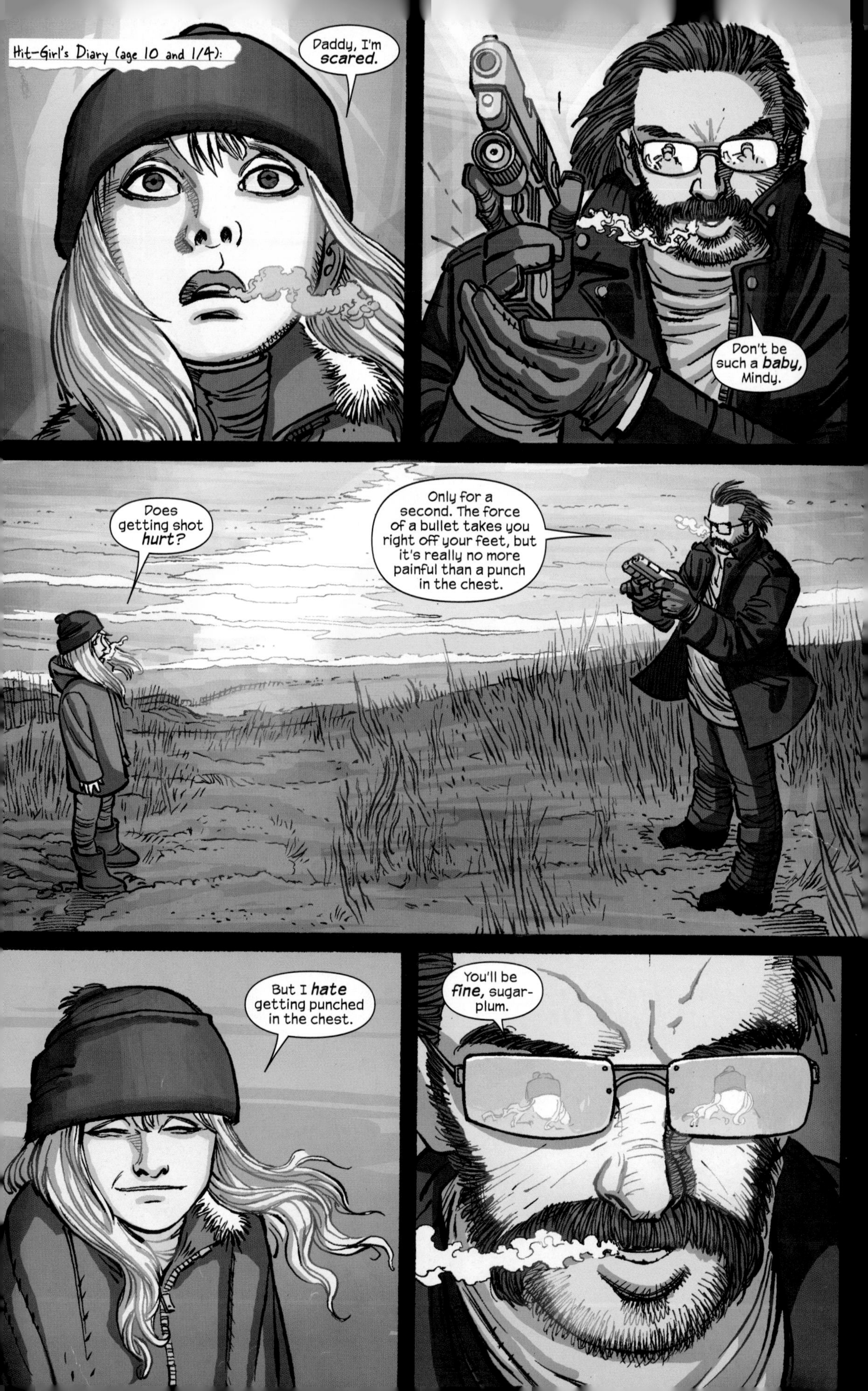
Hit-Girl's Diary (age 10 and 1/4):
Daddy, I'm *scared.*
Don't be such a *baby,* Mindy.
Does getting shot *hurt?*
Only for a second. The force of a bullet takes you right off your feet, but it's really no more painful than a punch in the chest.
But I *hate* getting punched in the chest.
You'll be *fine,* sugar-plum.

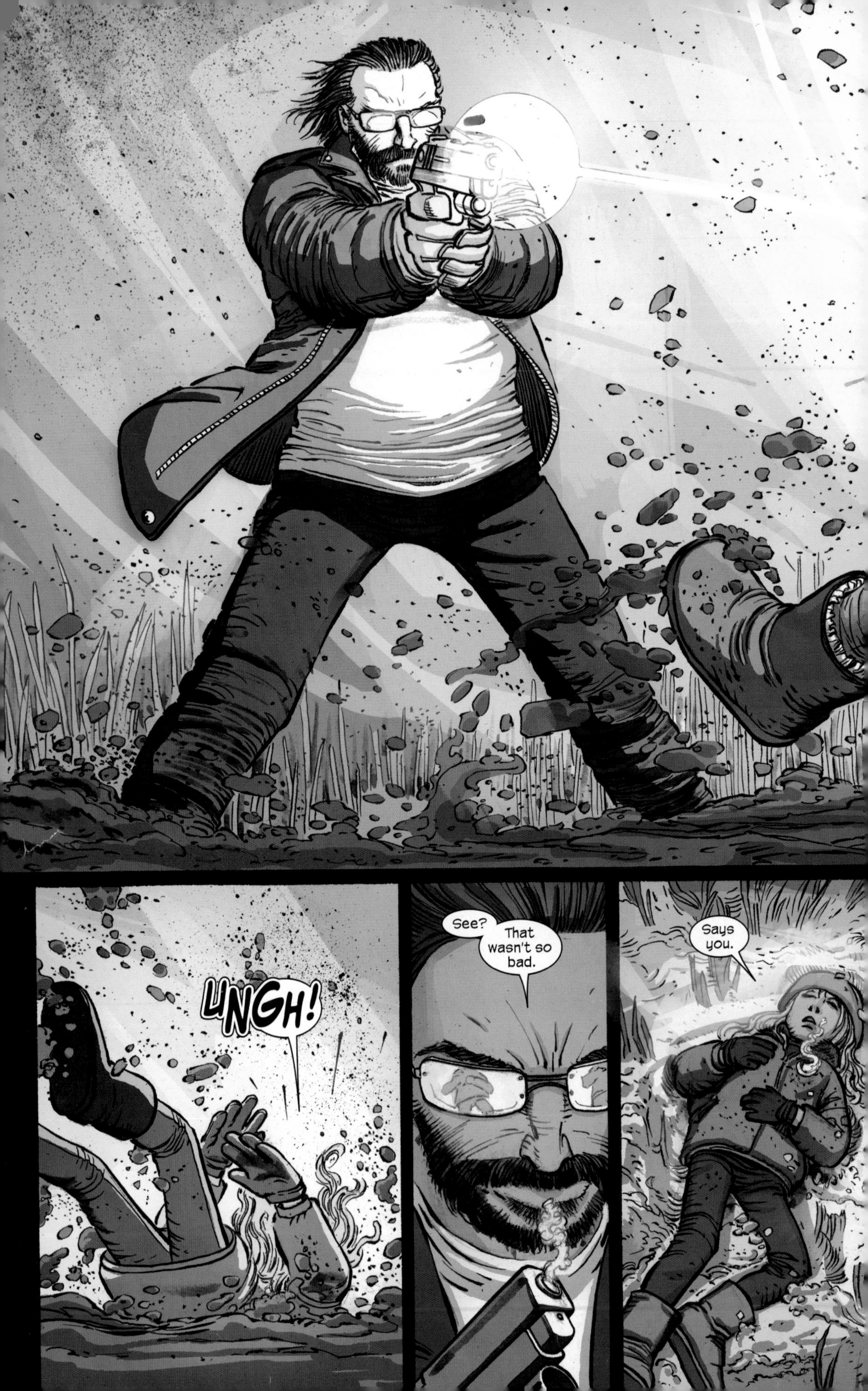
UNGH!
See?
That wasn't so bad.
Says you.

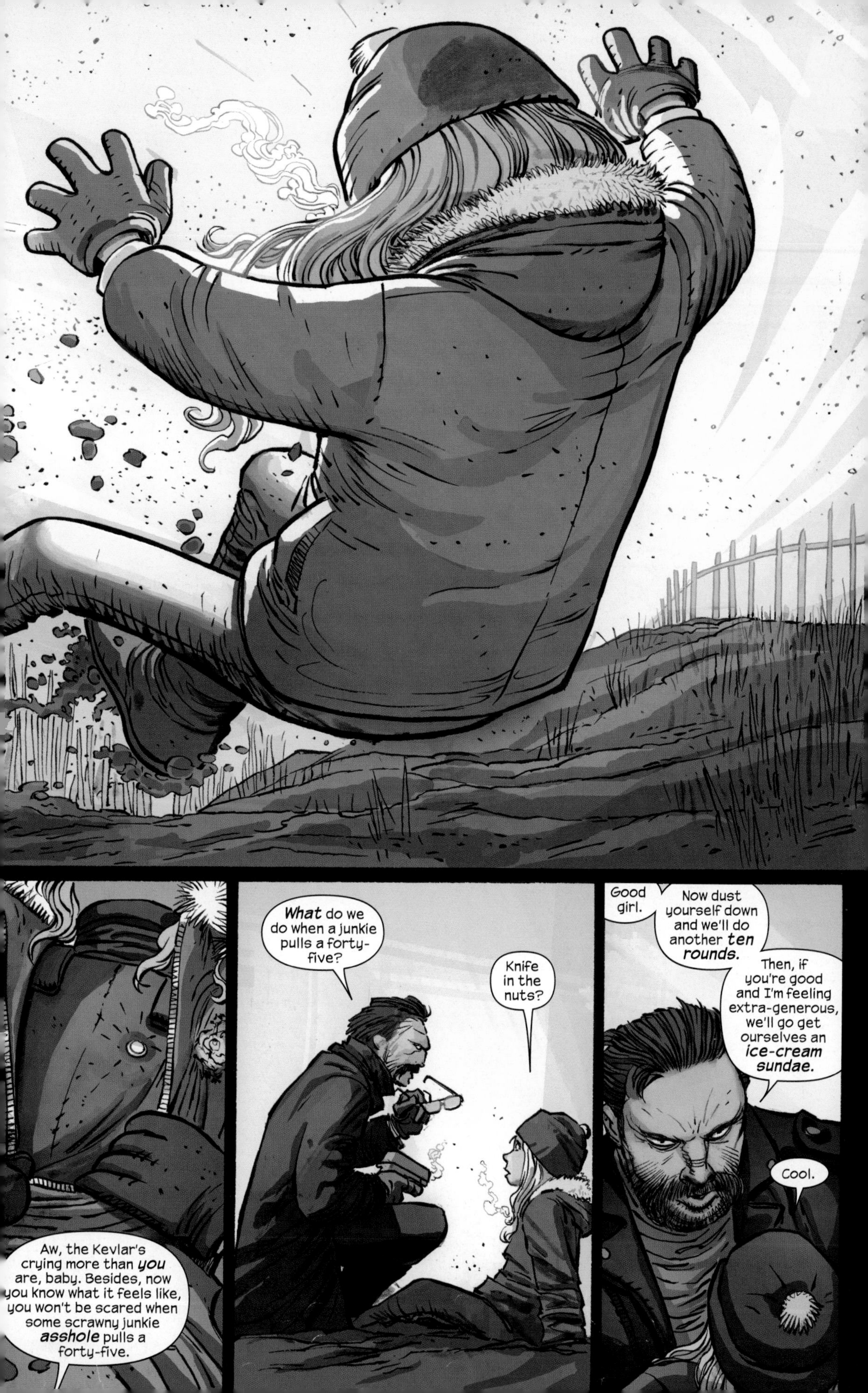
Aw, the Kevlar's crying more than *you* are, baby. Besides, now you know what it feels like, you won't be scared when some scrawny junkie *asshole* pulls a forty-five.
What do we do when a junkie pulls a forty-five?
Knife in the nuts?
Good girl.
Now dust yourself down and we'll do another *ten rounds.*
Then, if you're good and I'm feeling extra-generous, we'll go get ourselves an *ice-cream sundae.*
Cool.

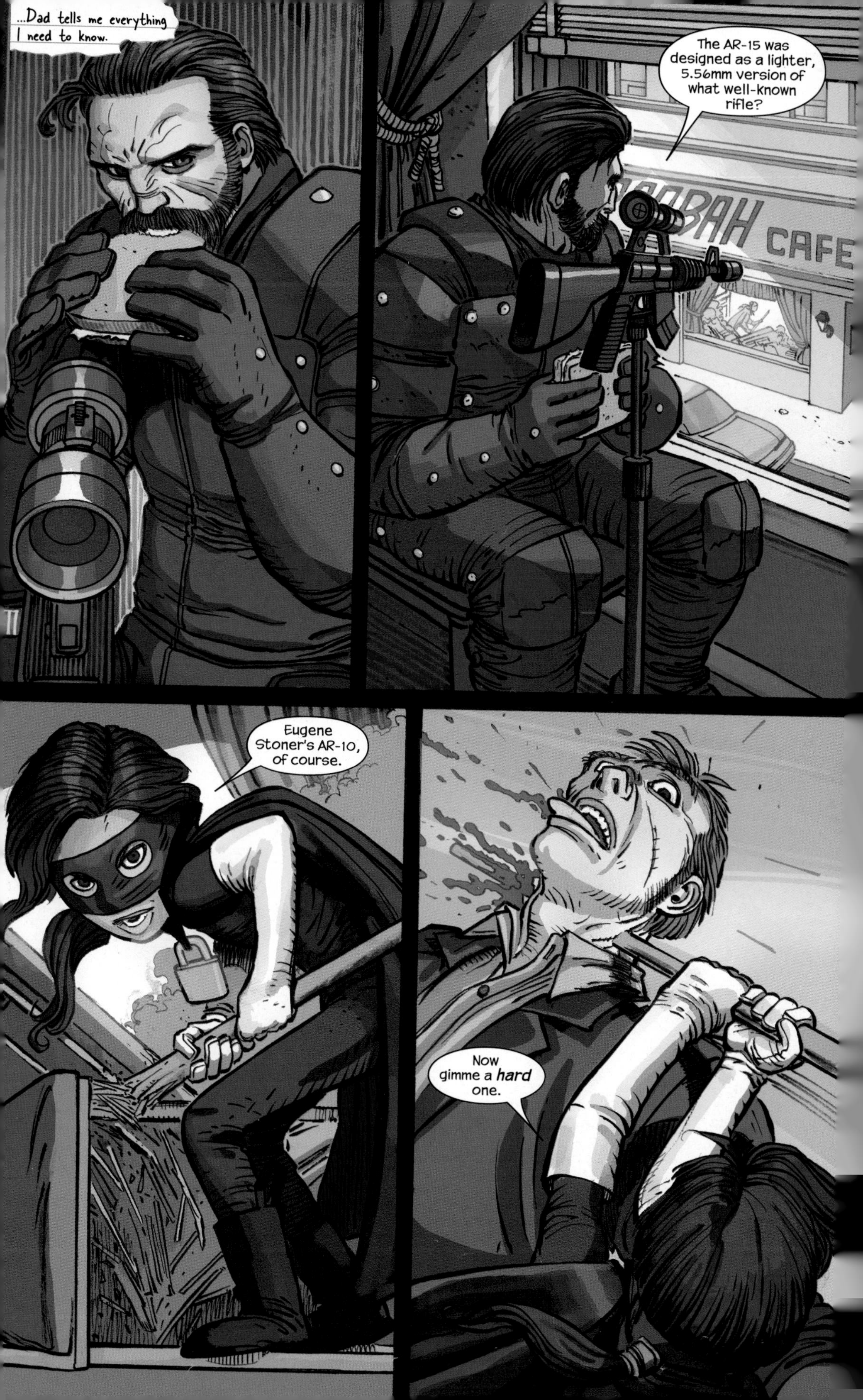
...Dad tells me everything I need to know.
The AR-15 was designed as a lighter, 5.56mm version of what well-known rifle?
CAFE
Eugene Stoner's AR-10, of course.
Now gimme a *hard* one.

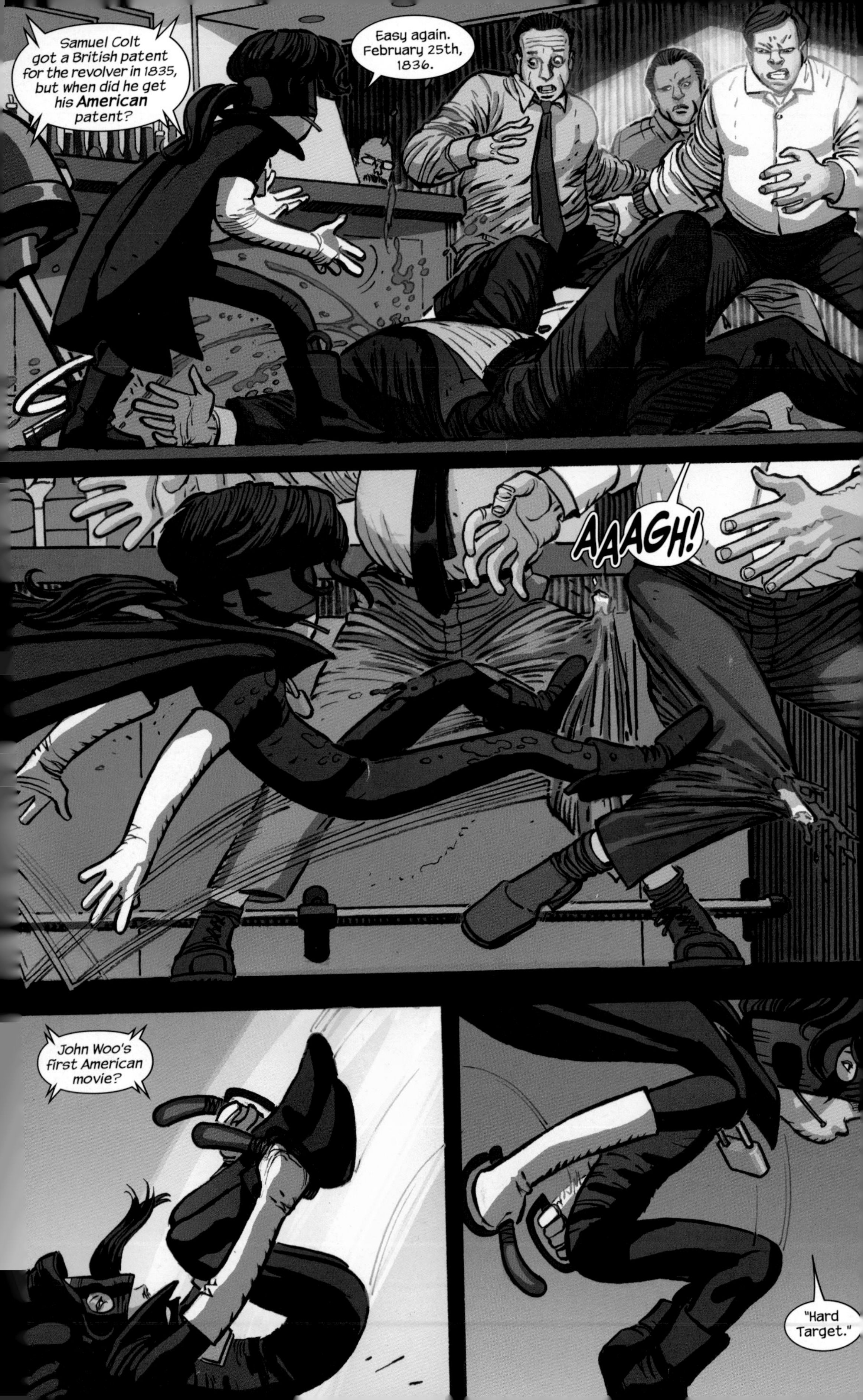
Samuel Colt got a British patent for the revolver in 1835, but when did he get his **American** patent?
Easy again. February 25th, 1836.
AAAGH!
John Woo's first American movie?
"Hard Target."

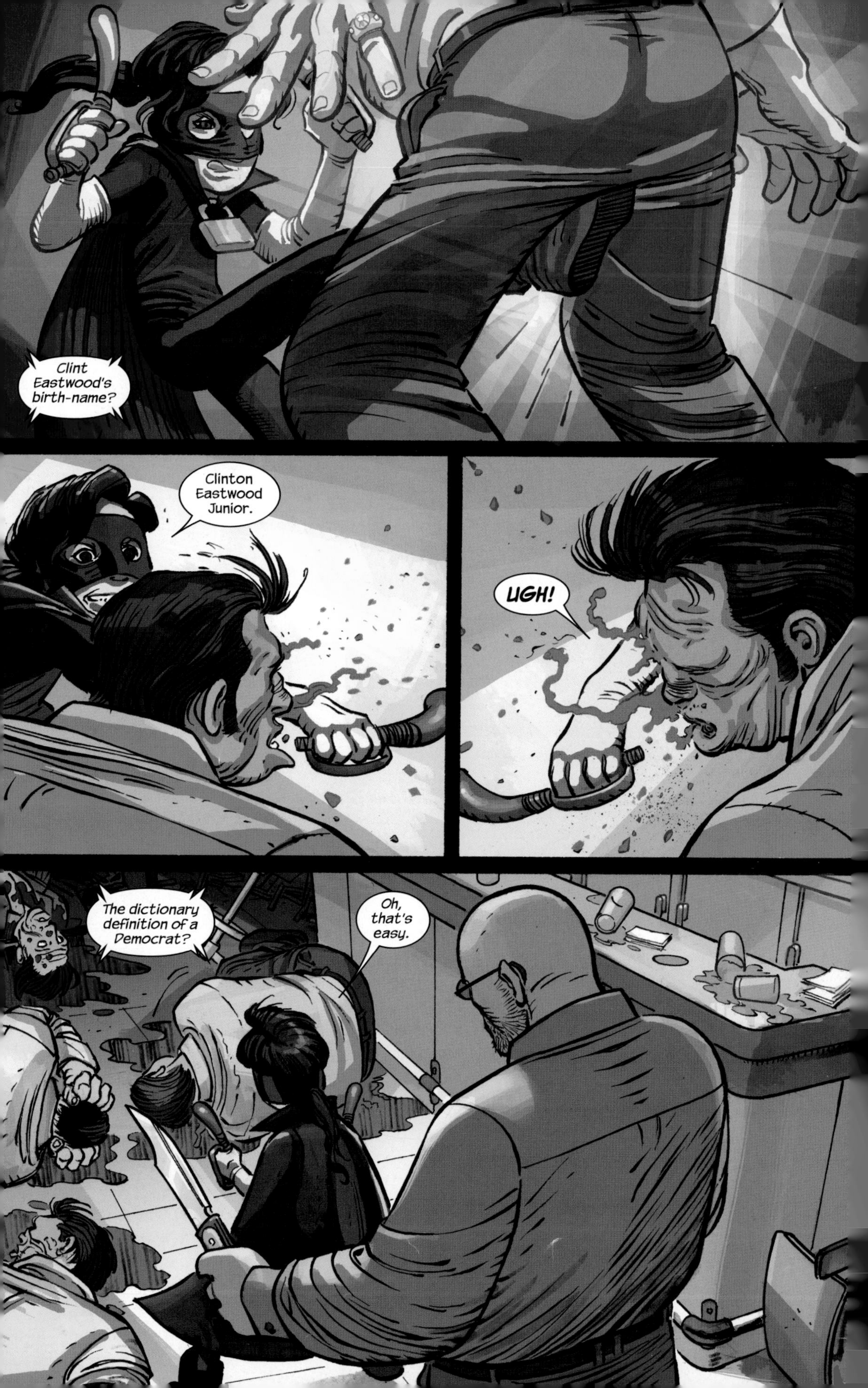
Clint Eastwood's birth-name?
Clinton Eastwood Junior.
UGH!
The dictionary definition of a Democrat?
Oh, that's easy.

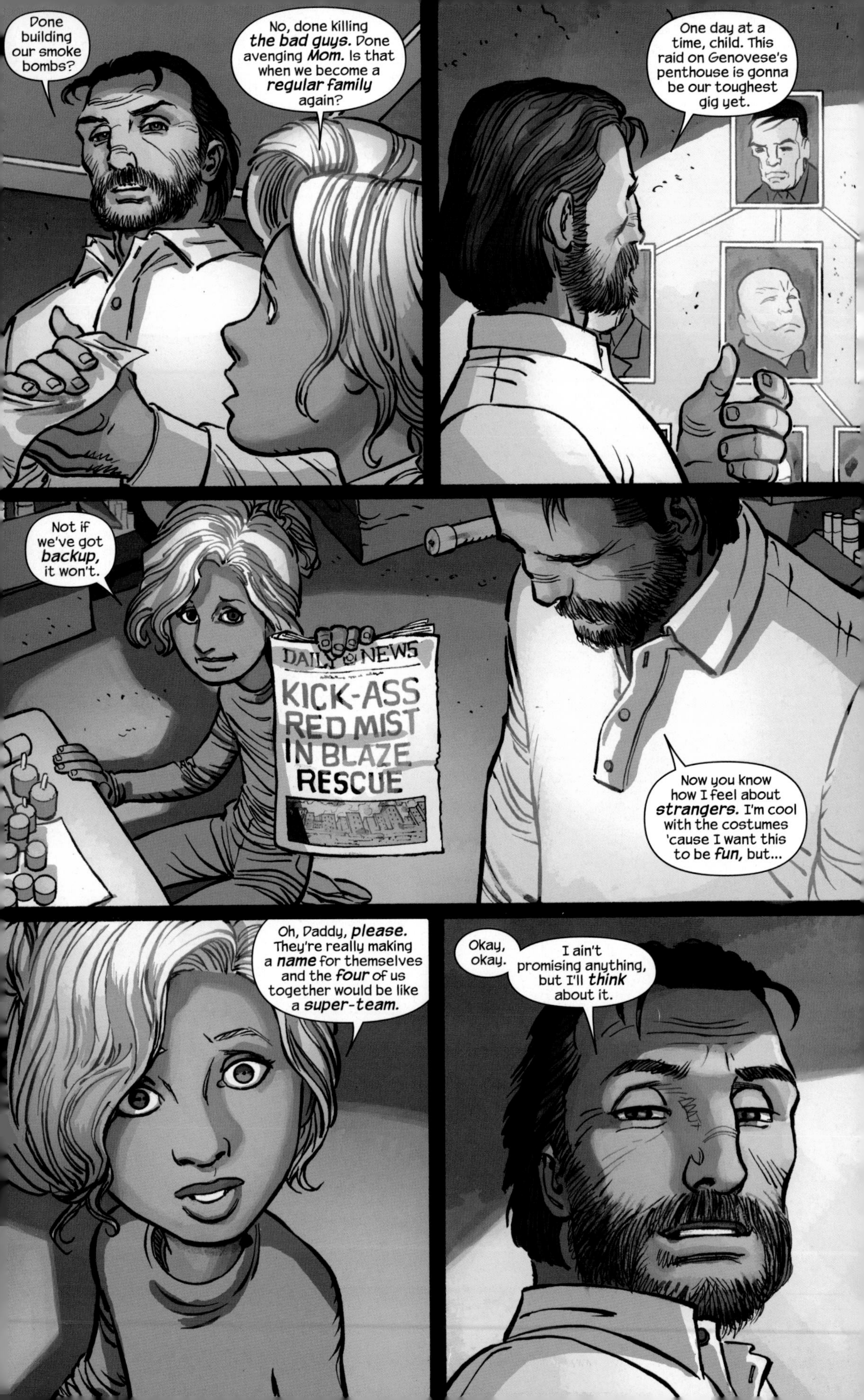
Done building our smoke bombs?
No, done killing **the bad guys.** Done avenging **Mom.** Is that when we become a **regular family** again?
One day at a time, child. This raid on Genovese's penthouse is gonna be our toughest gig yet.
Not if we've got **backup,** it won't.
DAILY NEWS
KICK-ASS RED MIST IN BLAZE RESCUE
Now you know how I feel about **strangers.** I'm cool with the costumes 'cause I want this to be **fun,** but...
Oh, Daddy, **please.** They're really making a **name** for themselves and the **four** of us together would be like a **super-team.**
Okay, okay.
I ain't promising anything, but I'll **think** about it.

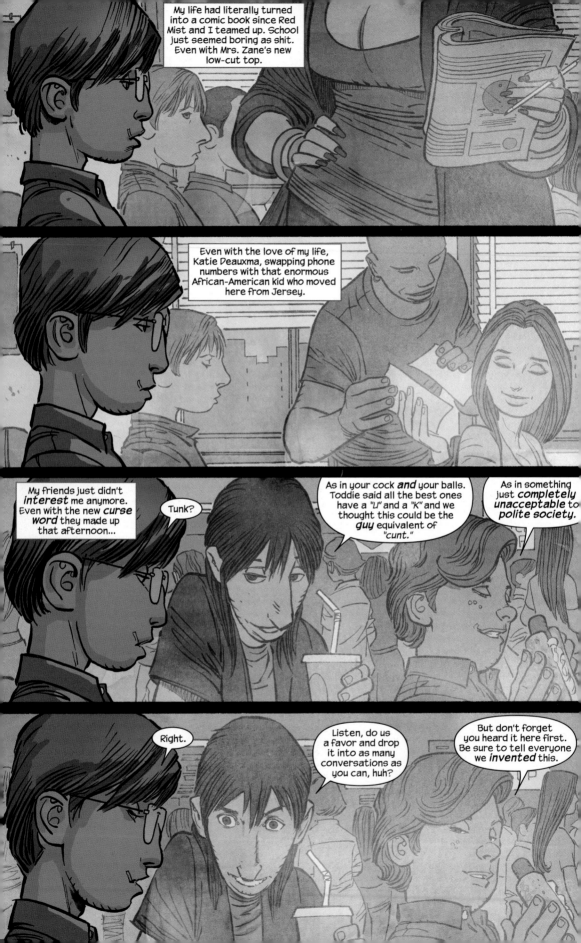

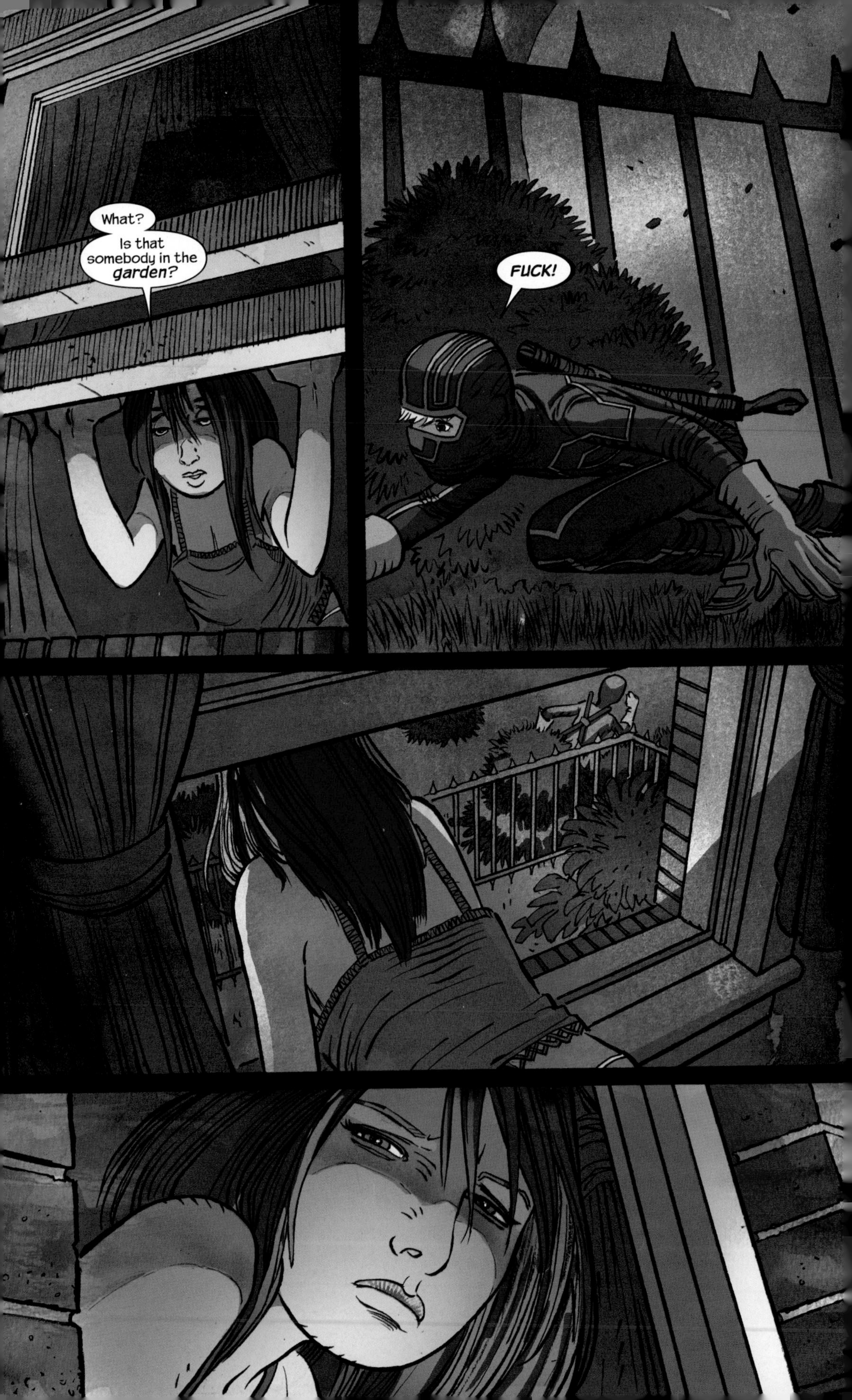
What? Is that somebody in the *garden*?
FUCK!

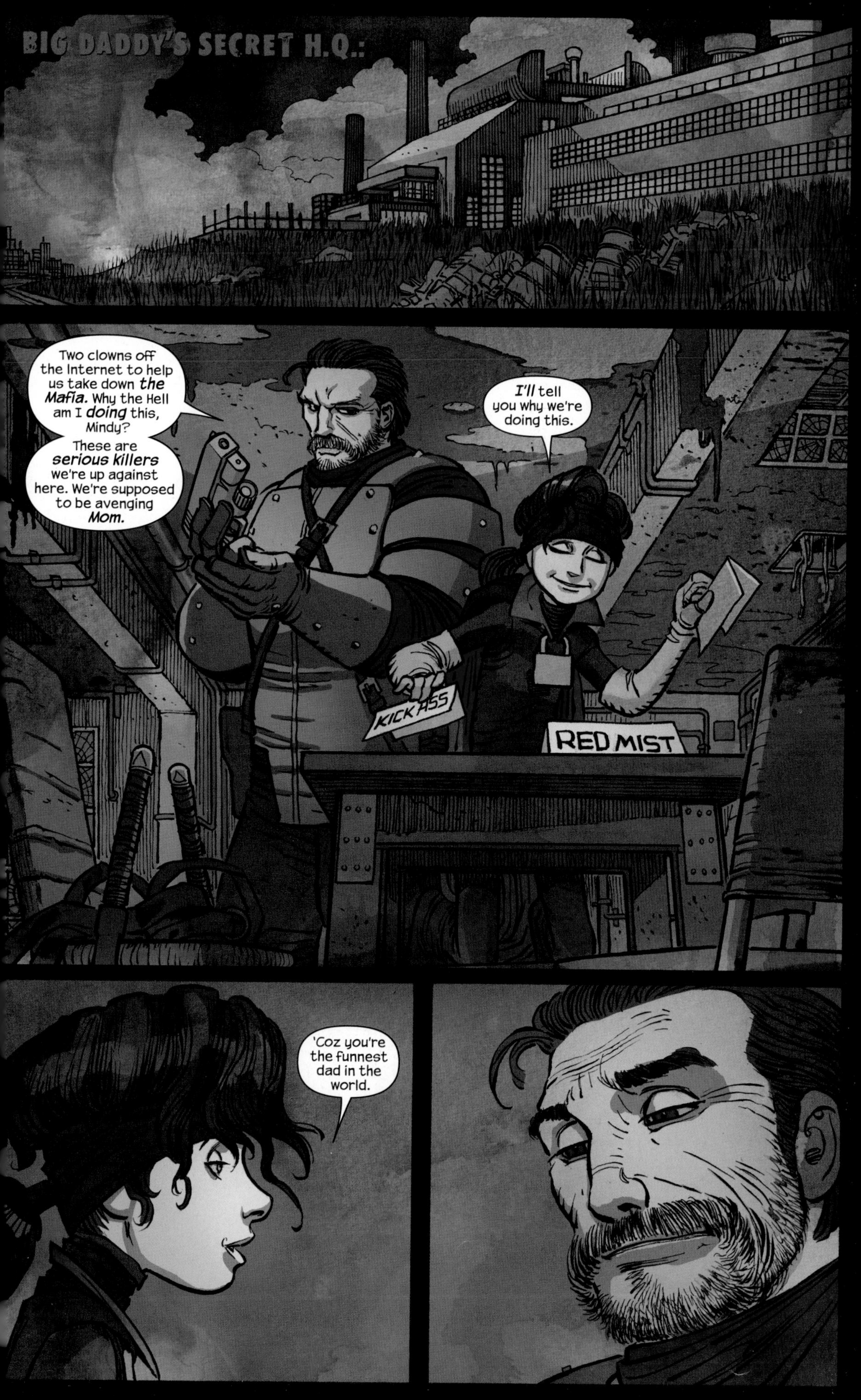
BIG DADDY'S SECRET H.Q.:
Two clowns off the Internet to help us take down *the Mafia.* Why the Hell am I *doing* this, Mindy?
These are *serious killers* we're up against here. We're supposed to be avenging *Mom.*
I'll tell you why we're doing this.
KICK ASS
RED MIST
'Coz you're the funnest dad in the world.

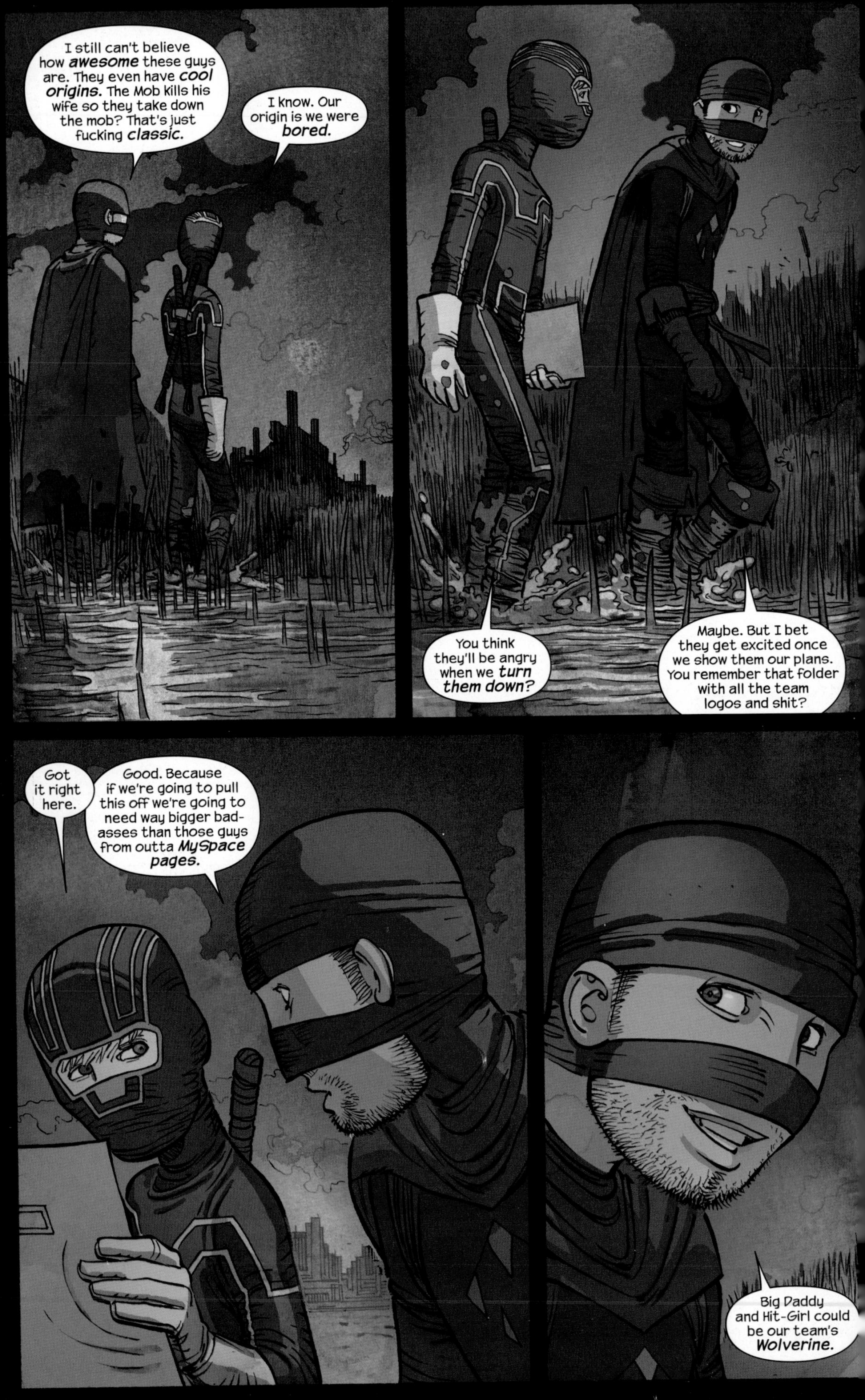
I still can't believe how awesome these guys are. They even have cool origins. The Mob kills his wife so they take down the mob? That's just fucking classic.
I know. Our origin is we were bored.
You think they'll be angry when we turn them down?
Maybe. But I bet they get excited once we show them our plans. You remember that folder with all the team logos and shit?
Got it right here.
Good. Because if we're going to pull this off we're going to need way bigger bad-asses than those guys from outta MySpace pages.
Big Daddy and Hit-Girl could be our team's Wolverine.

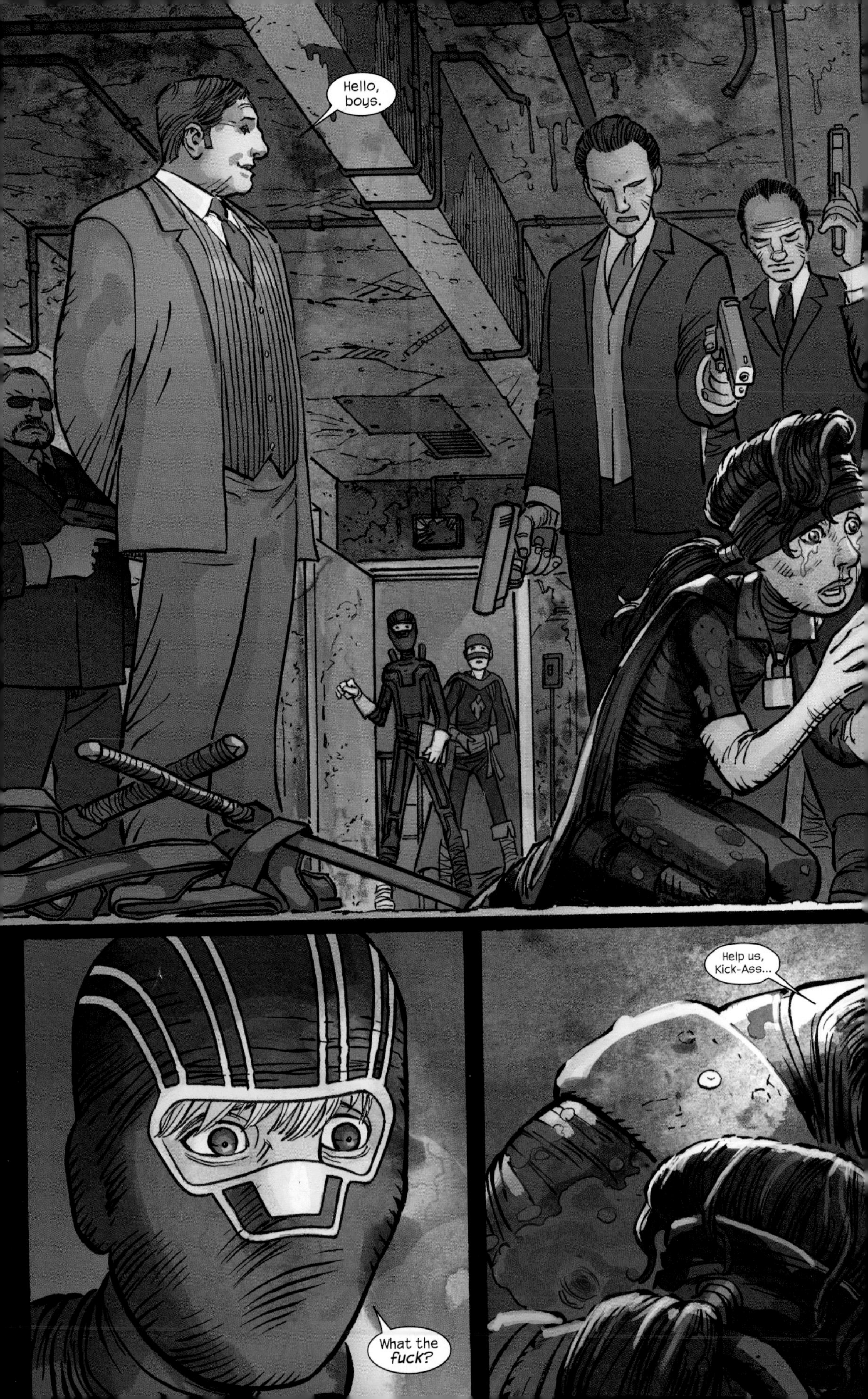
Hello, boys.
What the fuck?
Help us, Kick-Ass...

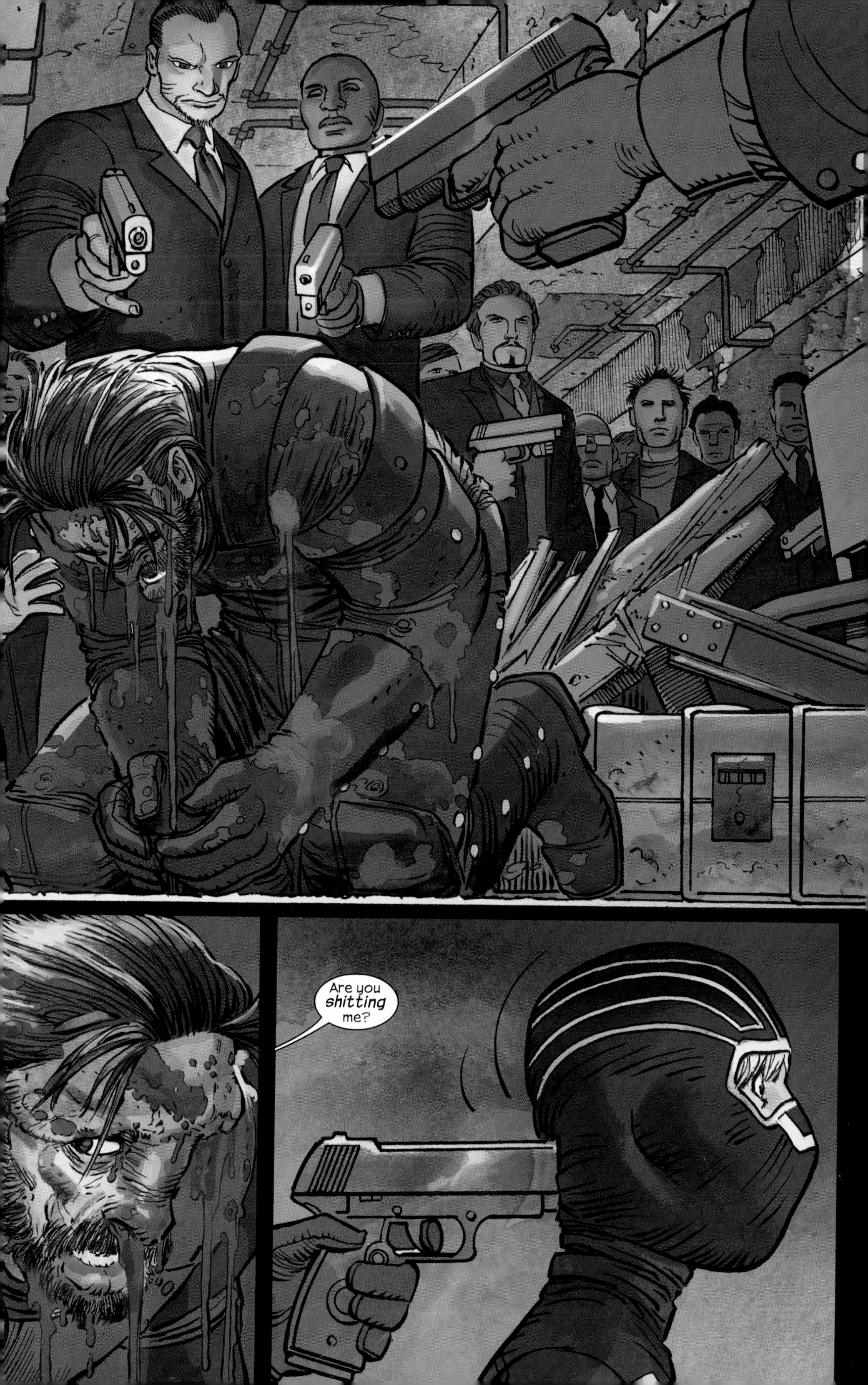
Are you shitting me?

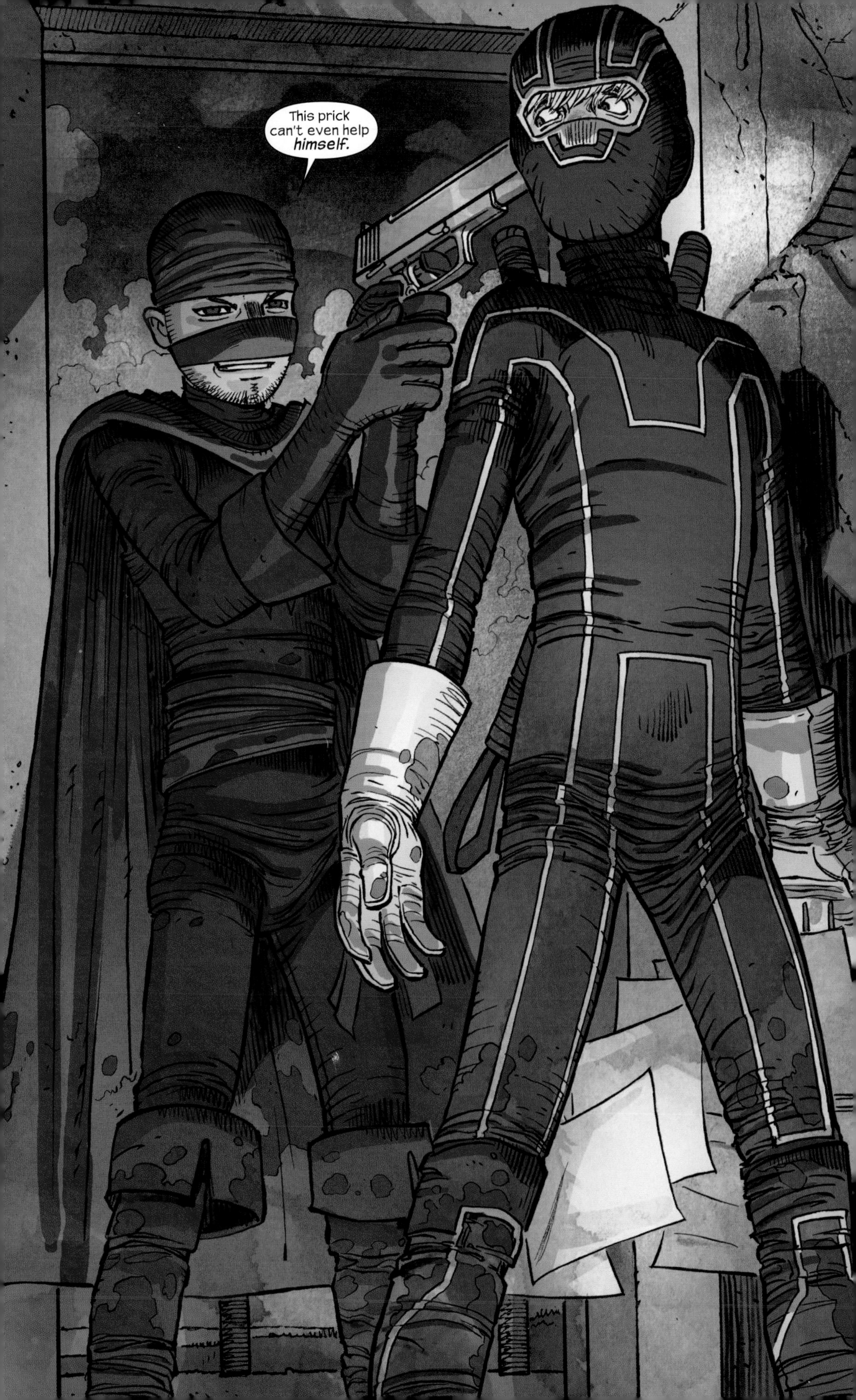
This prick can't even help *himself*.

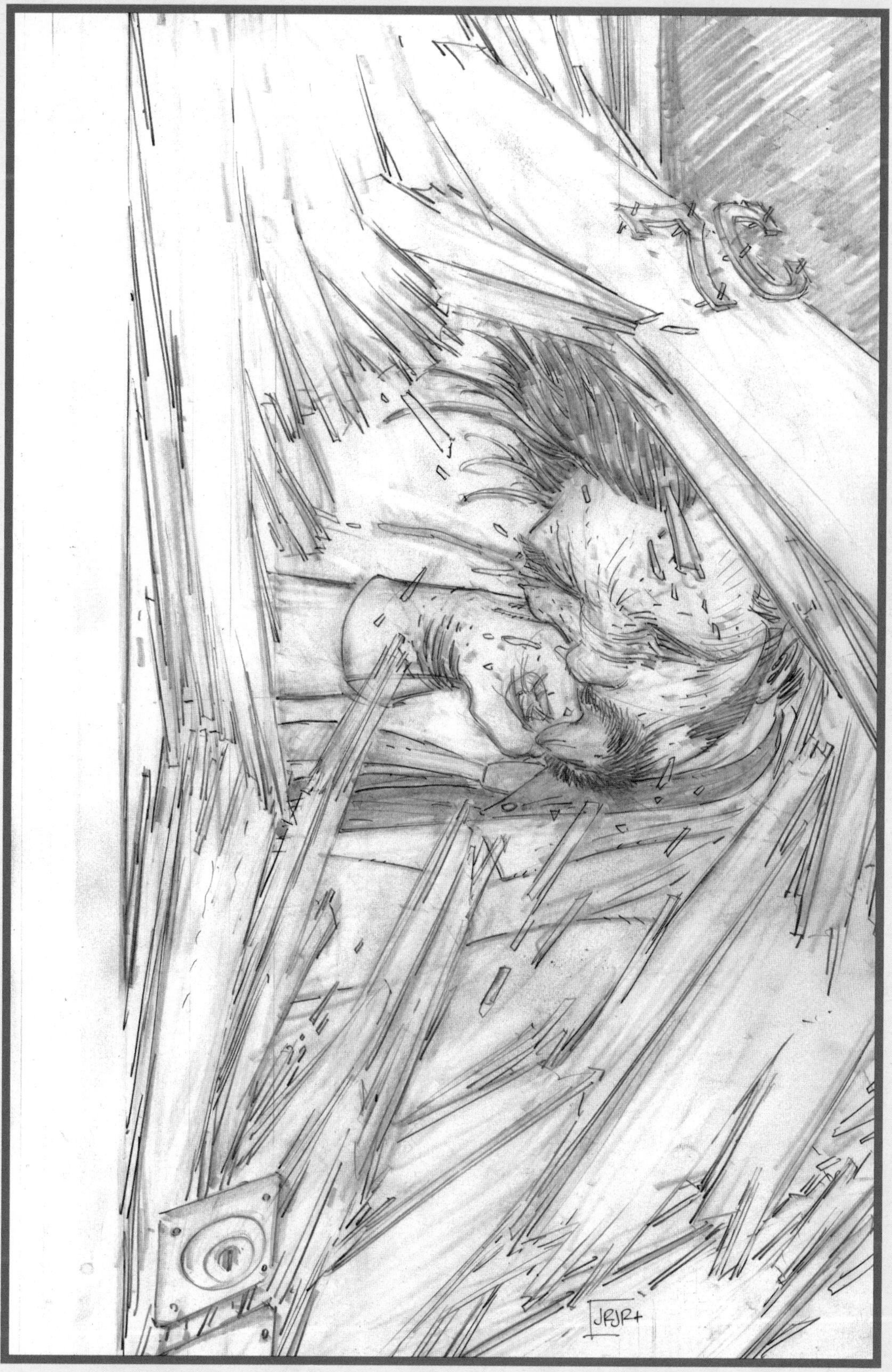
JRJR+

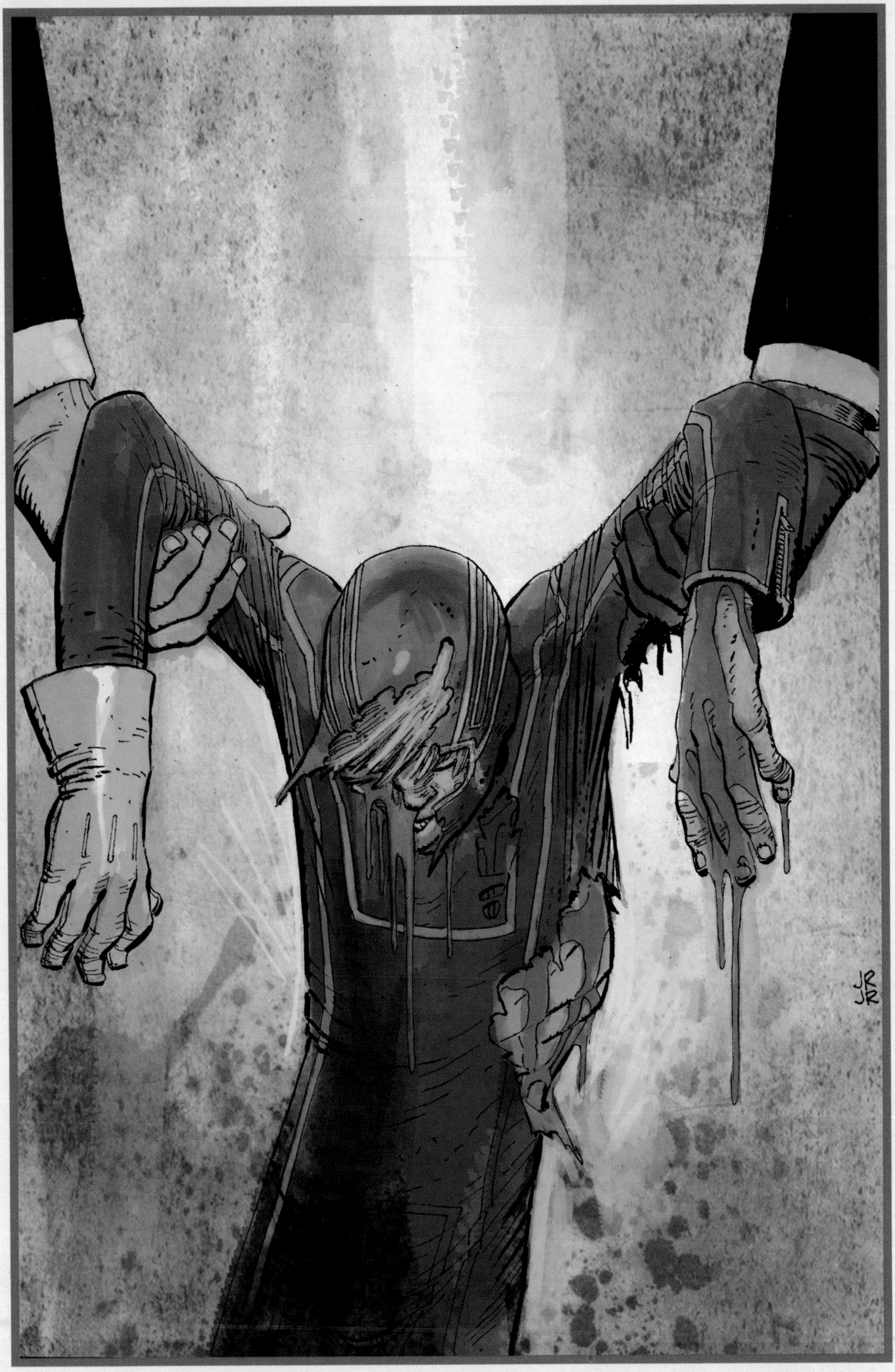
JR
JR

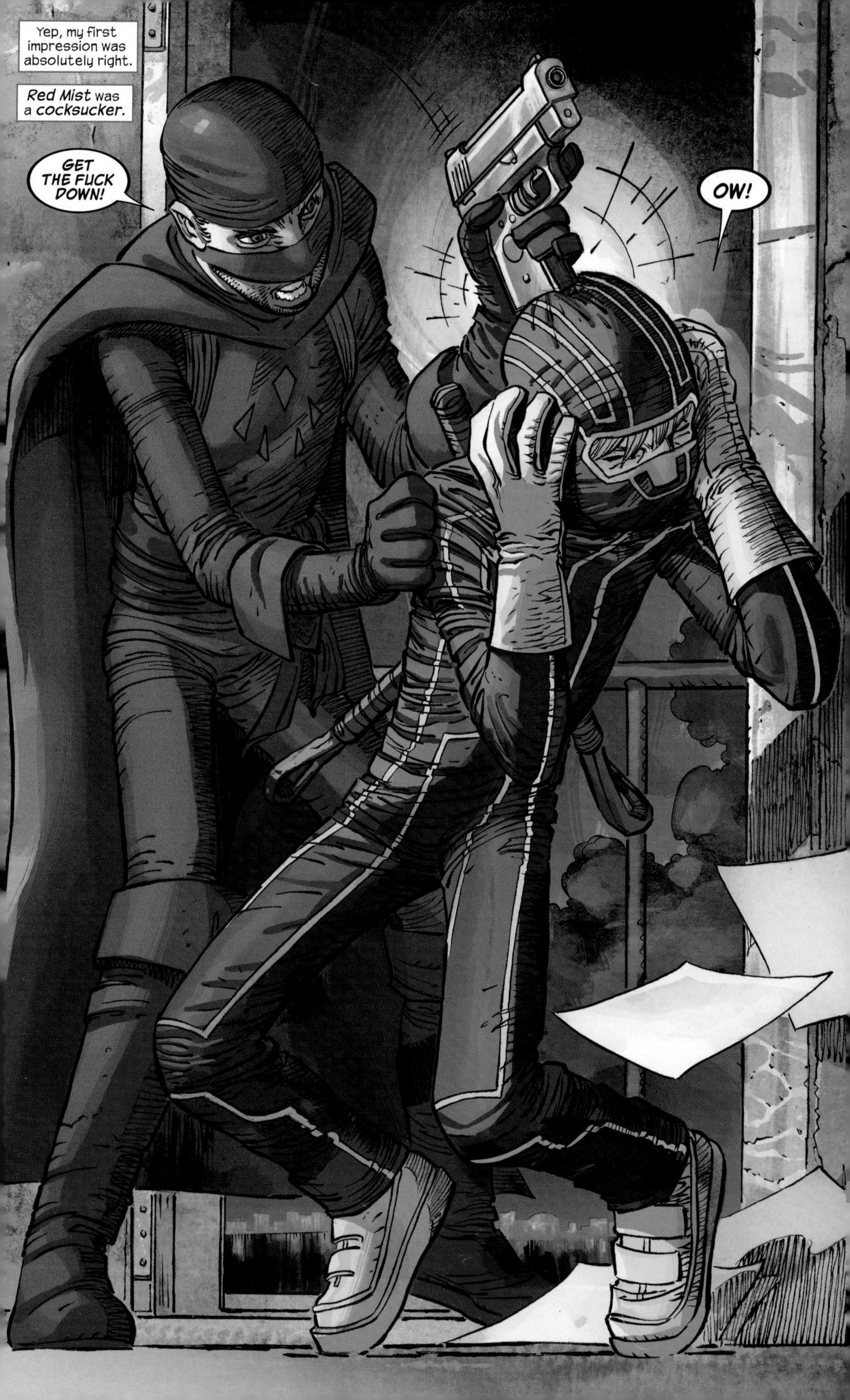
Yep, my first impression was absolutely right.
Red Mist was a cocksucker.
GET THE FUCK DOWN!
OW!

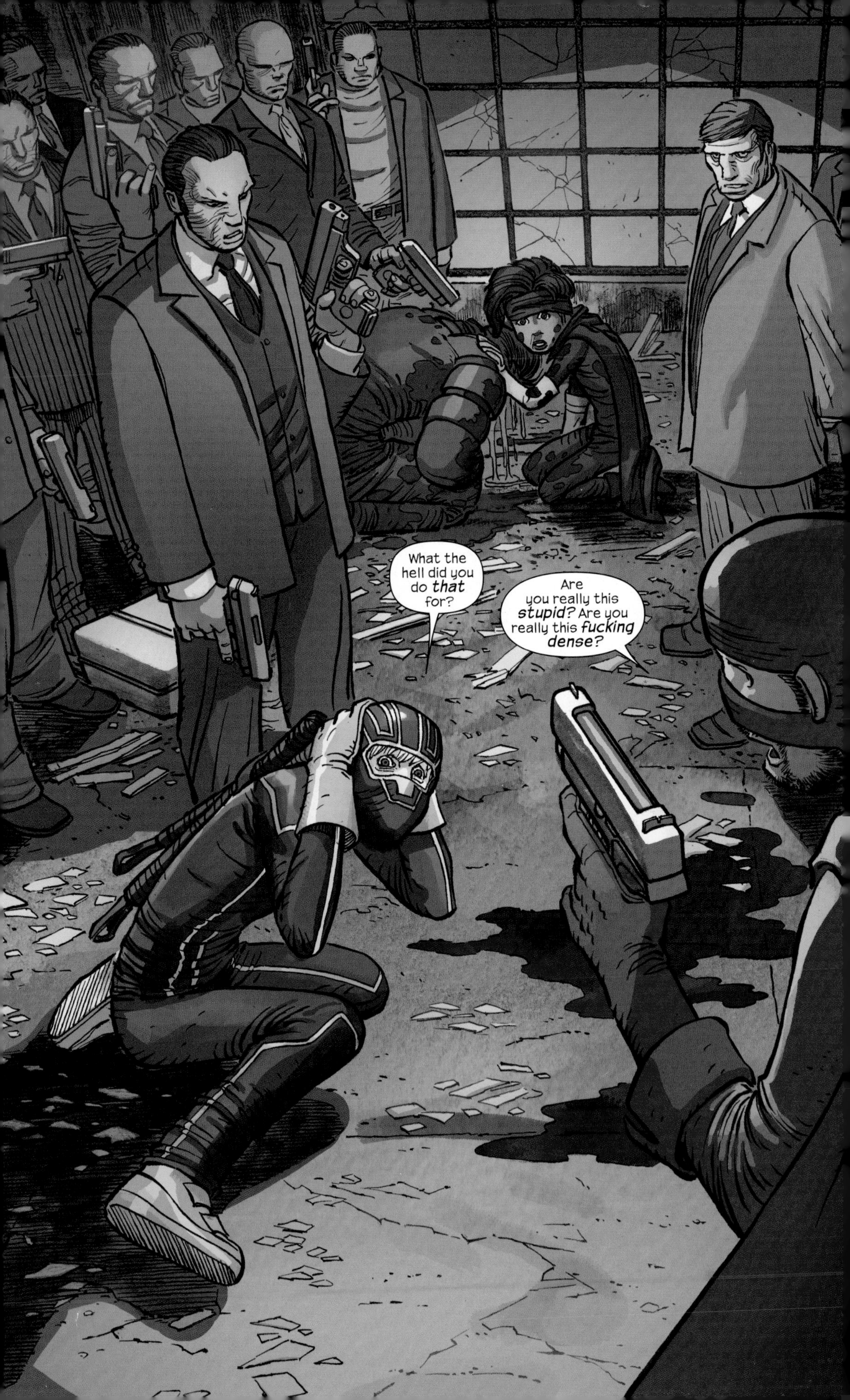

What the hell did you do *that* for?
Are you really this *stupid?* Are you really this *fucking dense?*

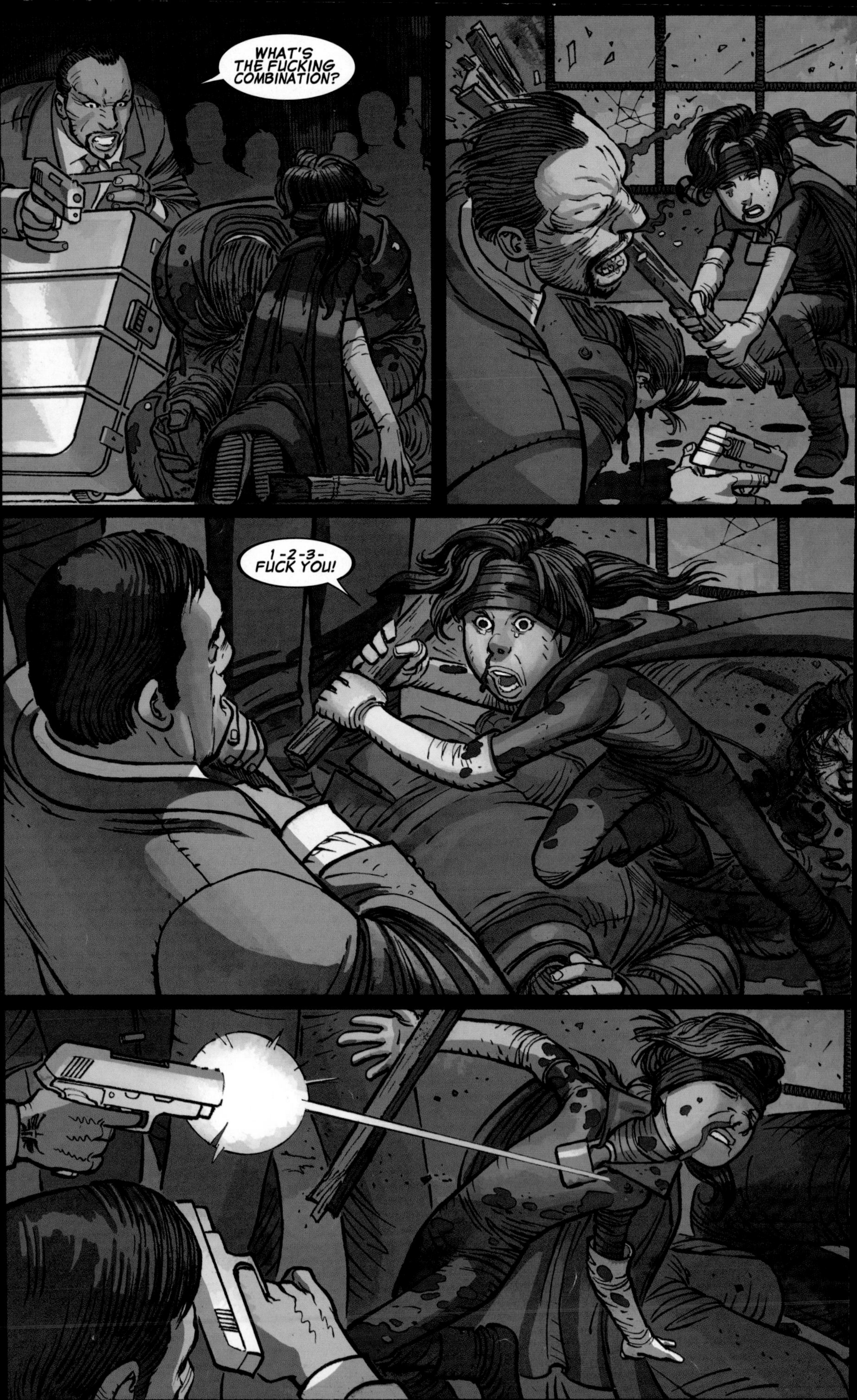
WHAT'S THE FUCKING COMBINATION?
1-2-3- FUCK YOU!

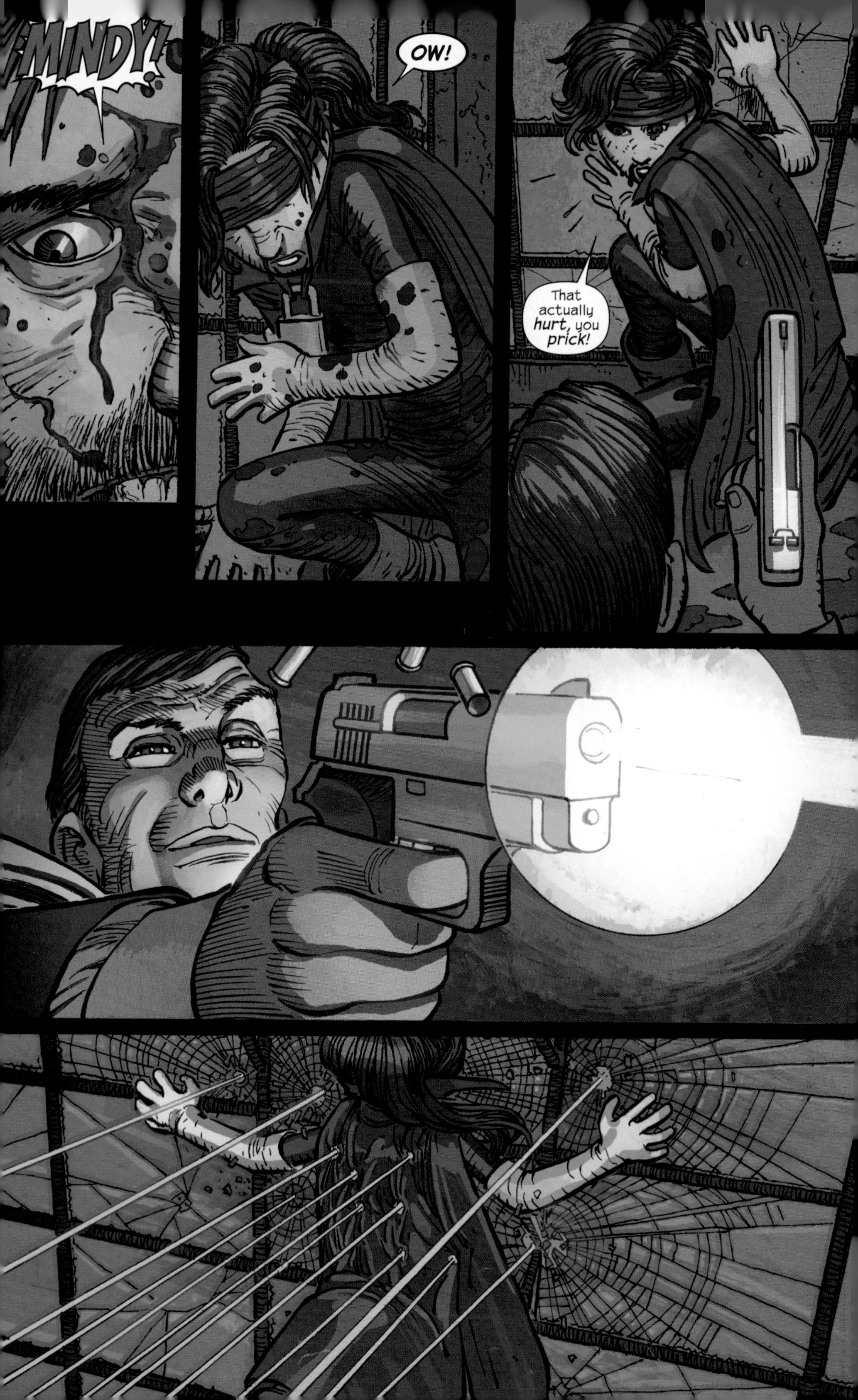
MINDY!
OW!
That actually hurt, you prick!

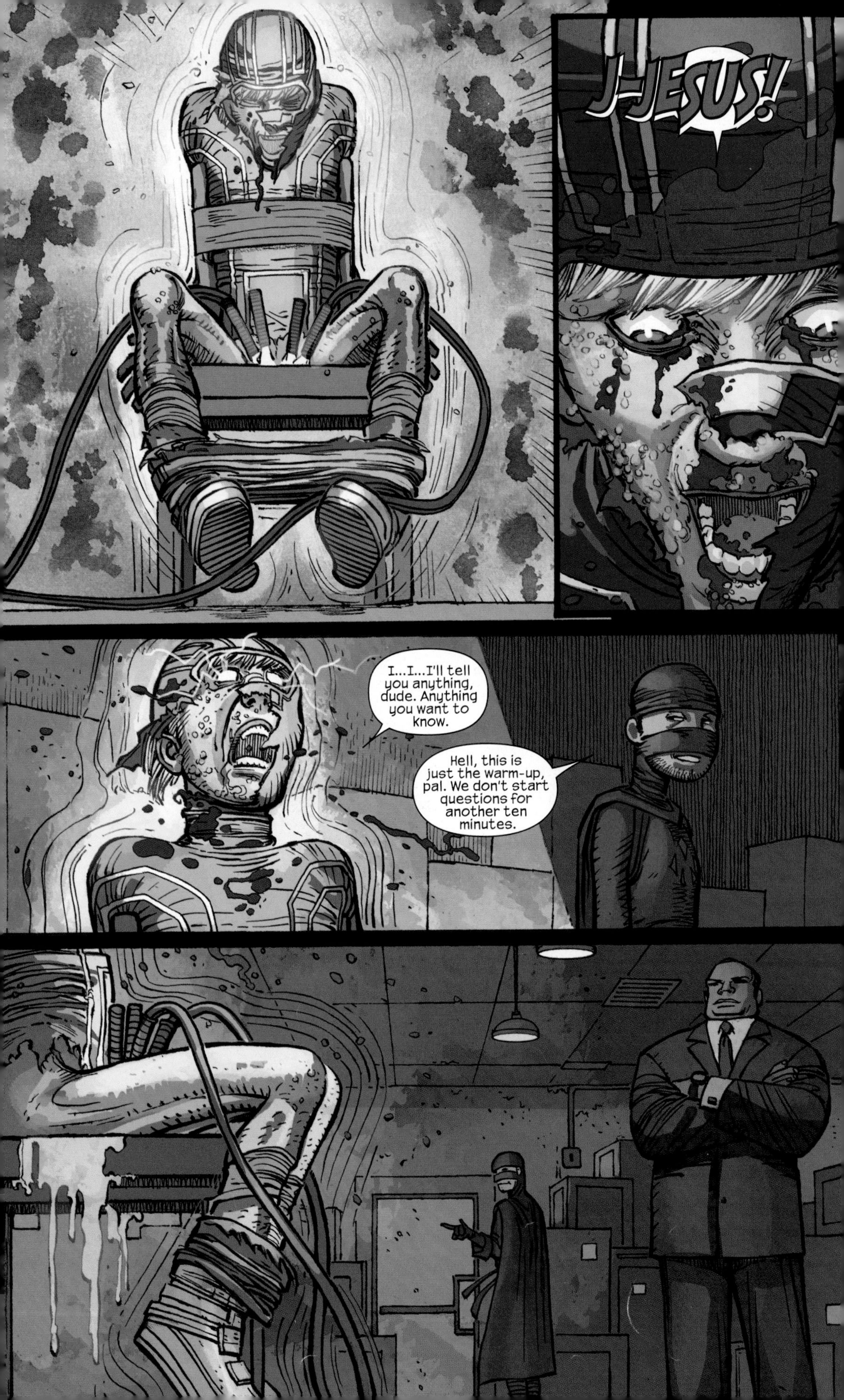
J-JESUS!
I...I...I'll tell you anything, dude. Anything you want to know.
Hell, this is just the warm-up, pal. We don't start questions for another ten minutes.

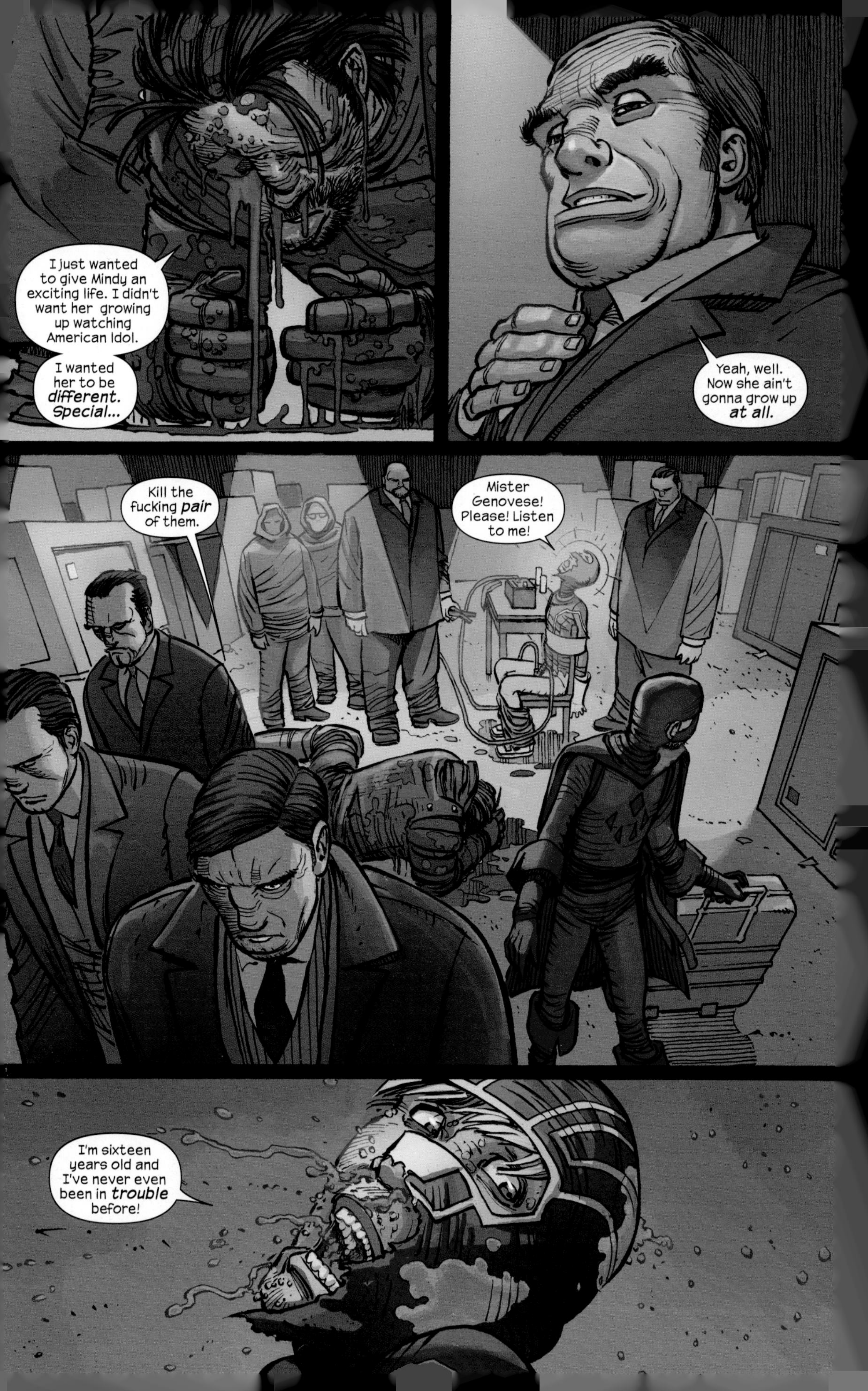

I just wanted to give Mindy an exciting life. I didn't want her growing up watching American Idol.
I wanted her to be *different*. *Special*...
Yeah, well. Now she ain't gonna grow up *at all*.
Kill the fucking *pair* of them.
Mister Genovese! Please! Listen to me!
I'm sixteen years old and I've never even been in *trouble* before!

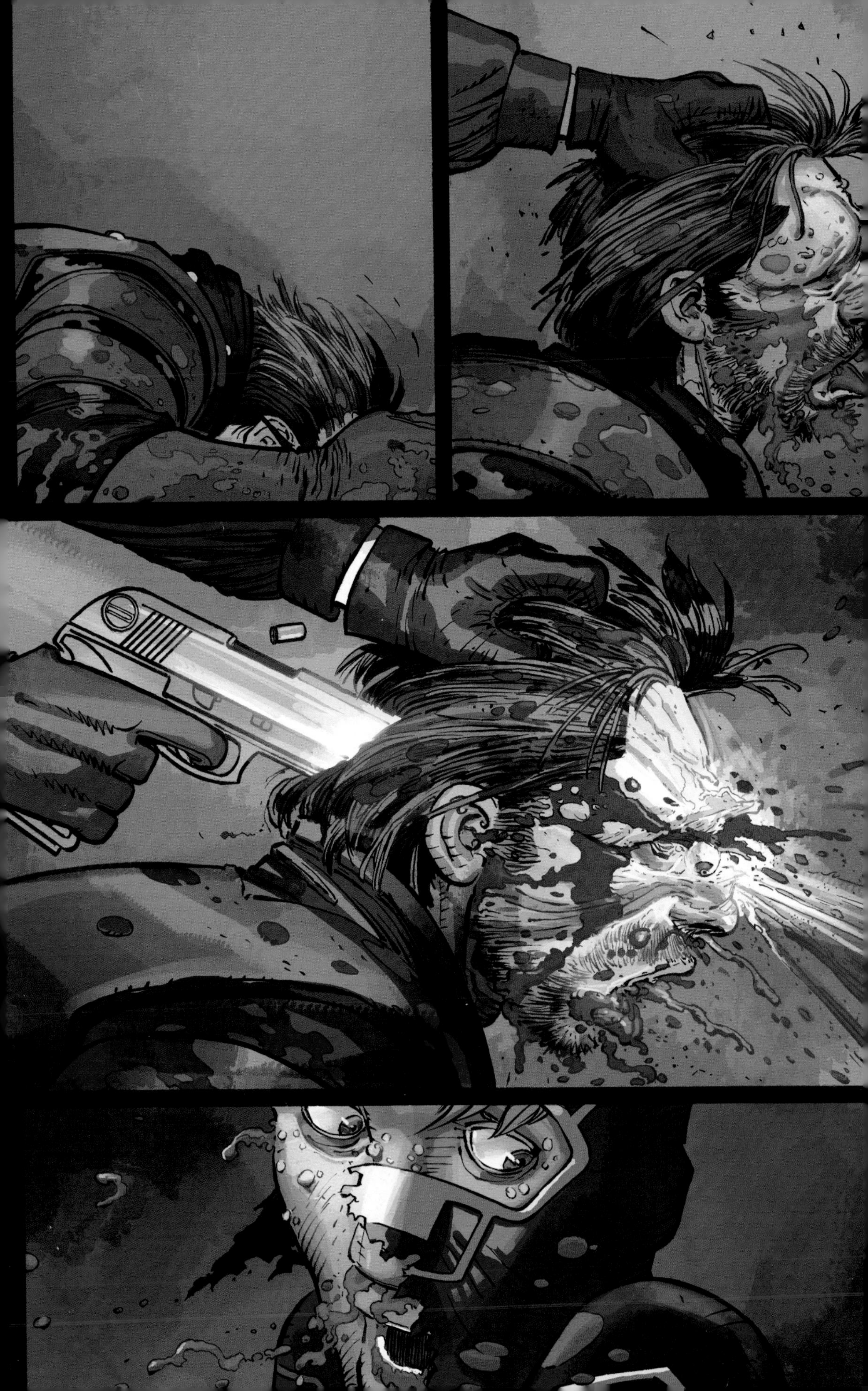

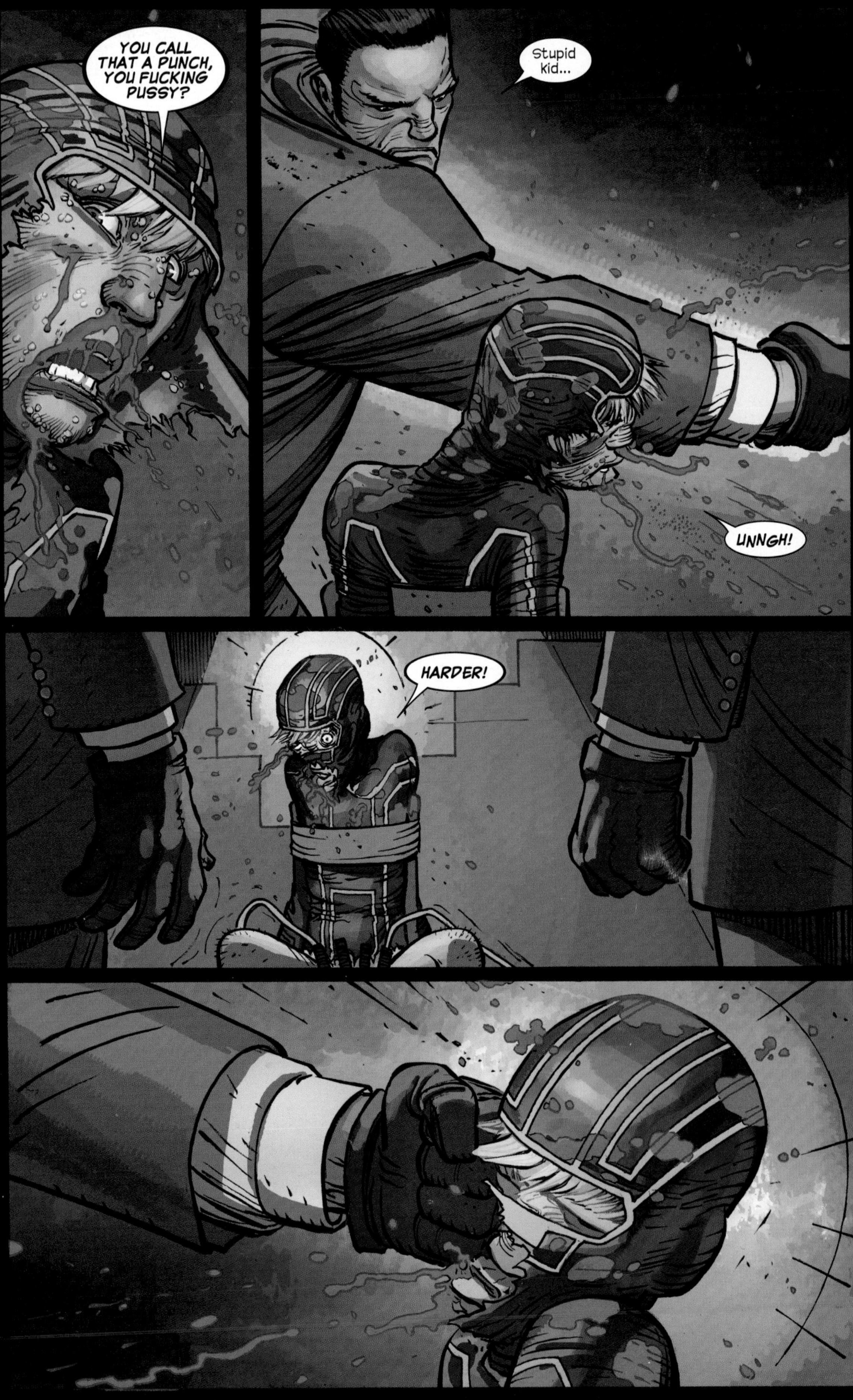
YOU CALL THAT A PUNCH, YOU FUCKING PUSSY?
Stupid kid...
UNNGH!
HARDER!

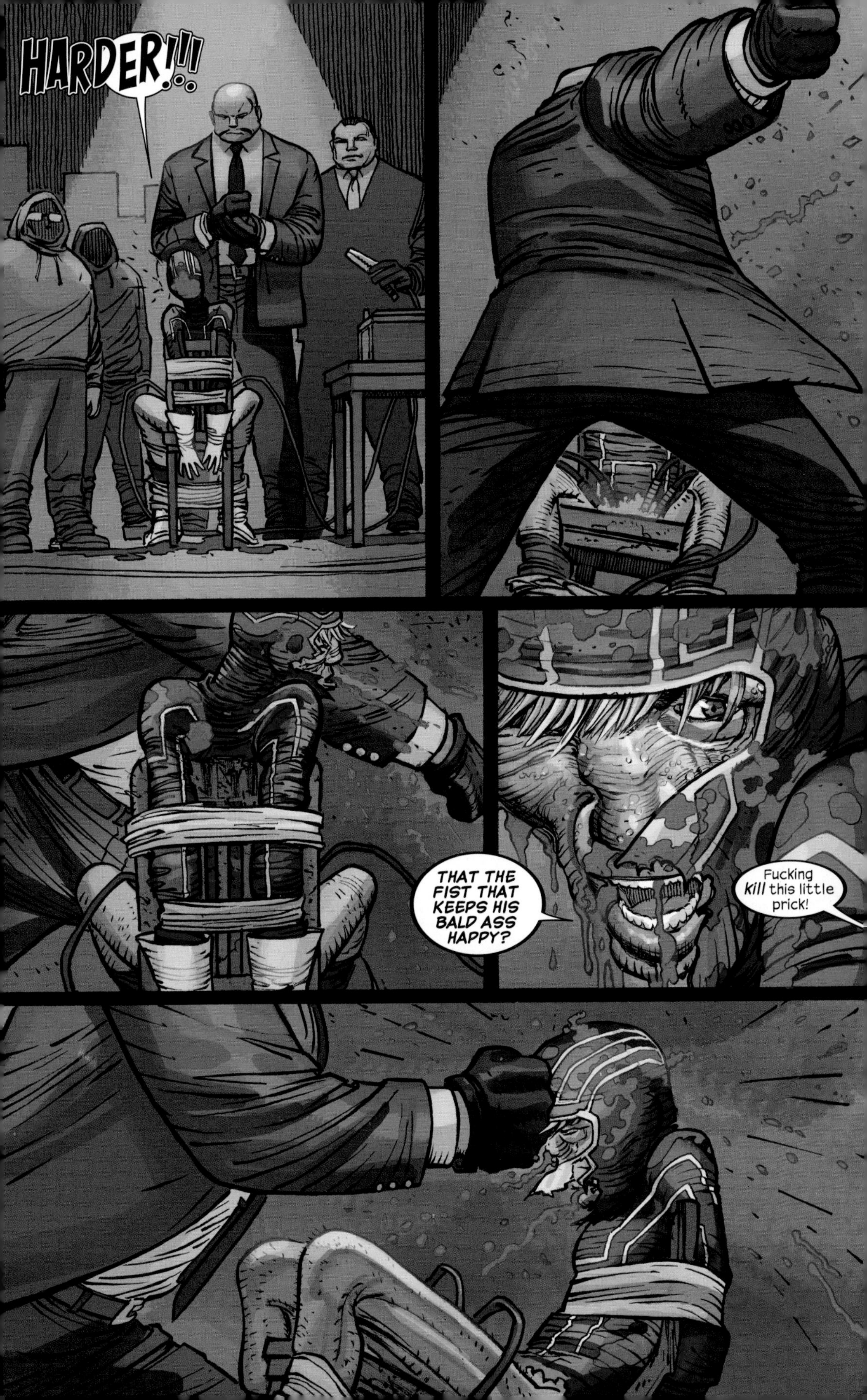
HARDER!!!
THAT THE FIST THAT KEEPS HIS BALD ASS HAPPY?
Fucking *kill* this little prick!

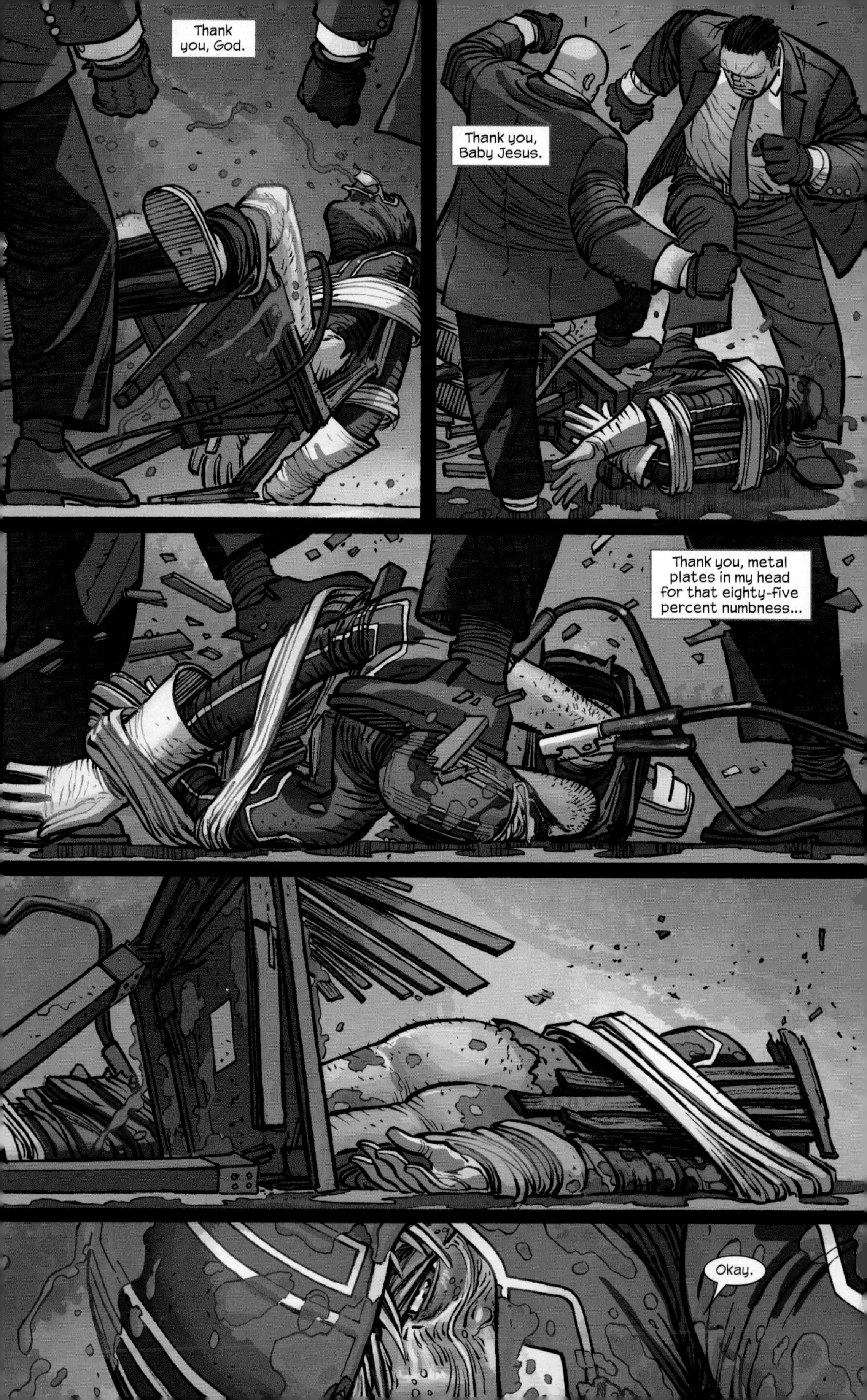
Thank you, God.
Thank you, Baby Jesus.
Thank you, metal plates in my head for that eighty-five percent numbness...
Okay.

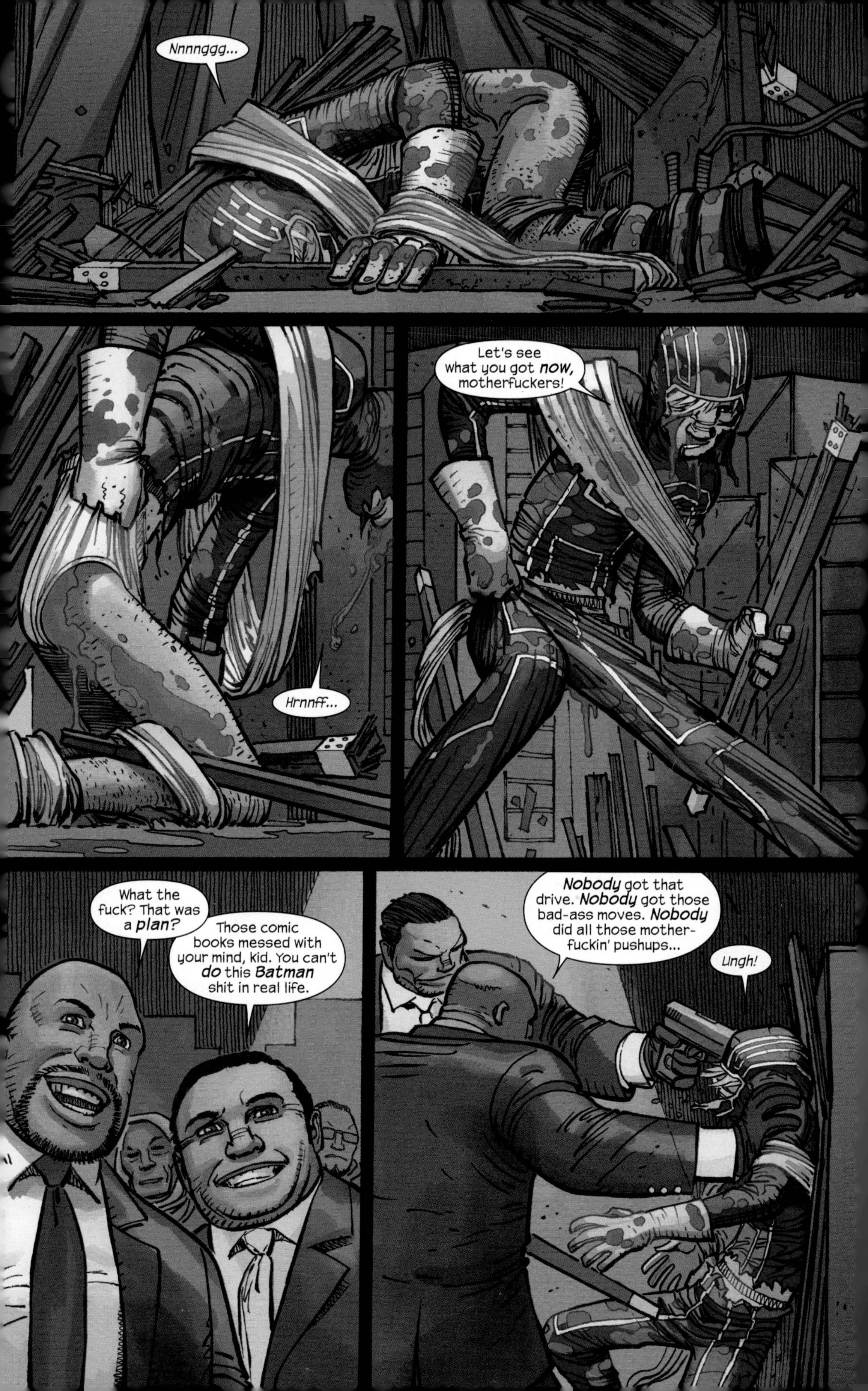
Nnnnggg...
Hrnnff...
Let's see what you got **now,** motherfuckers!
What the fuck? That was a *plan?*
Those comic books messed with your mind, kid. You can't ***do*** this ***Batman*** shit in real life.
Nobody got that drive. ***Nobody*** got those bad-ass moves. ***Nobody*** did all those mother-fuckin' pushups...
Ungh!

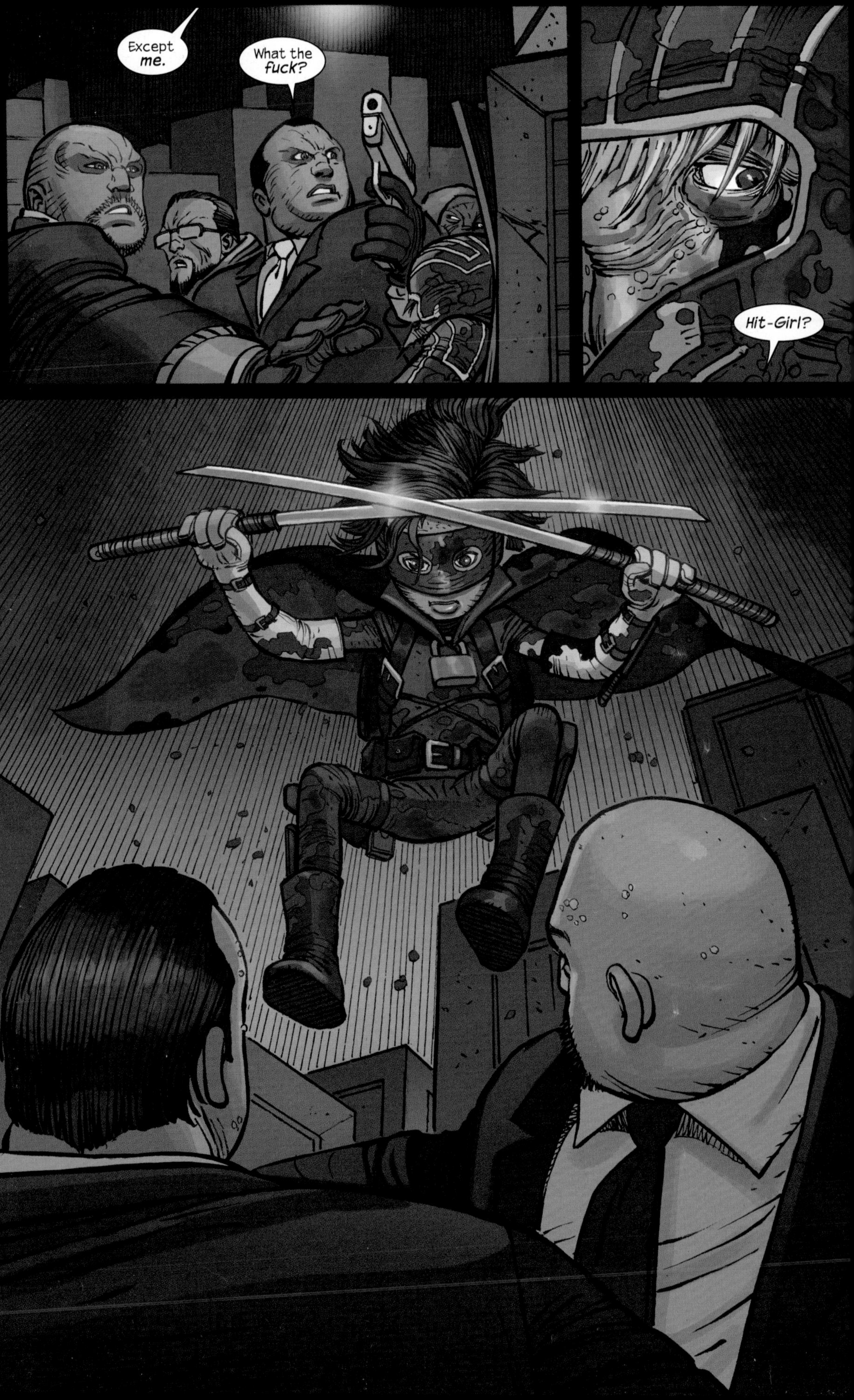
Except me.
What the fuck?
Hit-Girl?

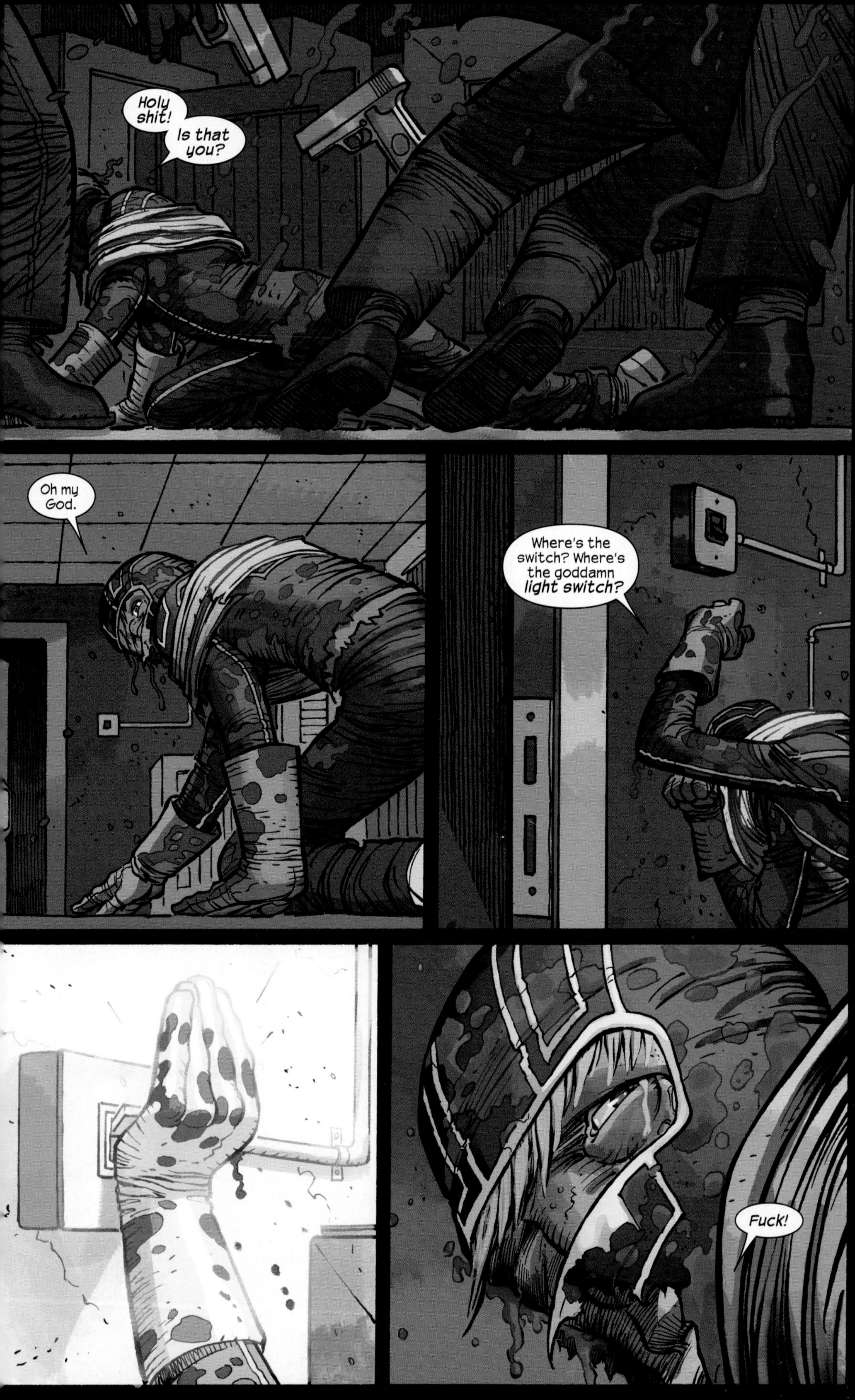
Holy shit!
Is that you?
Oh my God.
Where's the switch? Where's the goddamn *light switch?*
Fuck!

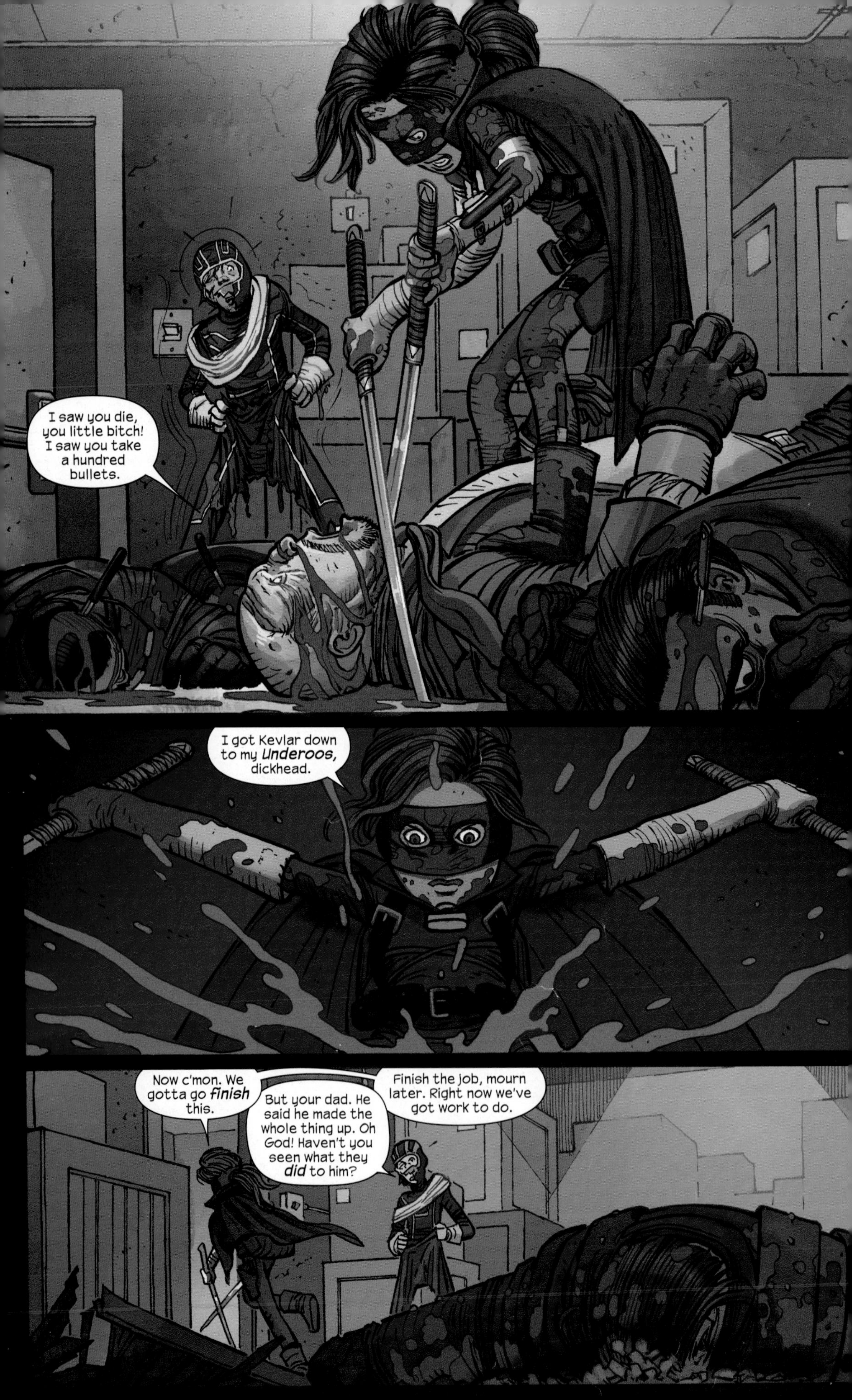
I saw you die, you little bitch! I saw you take a hundred bullets.
I got Kevlar down to my *Underoos,* dickhead.
Now c'mon. We gotta go *finish* this.
But your dad. He said he made the whole thing up. Oh God! Haven't you seen what they *did* to him?
Finish the job, mourn later. Right now we've got work to do.

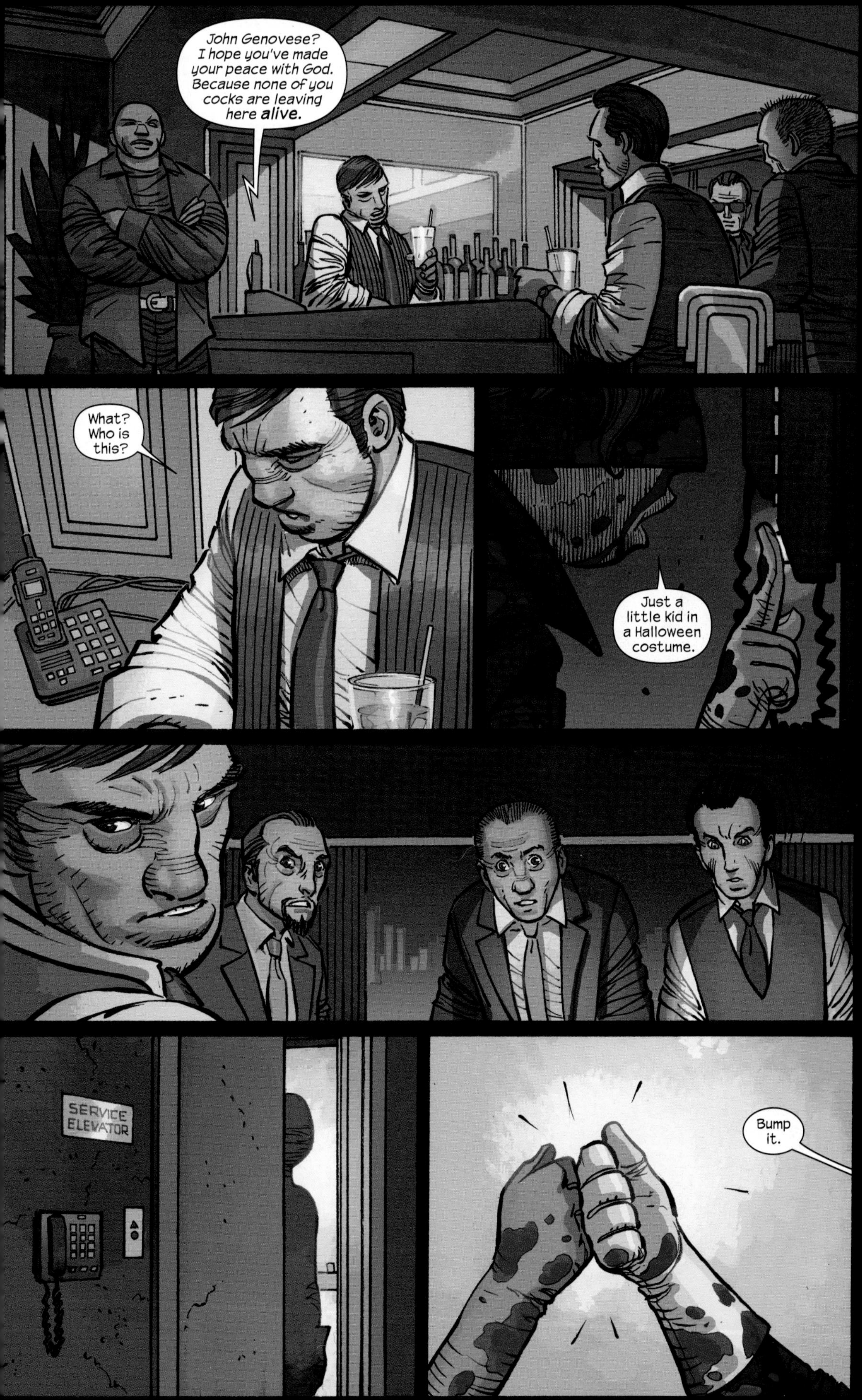
John Genovese? I hope you've made your peace with God. Because none of you cocks are leaving here alive.
What? Who is this?
Just a little kid in a Halloween costume.
SERVICE ELEVATOR
Bump it.

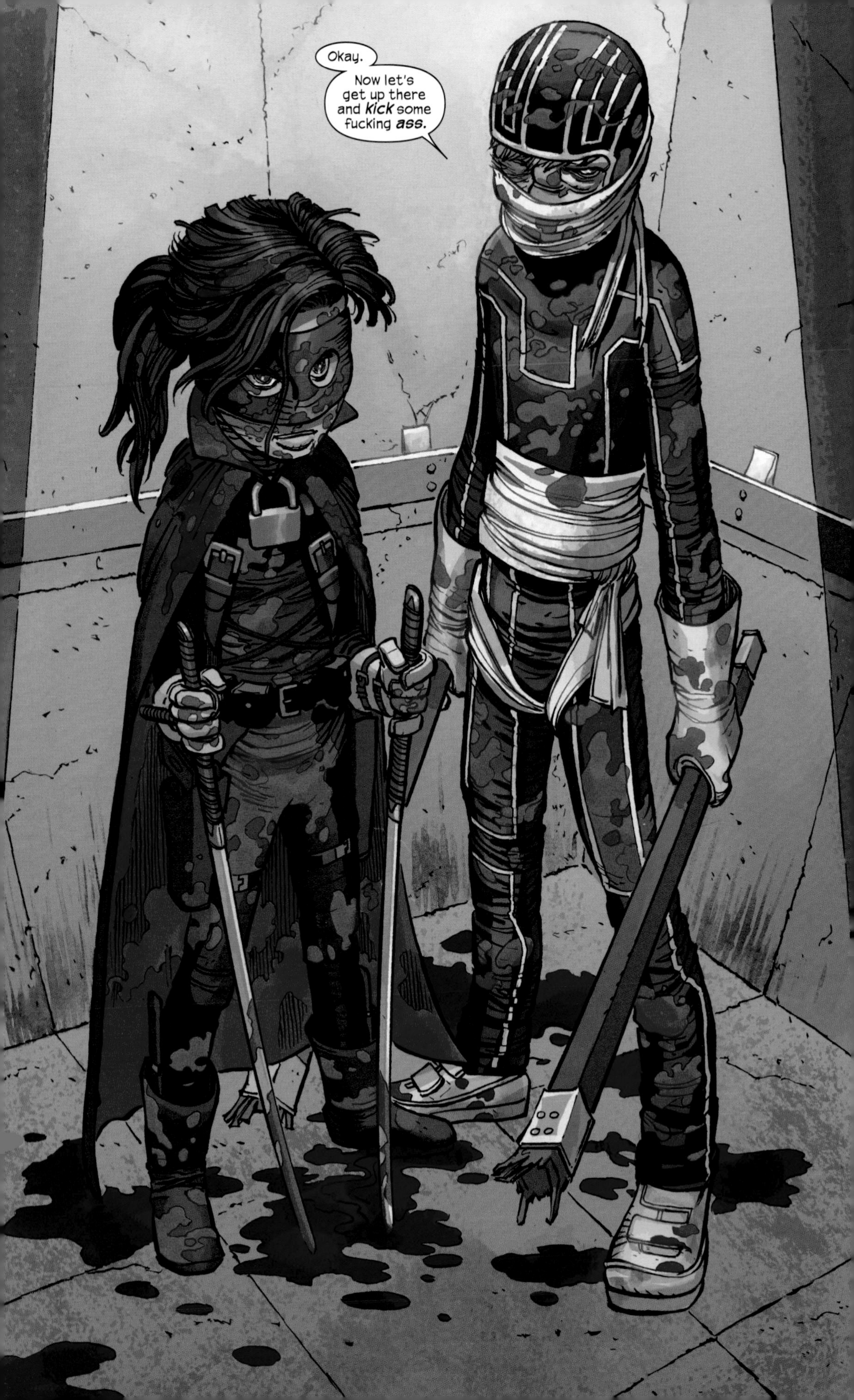
Okay.
Now let's get up there and *kick* some fucking *ass.*

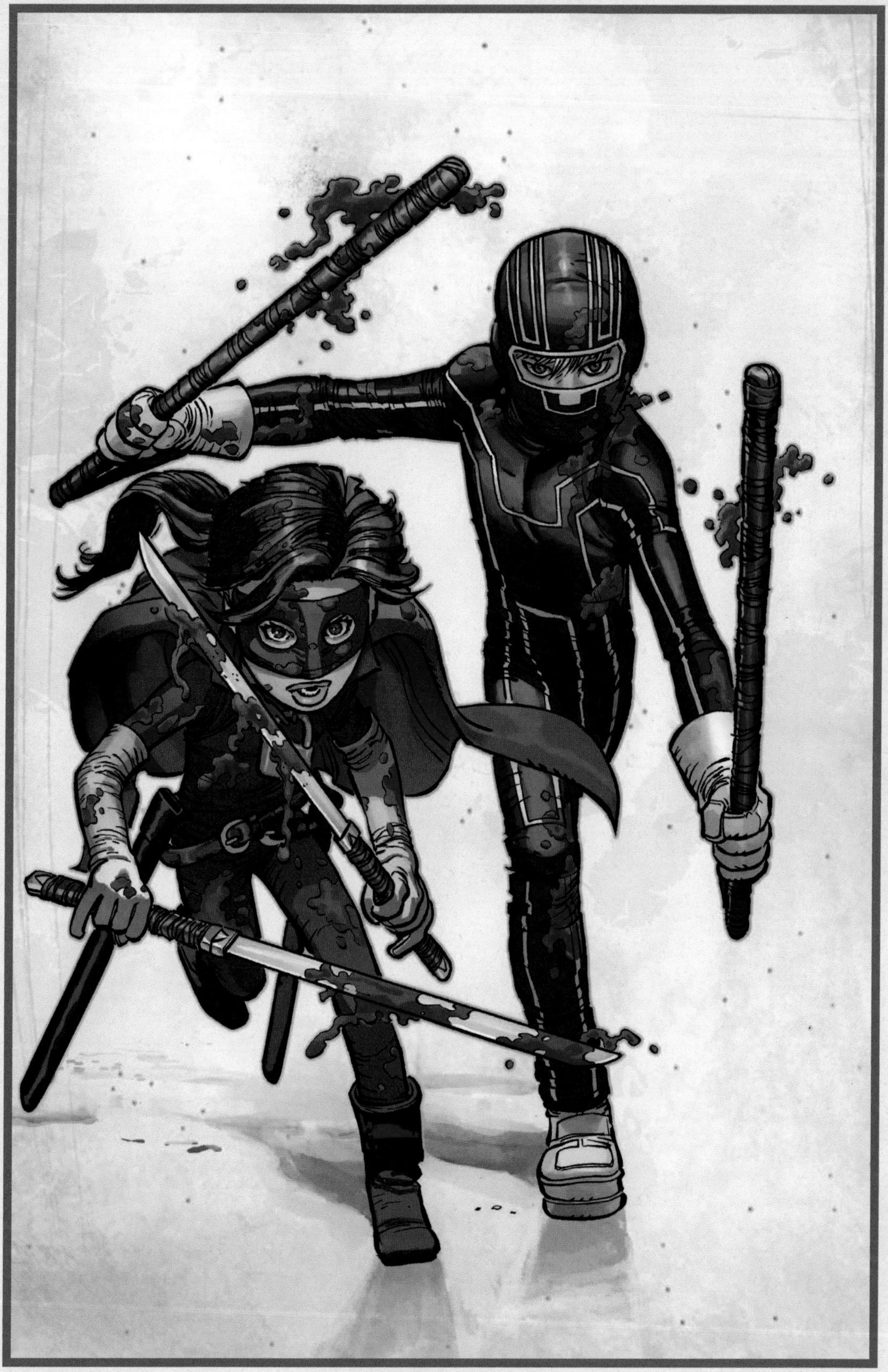

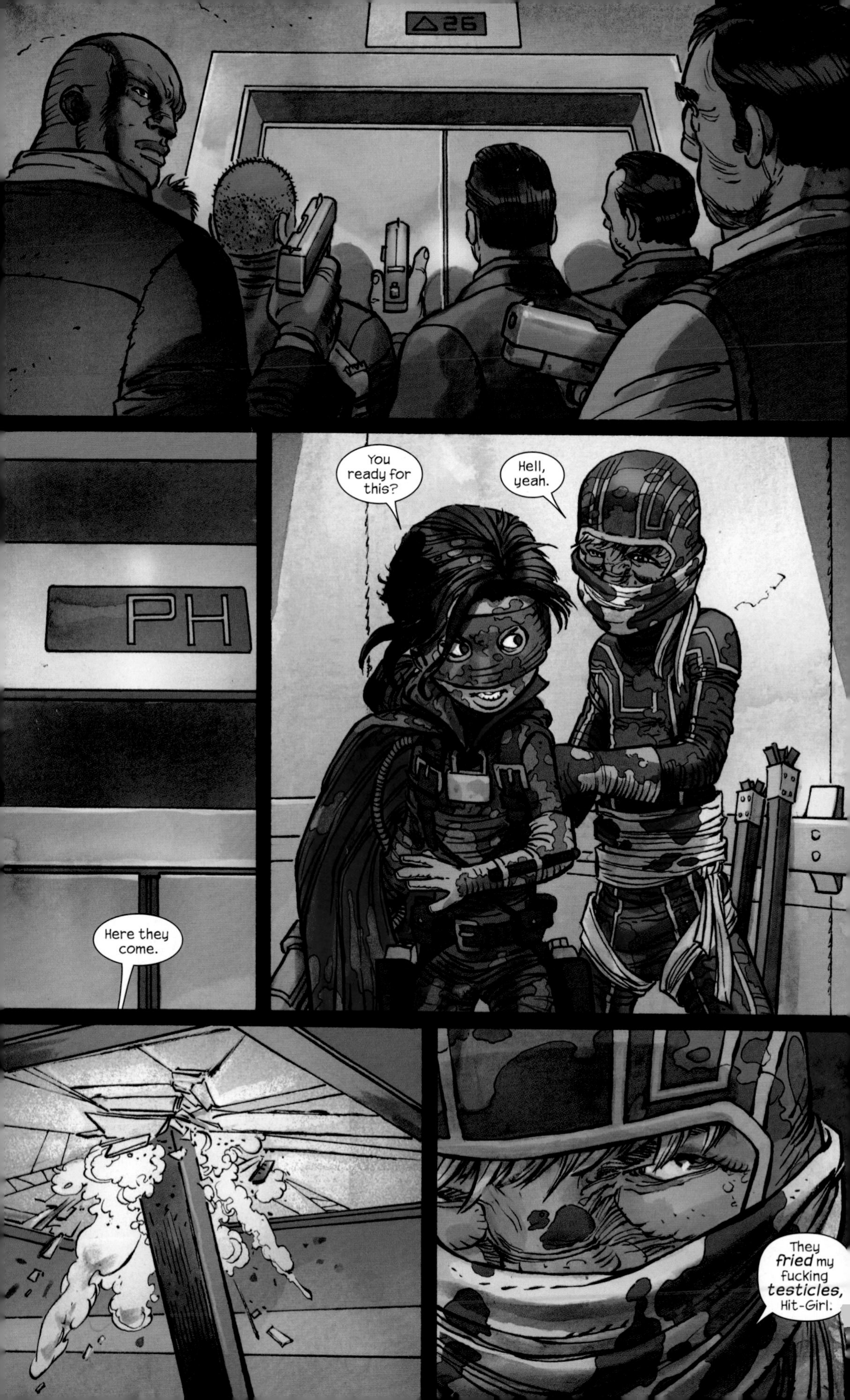
26
PH
You ready for this?
Hell, yeah.
Here they come.
They *fried* my fucking *testicles,* Hit-Girl.

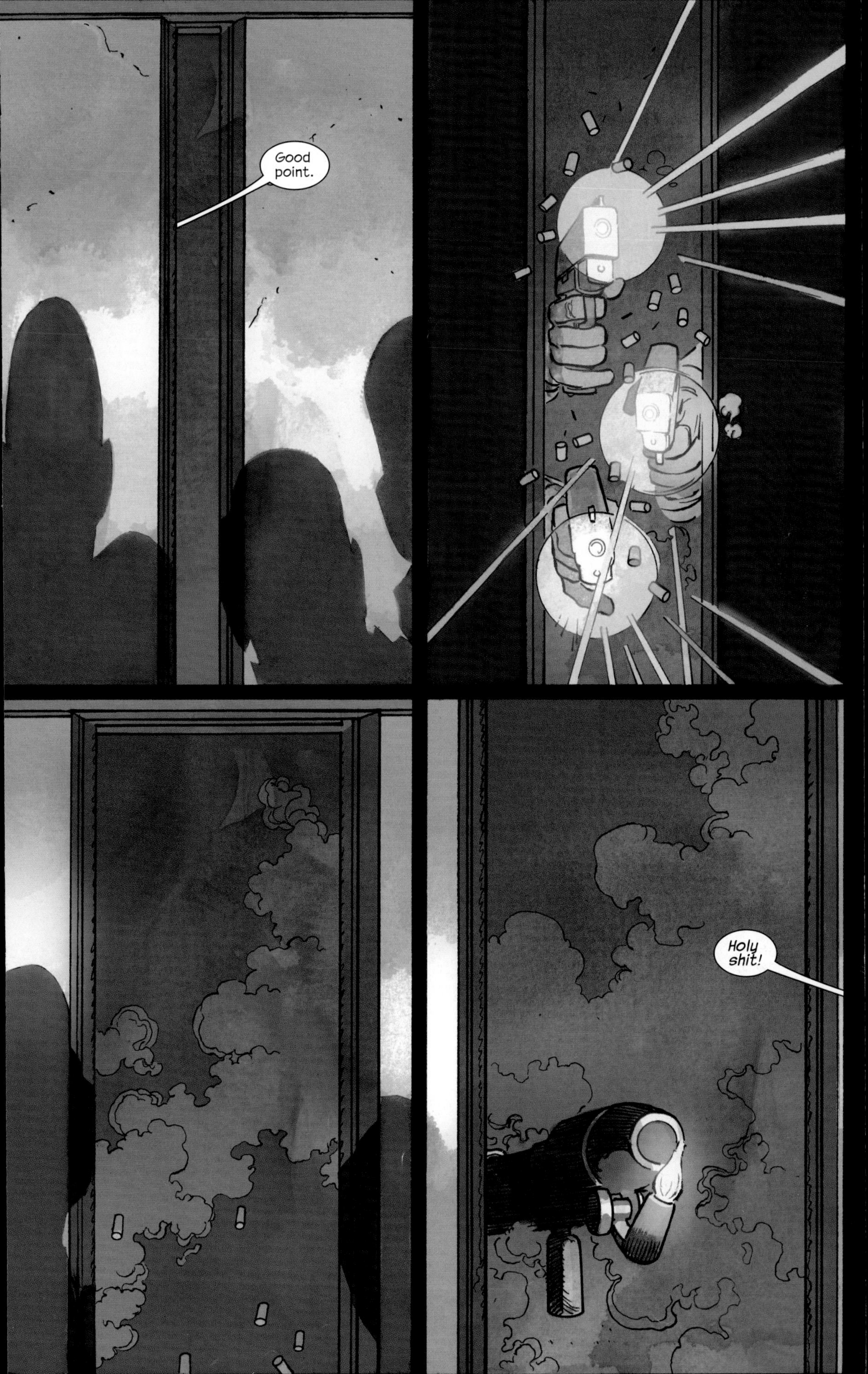
Good point.
Holy shit!

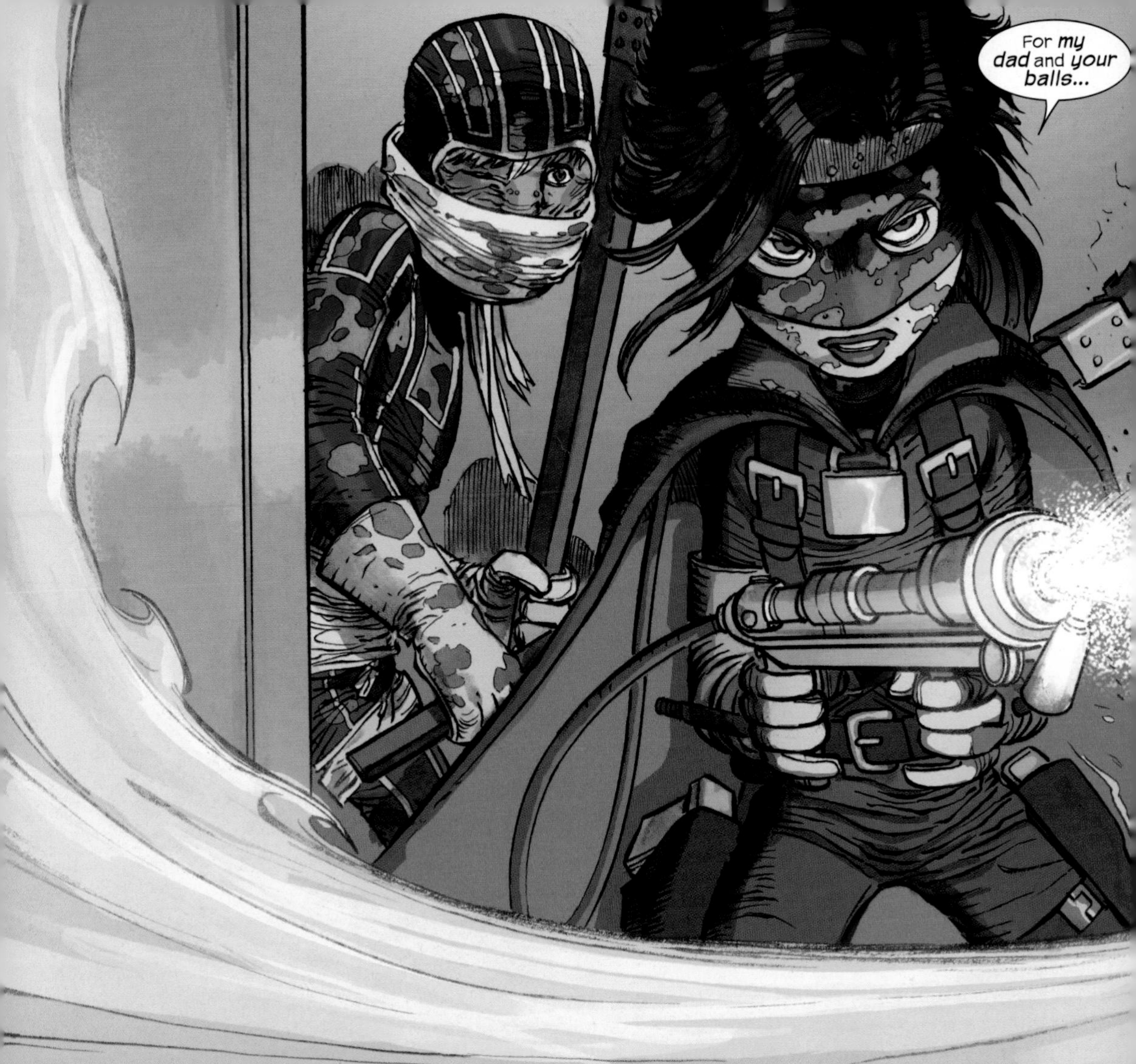
For my dad and your balls...

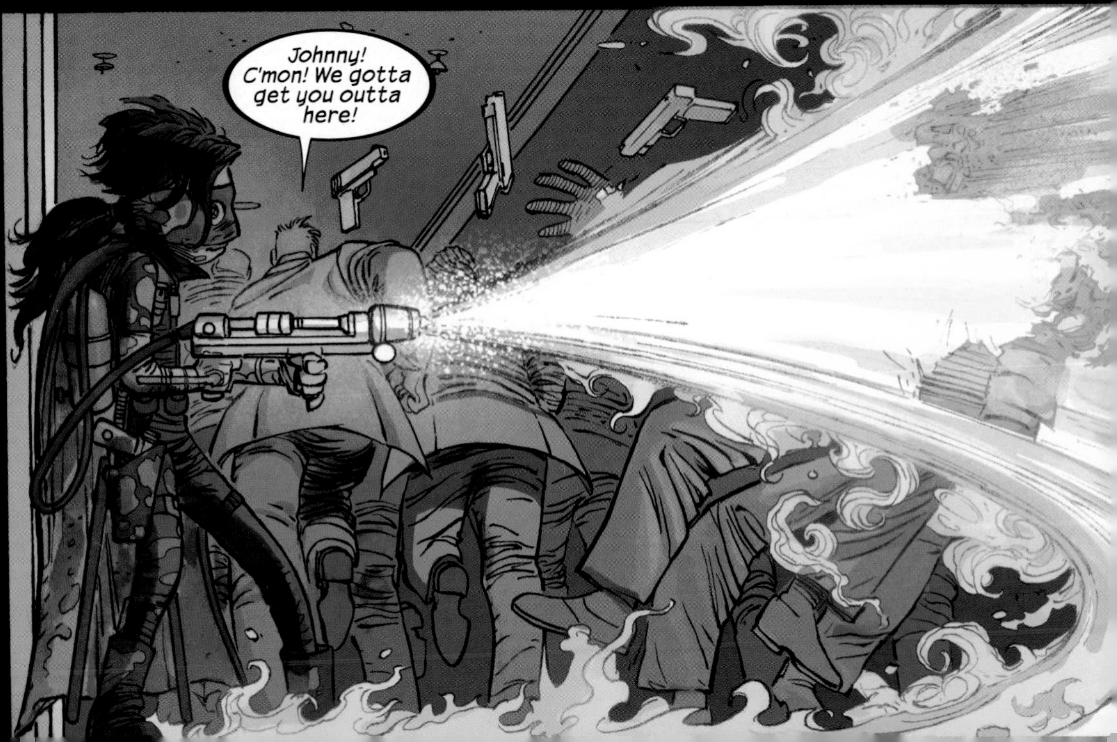
Johnny! C'mon! We gotta get you outta here!

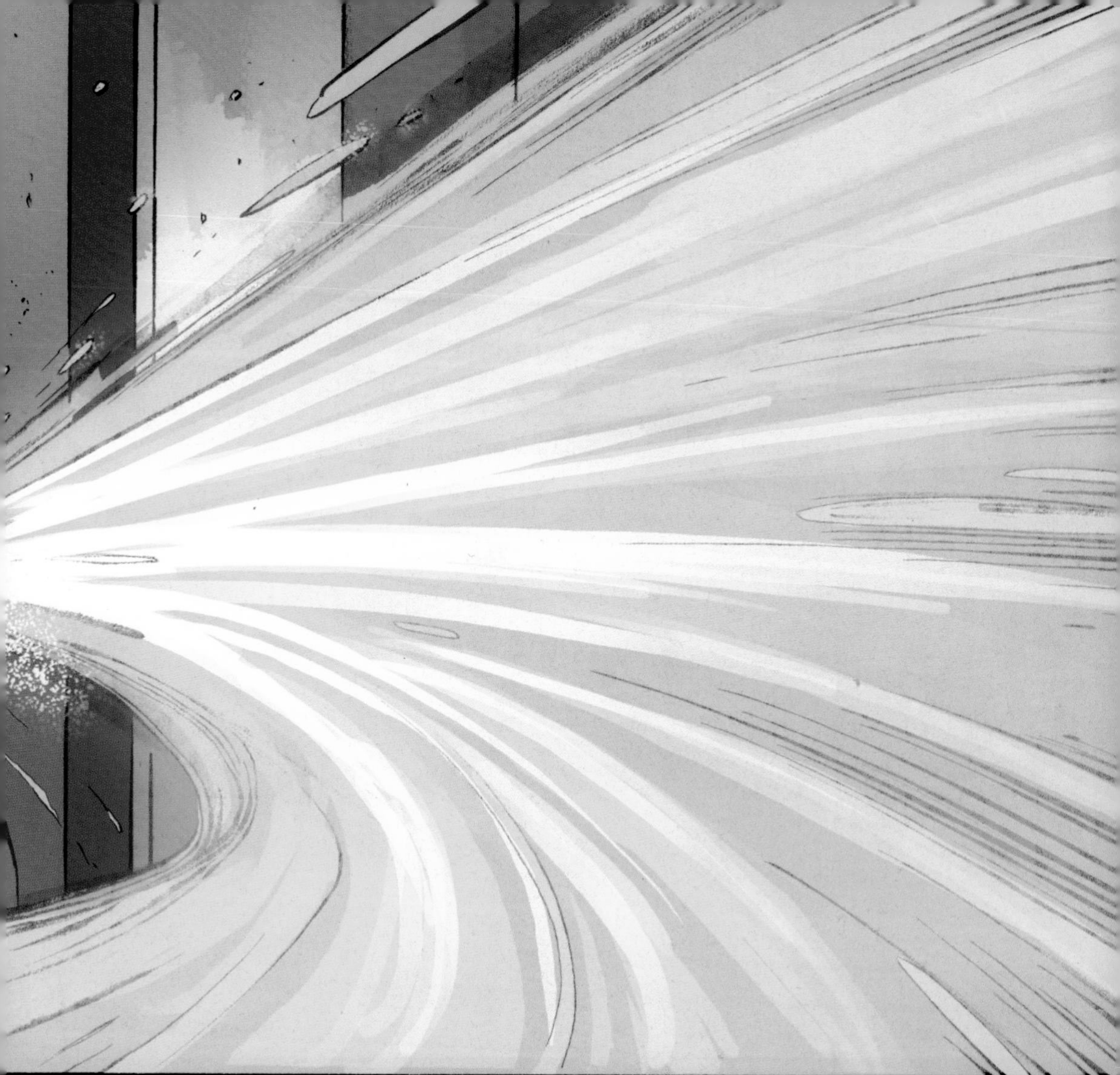
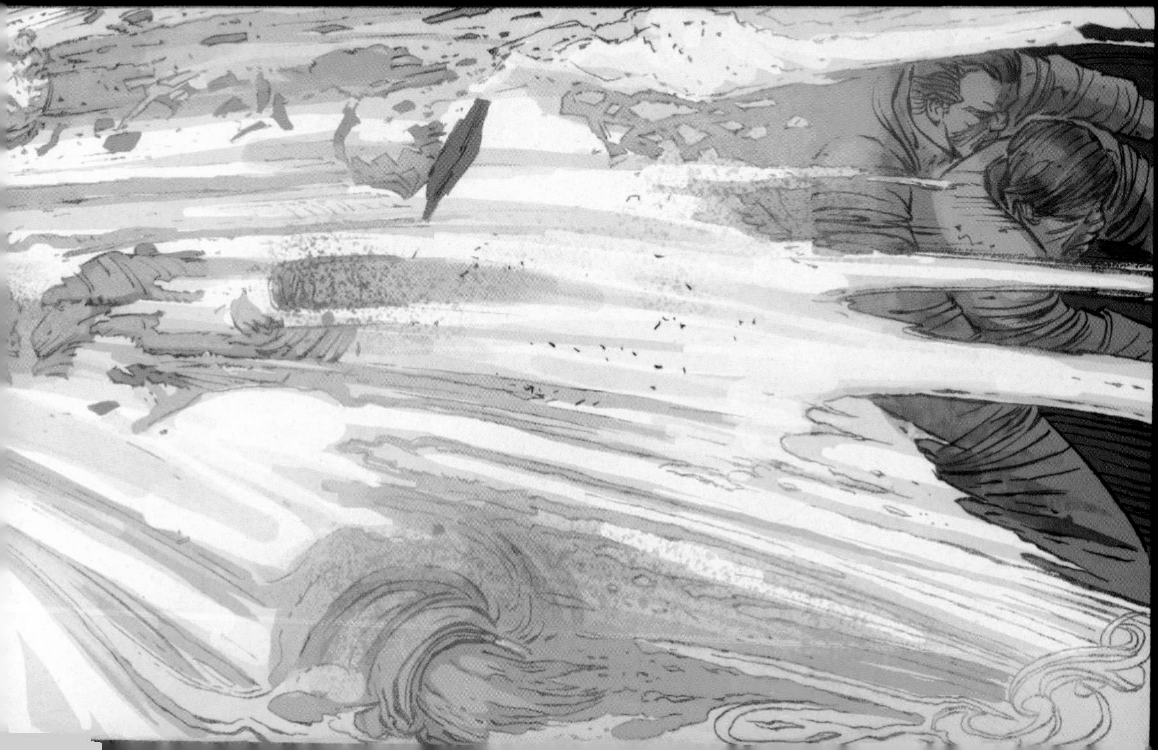

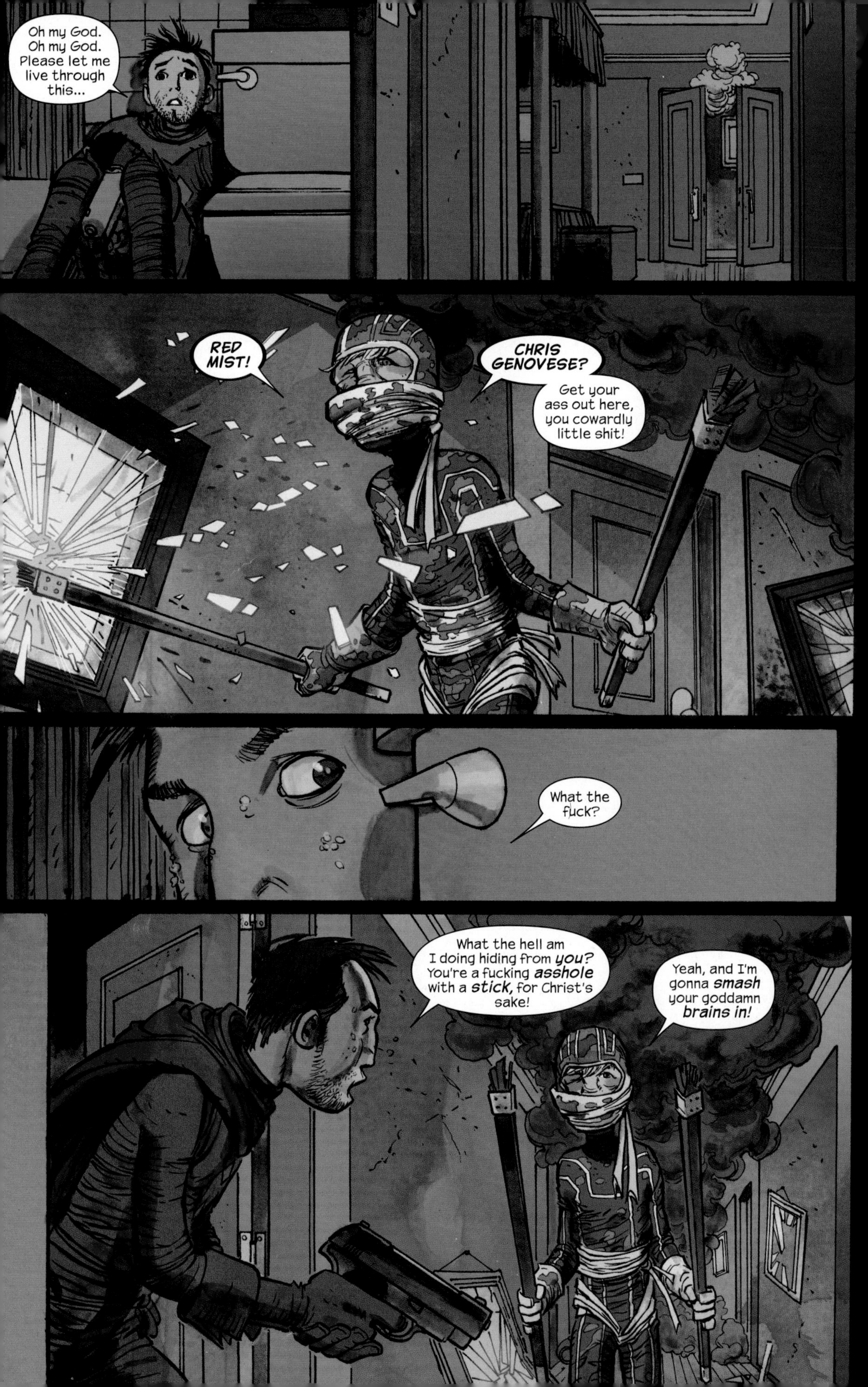
Oh my God. Oh my God. Please let me live through this...
RED MIST!
CHRIS GENOVESE?
Get your ass out here, you cowardly little shit!
What the fuck?
What the hell am I doing hiding from *you*? You're a fucking *asshole* with a *stick*, for Christ's sake!
Yeah, and I'm gonna *smash* your goddamn *brains in*!

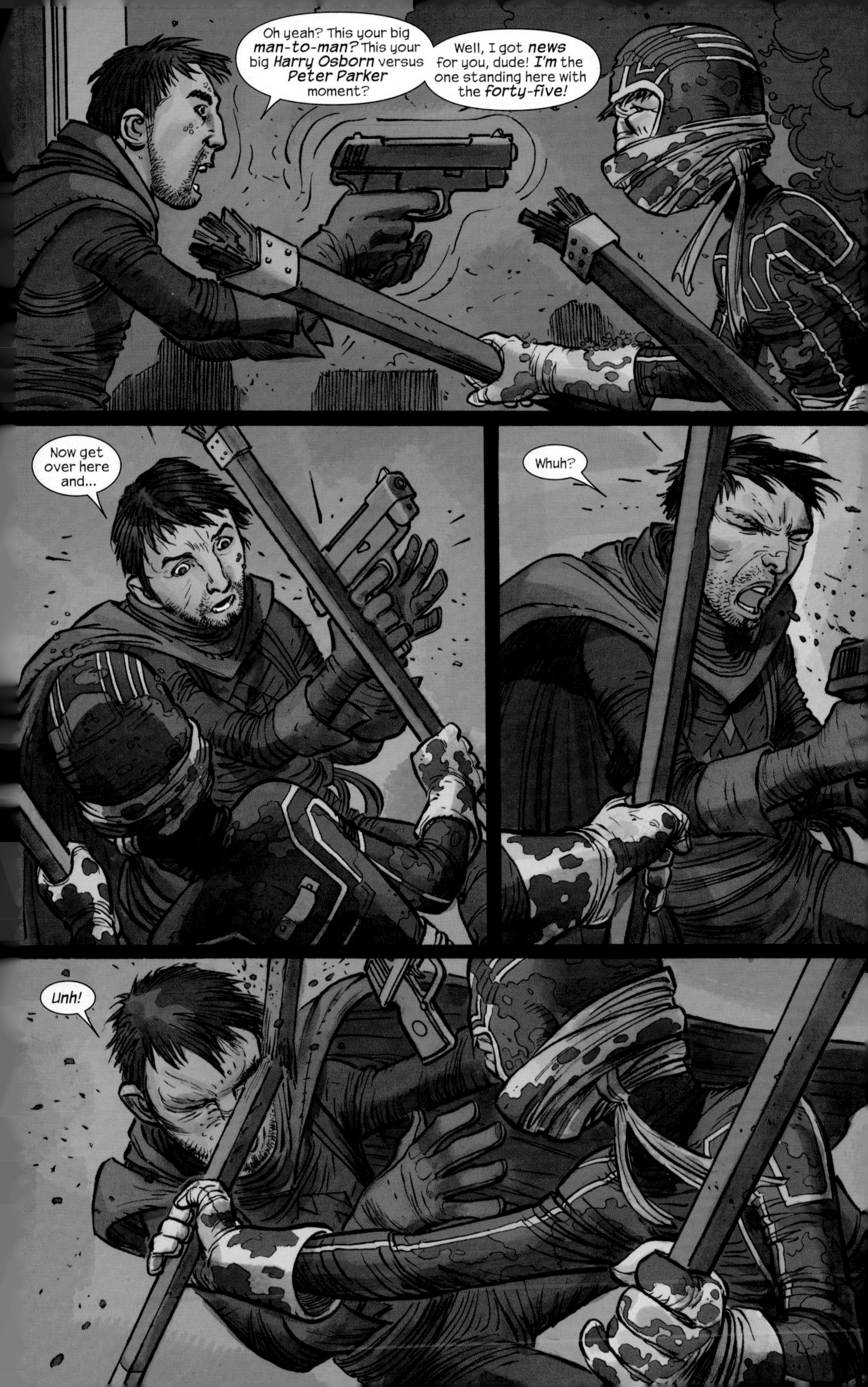
Oh yeah? This your big man-to-man? This your big Harry Osborn versus Peter Parker moment?
Well, I got news for you, dude! I'm the one standing here with the forty-five!
Now get over here and...
Whuh?
Unh!

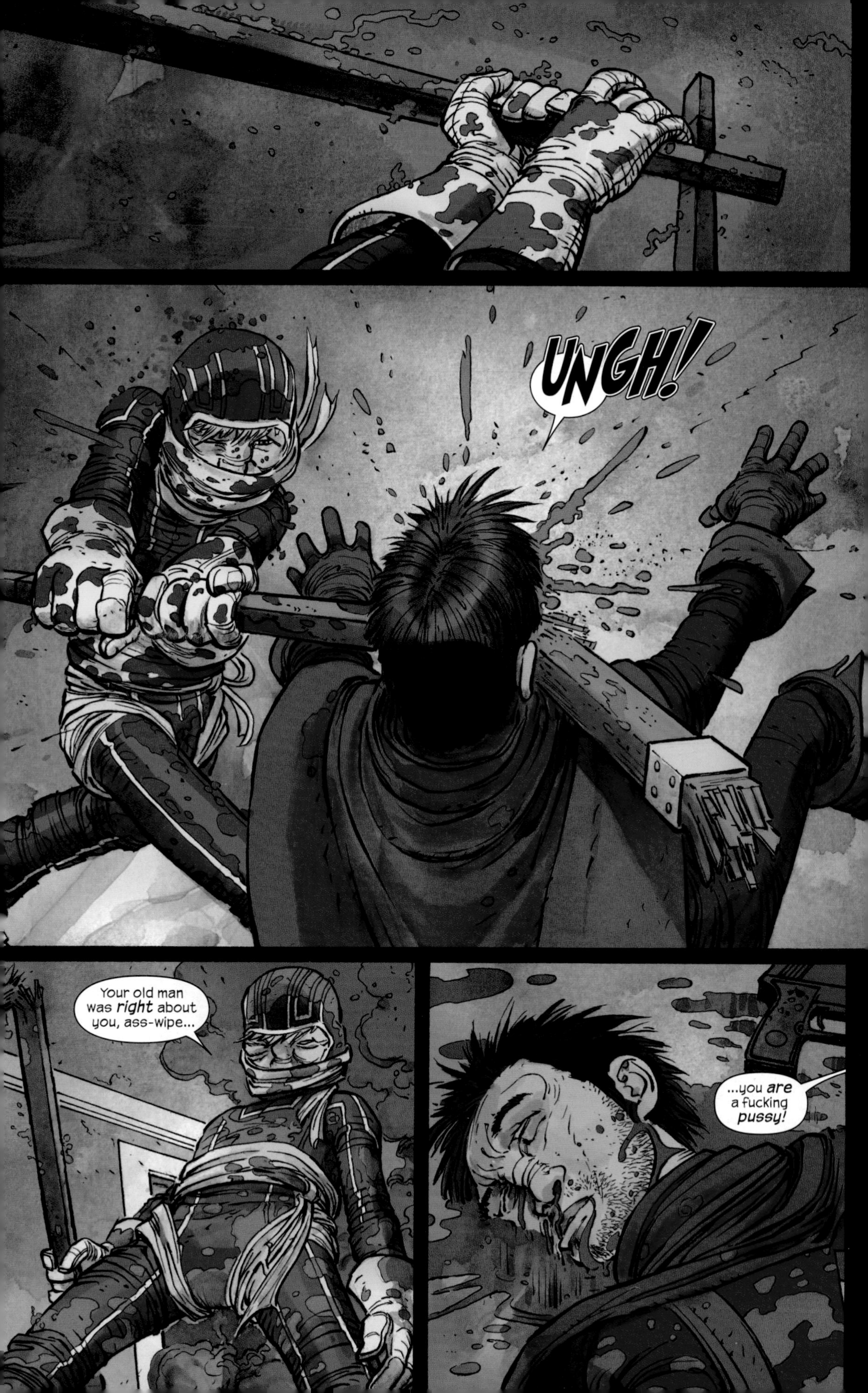
UNGH!
Your old man was right about you, ass-wipe...
...you are a fucking pussy!

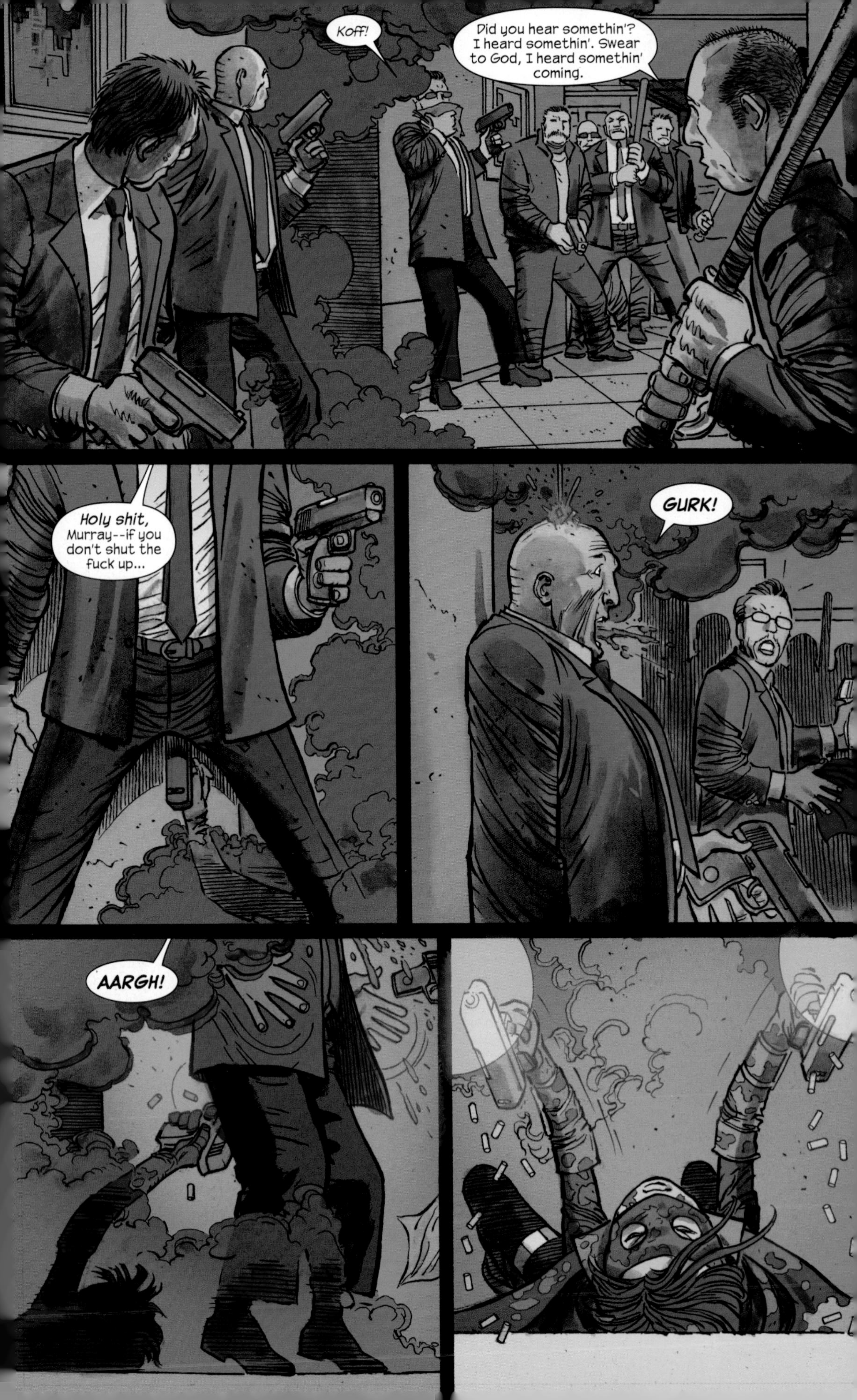
Koff!
Did you hear somethin'? I heard somethin'. Swear to God, I heard somethin' coming.
Holy shit, Murray--if you don't shut the fuck up...
GURK!
AARGH!

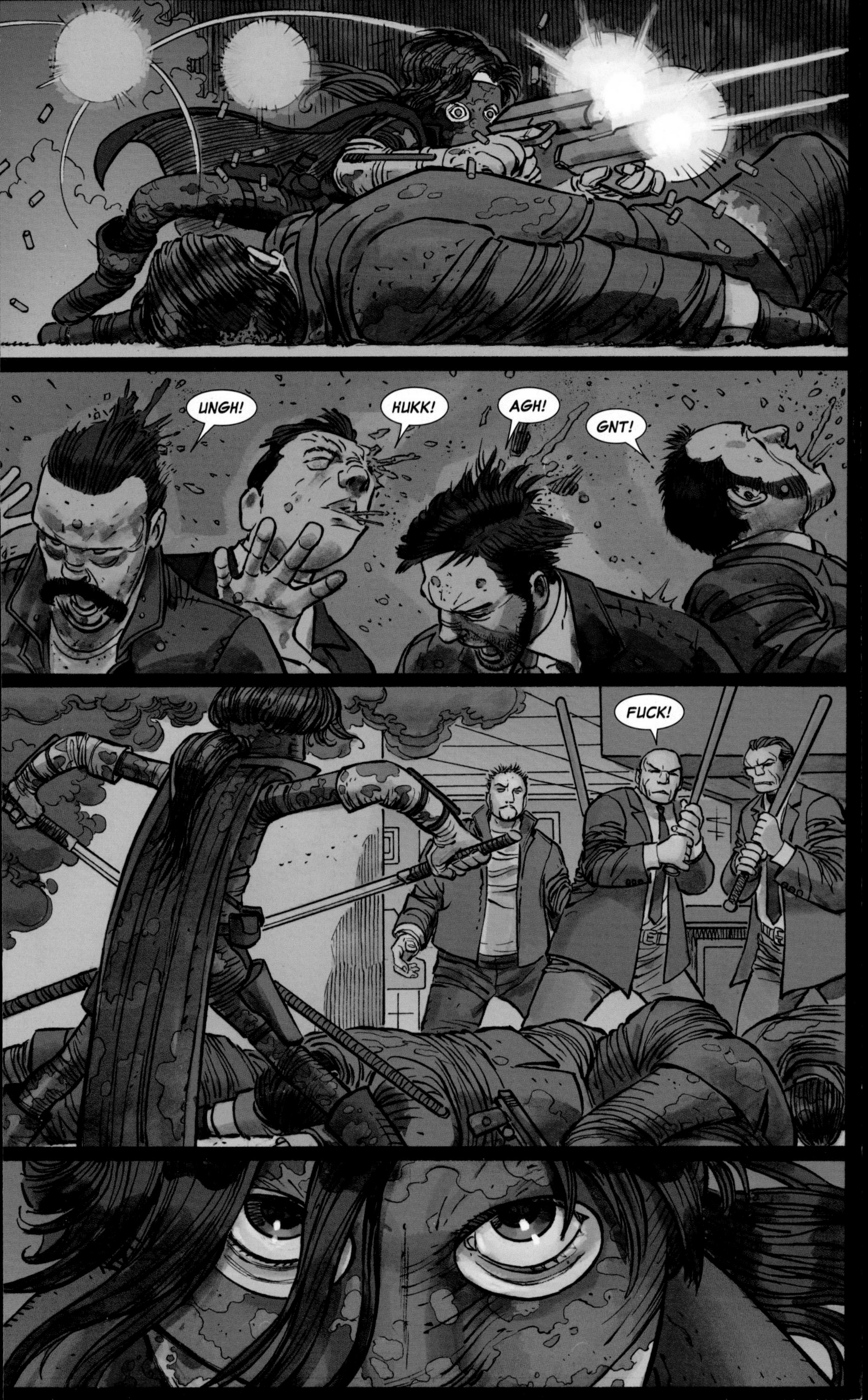
UNGH!
HUKK!
AGH!
GNT!
FUCK!

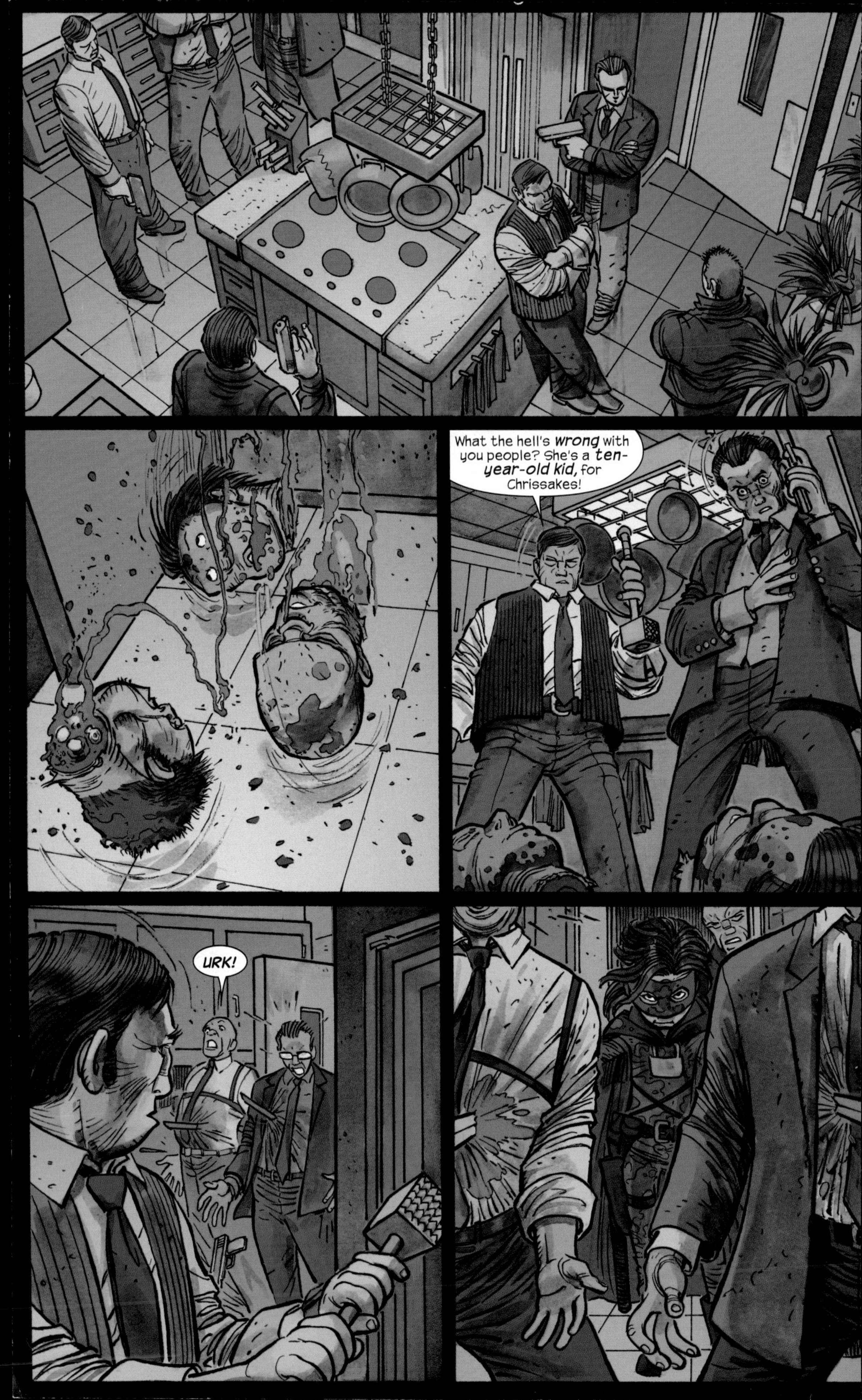
What the hell's wrong with you people? She's a ten-year-old kid, for Chrissakes!
URK!

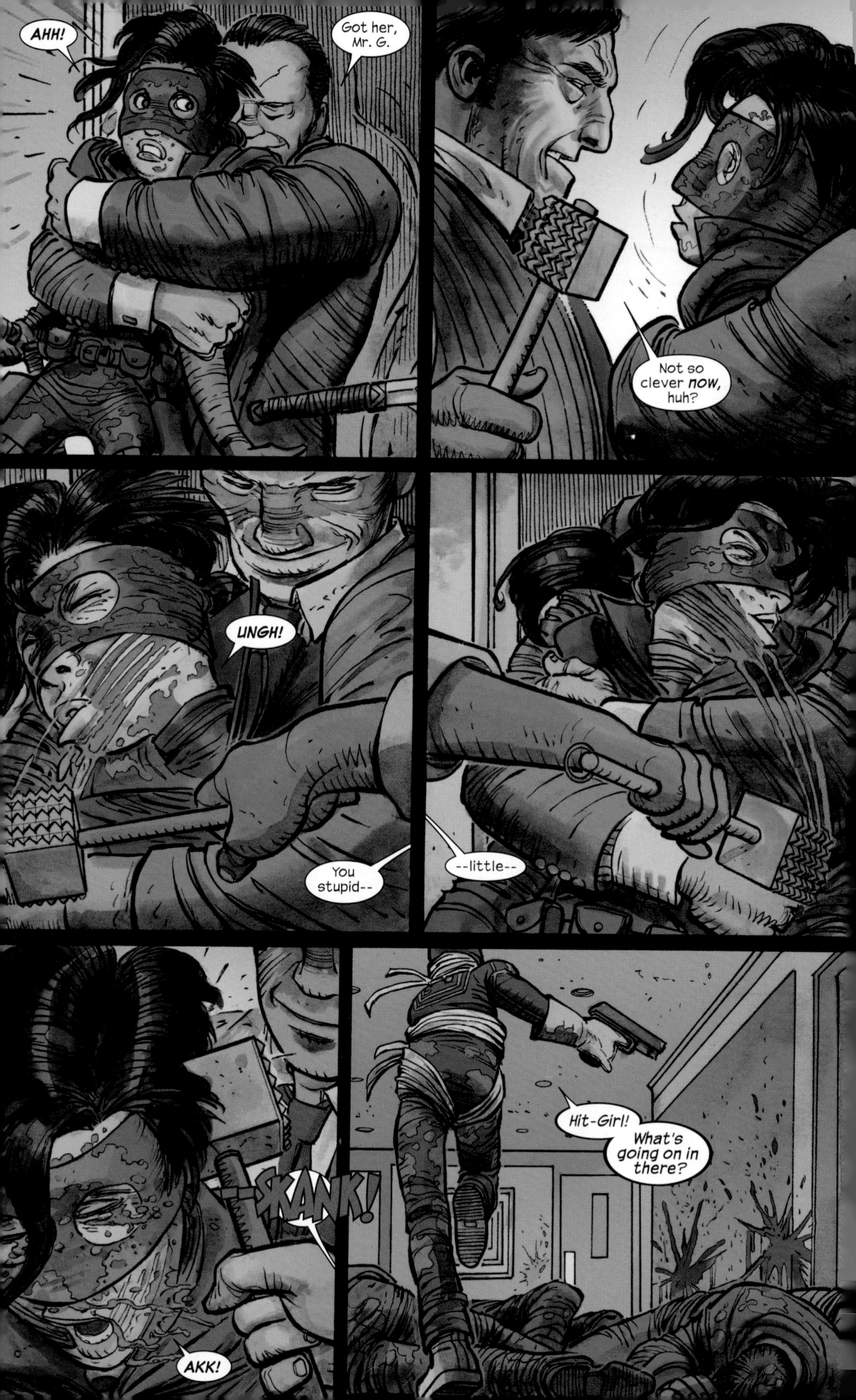
AHH!
Got her, Mr. G.
Not so clever NOW, huh?
UNGH!
You stupid--
--little--
SKANK!
AKK!
Hit-Girl!
What's going on in there?

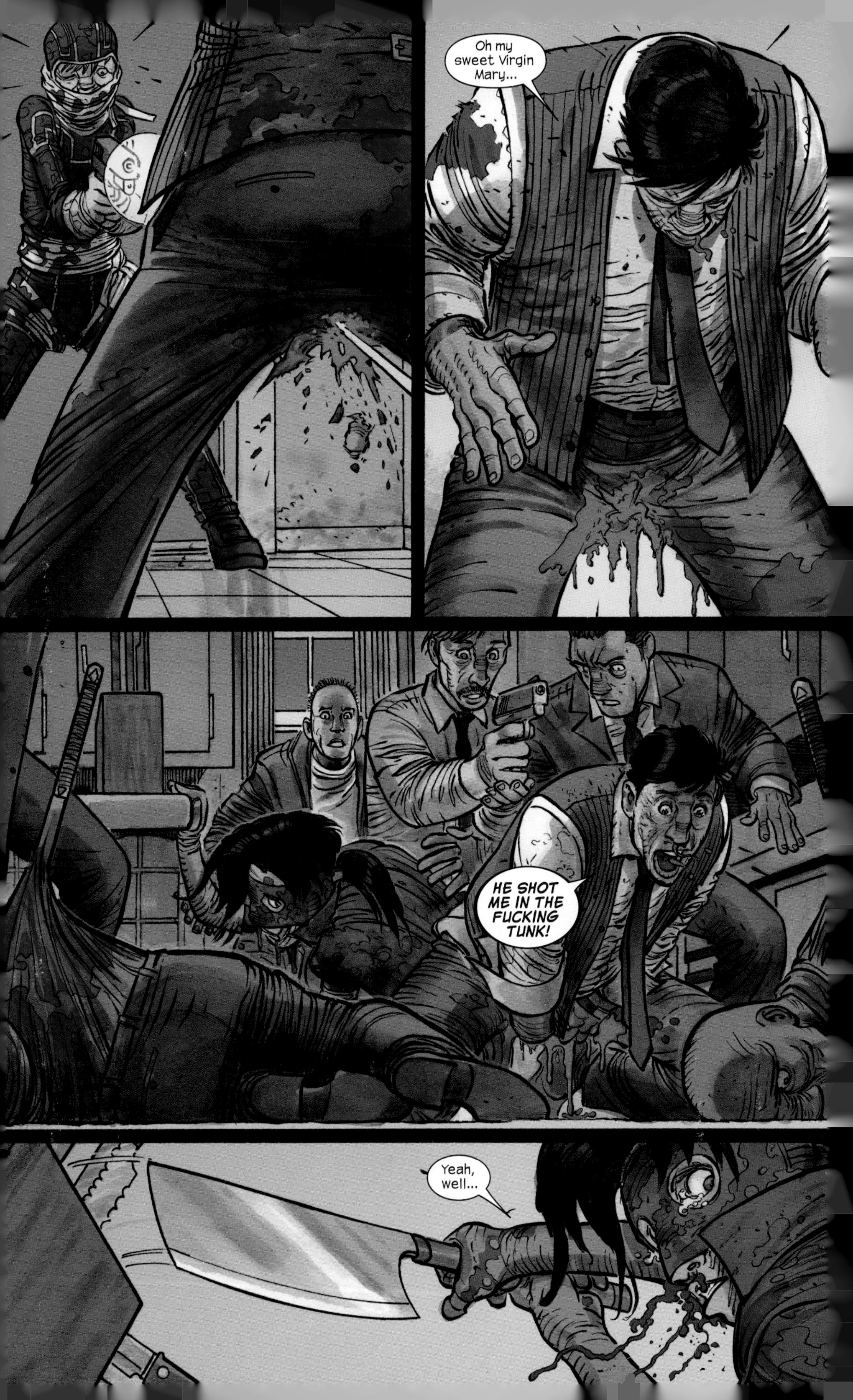
Oh my sweet Virgin Mary...
HE SHOT ME IN THE FUCKING TUNK!
Yeah, well...

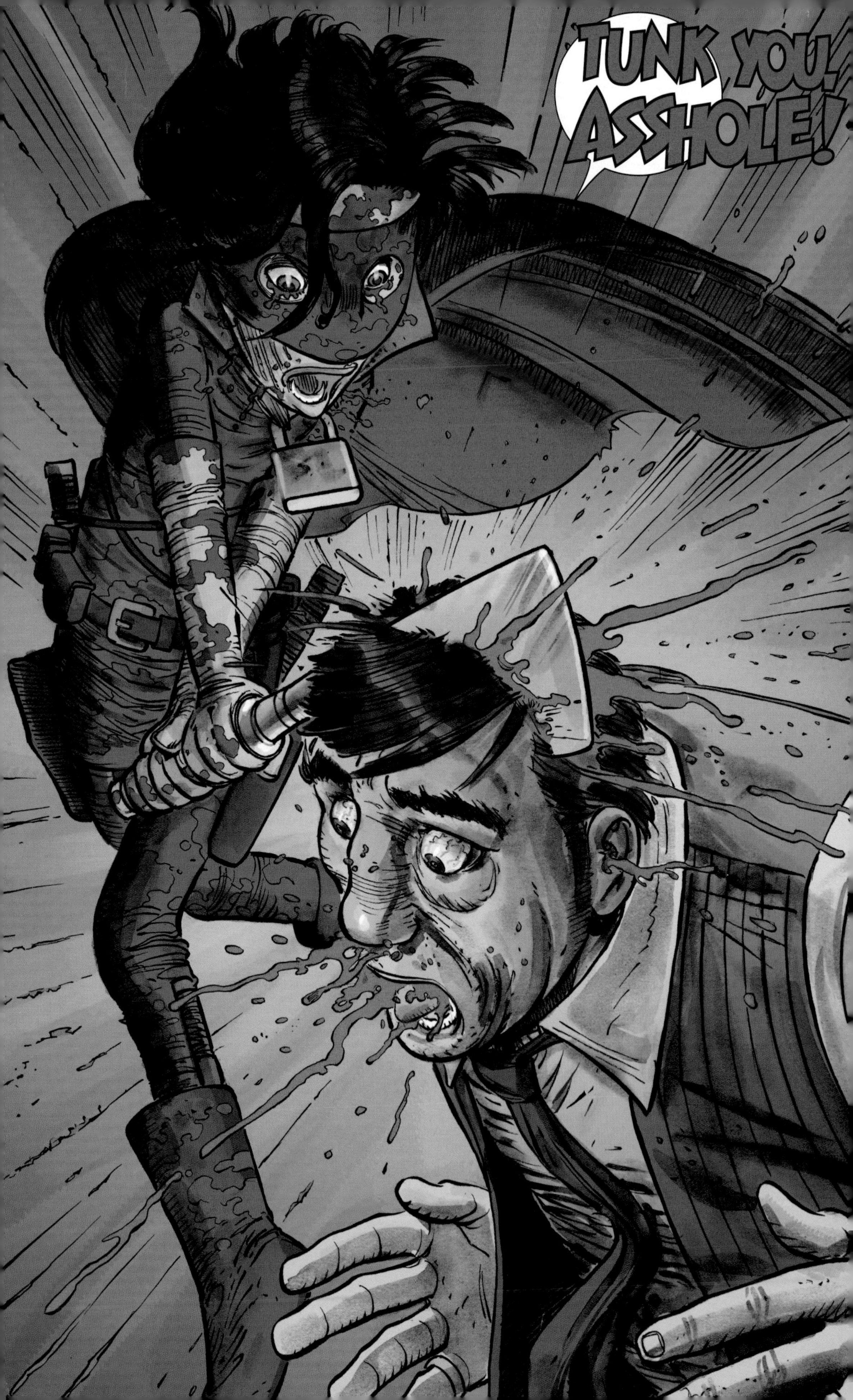
TUNK YOU, ASSHOLE!

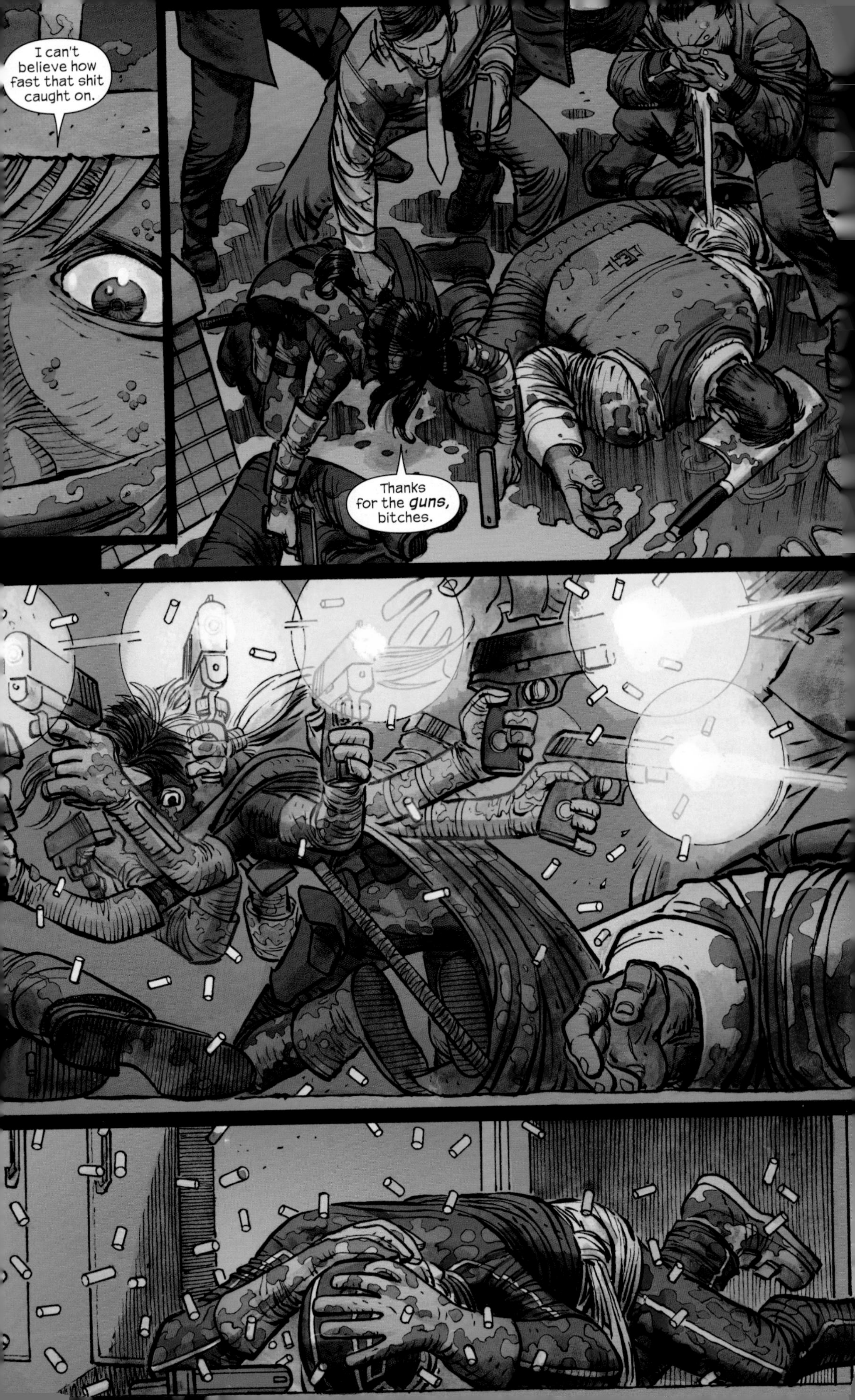
I can't believe how fast that shit caught on.
Thanks for the *guns,* bitches.

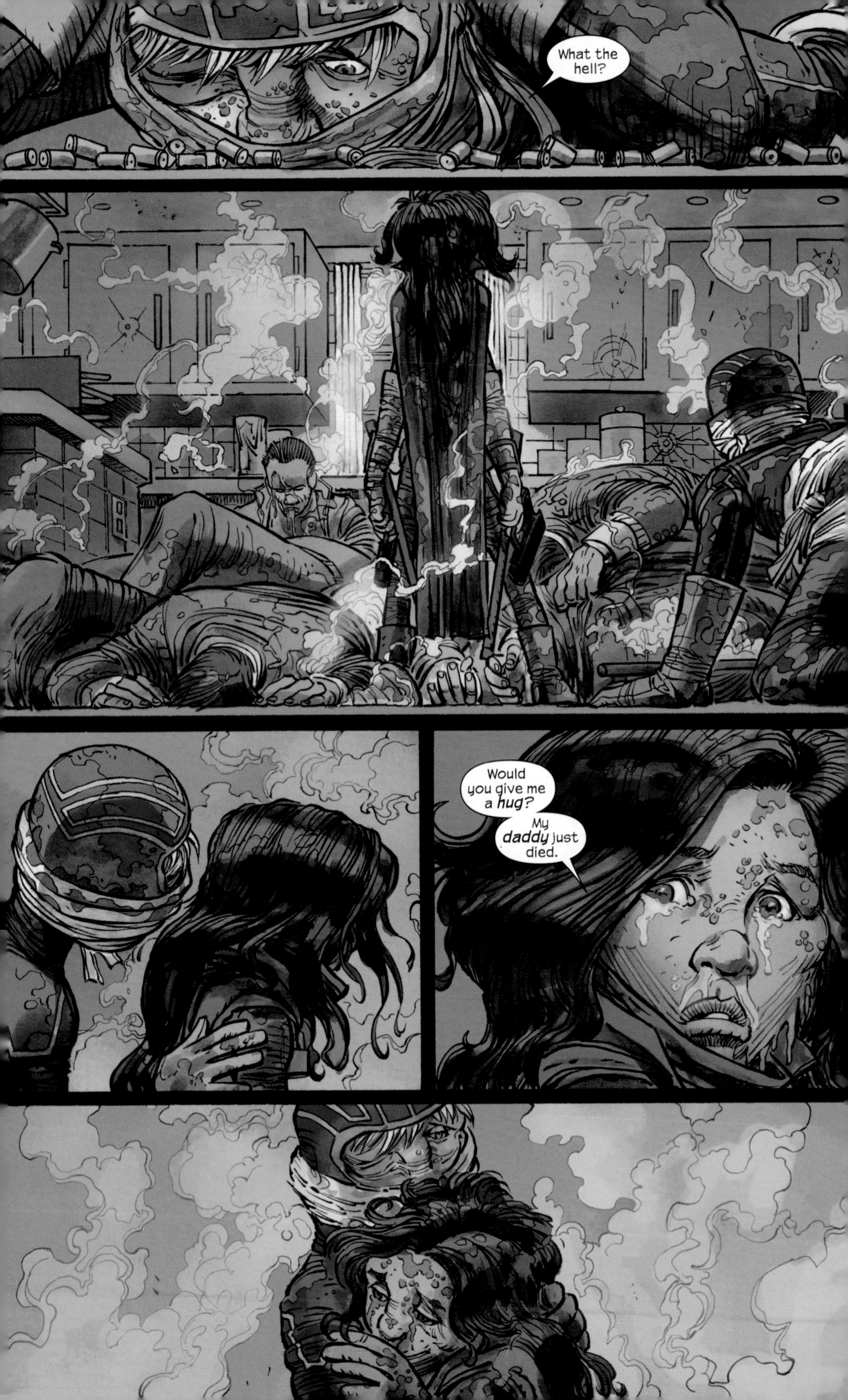
What the hell?
Would you give me a hug?
My daddy just died.

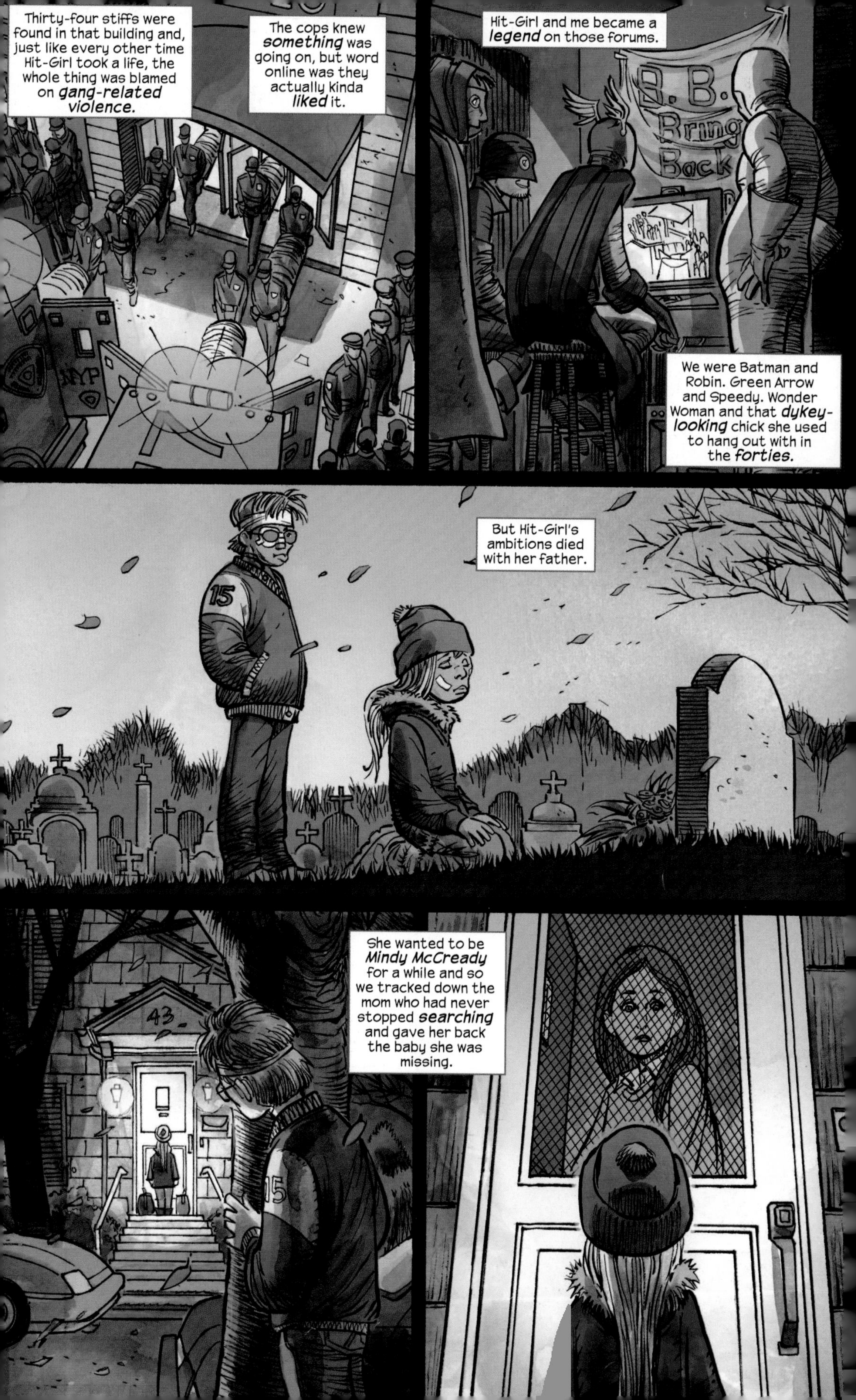
Thirty-four stiffs were found in that building and, just like every other time Hit-Girl took a life, the whole thing was blamed on *gang-related violence.*
The cops knew *something* was going on, but word online was they actually kinda *liked* it.
NYP
Hit-Girl and me became a *legend* on those forums.
B. B. Bring Back
We were Batman and Robin. Green Arrow and Speedy. Wonder Woman and that *dykey-looking* chick she used to hang out with in the *forties.*
But Hit-Girl's ambitions died with her father.
15
She wanted to be *Mindy McCready* for a while and so we tracked down the mom who had never stopped *searching* and gave her back the baby she was missing.
43
15

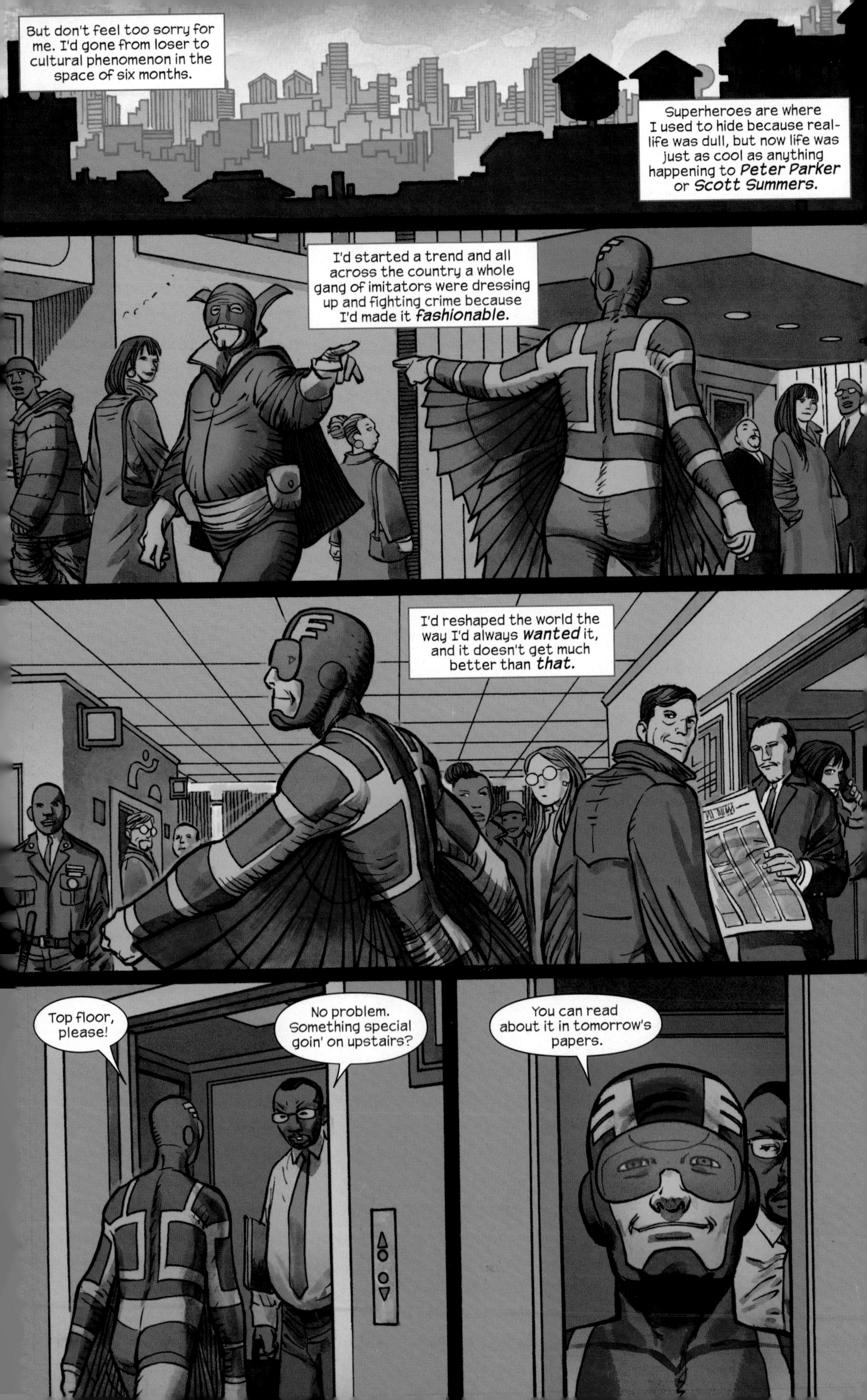
But don't feel too sorry for me. I'd gone from loser to cultural phenomenon in the space of six months.
Superheroes are where I used to hide because real-life was dull, but now life was just as cool as anything happening to *Peter Parker* or *Scott Summers.*
I'd started a trend and all across the country a whole gang of imitators were dressing up and fighting crime because I'd made it *fashionable.*
I'd reshaped the world the way I'd always *wanted* it, and it doesn't get much better than *that.*
Top floor, please!
No problem. Something special goin' on upstairs?
You can read about it in tomorrow's papers.

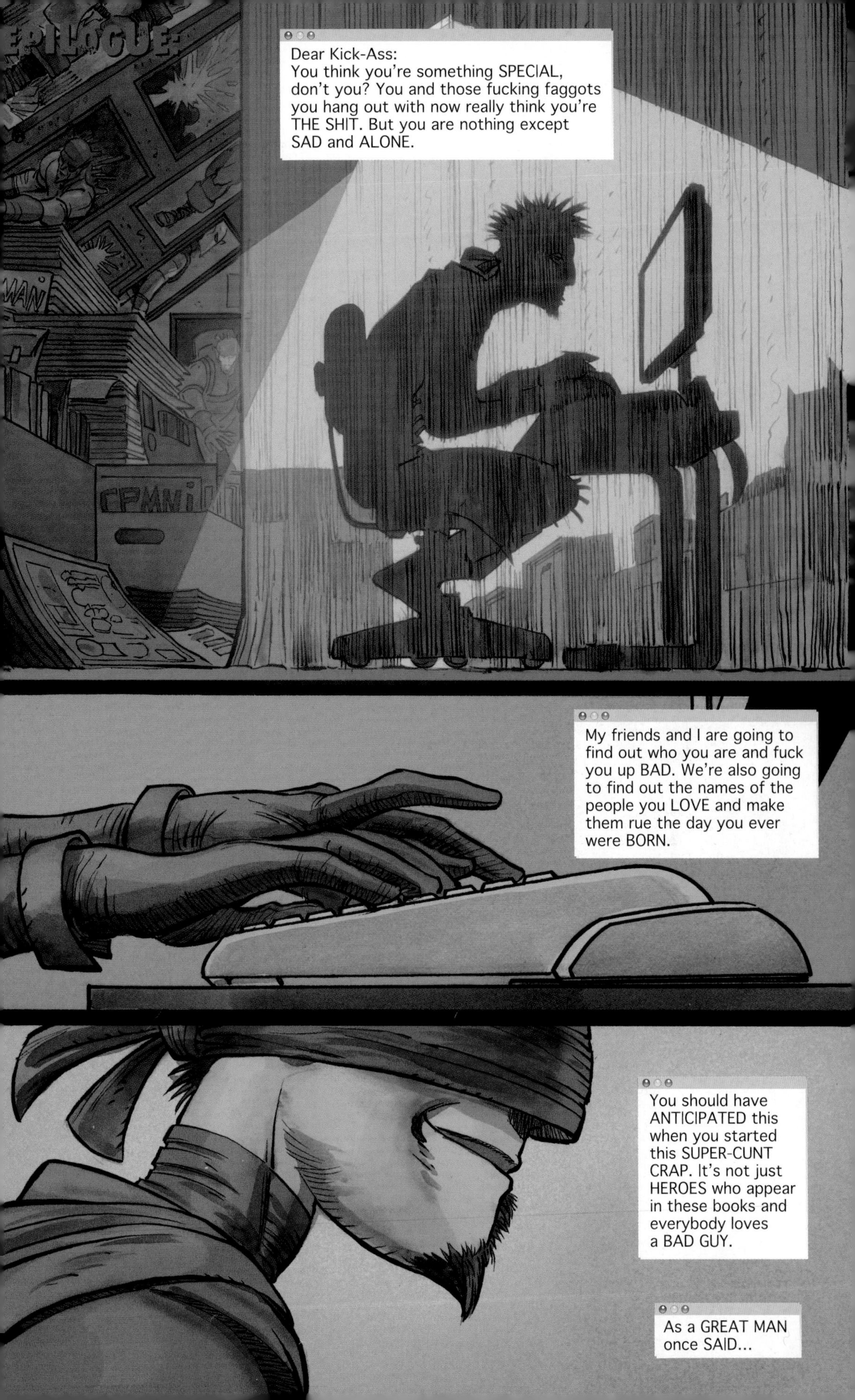
EPILOGUE:
Dear Kick-Ass:
You think you're something SPECIAL, don't you? You and those fucking faggots you hang out with now really think you're THE SHIT. But you are nothing except SAD and ALONE.
My friends and I are going to find out who you are and fuck you up BAD. We're also going to find out the names of the people you LOVE and make them rue the day you ever were BORN.
You should have ANTICIPATED this when you started this SUPER-CUNT CRAP. It's not just HEROES who appear in these books and everybody loves a BAD GUY.
As a GREAT MAN once SAID...

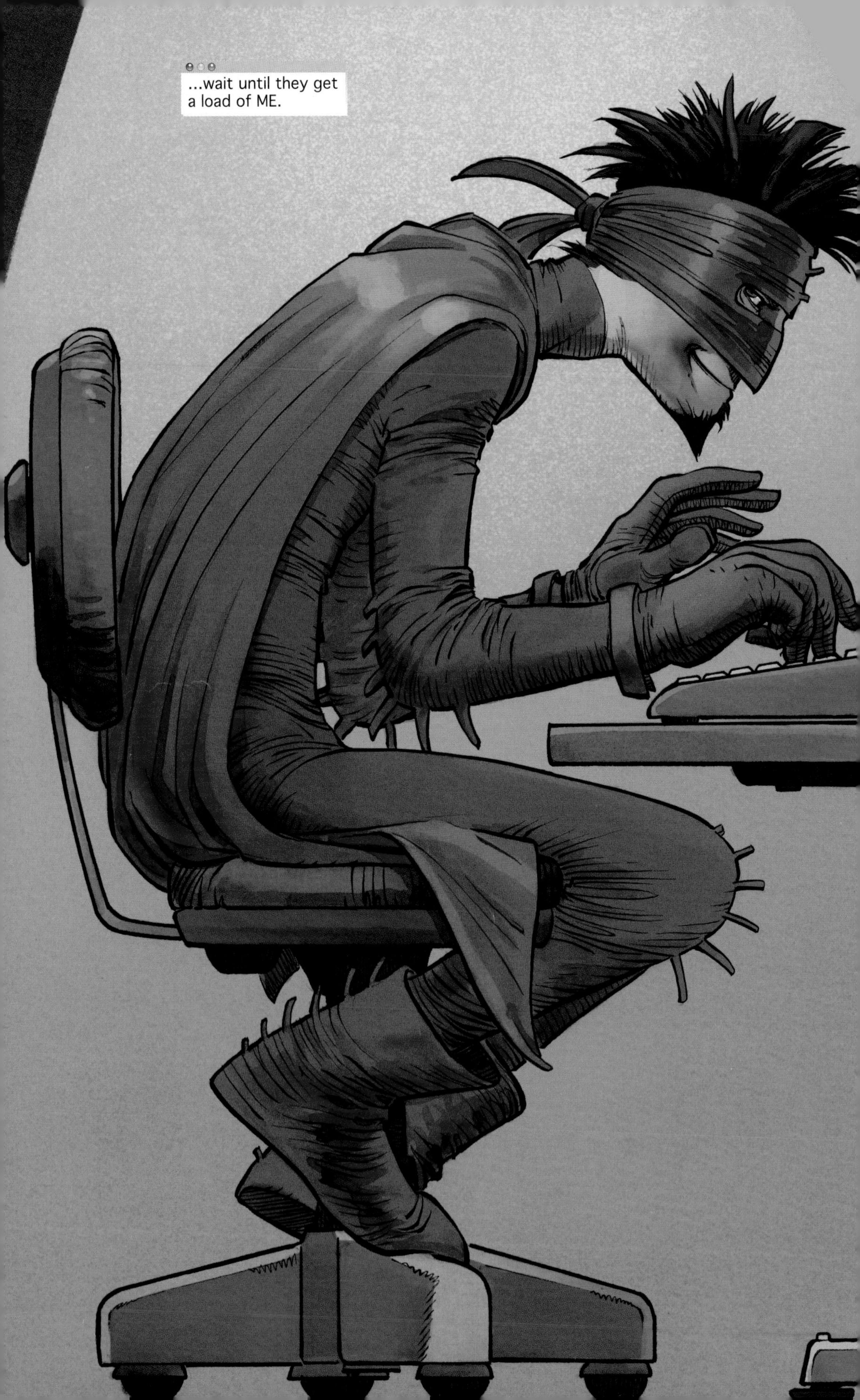
...wait until they get a load of ME.

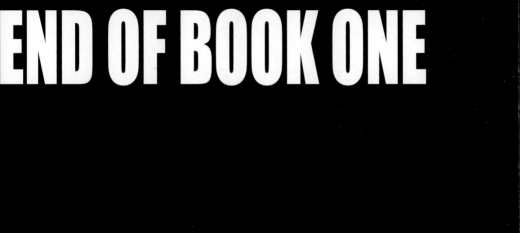

END OF BOOK ONE

KICK

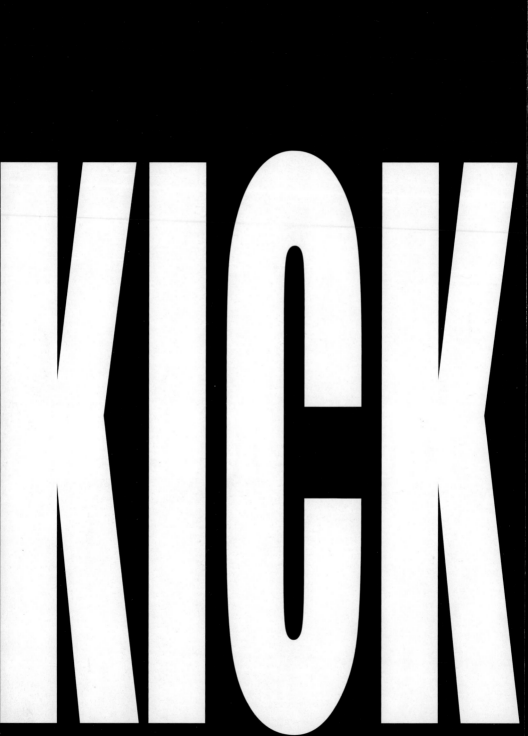

-ASS

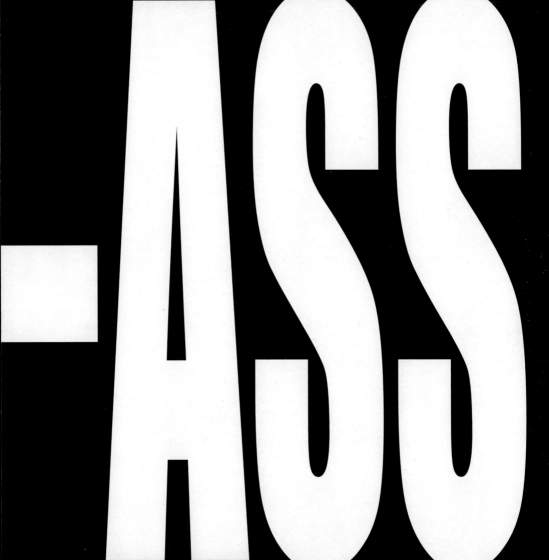

MARK MILLAR has been one of the key writers for Marvel Comics in the 21st century. Millar's first major contribution to Marvel was *Ultimate X-Men*, which achieved great creative and commercial success throughout his two-year run. Working with artist Bryan Hitch on *The Ultimates*, Millar surpassed his own success with that commercial and critical darling. Next, joining up with some of the industry's top creative talent, the Scottish writer took on two of Marvel's most iconic characters: Spider-Man and Wolverine. While working on creator-owned books like *Wanted*, turned into a Hollywood blockbuster staring Angelina Jolie, he penned *Civil War*, the epic miniseries that definitively reshaped the landscape of Marvel's heroes. More recently, Millar has reunited with Hitch on *Fantastic Four* and with *Civil War* artist Steve McNiven in both the pages of *Wolverine* and the upcoming *Nemesis*, as well as returning to the Ultimate Universe with *Ultimate Avengers*.

JOHN ROMITA JR. is a modern-day comic-art legend. A loyal Marvel artist since the late '70s, he has followed in his father's footsteps and helped keep the Romita name on the list of top-shelf talent. Timeless runs on *Iron Man, Uncanny X-Men, Amazing Spider-Man,* and *Daredevil* helped establish him as his own man artistically, and his art on *Wolverine* is arguably the decade's most explosive comic art—trumped perhaps only by his own work on the massive summer blockbuster event *World War Hulk*. JRJR has also paired with renowned writer Neil Gaiman for *The Eternals*, their reworking of the classic Marvel Comics characters, and has recently returned to *Amazing Spider-Man*; he will follow that up with another high-profile Marvel series.

TOM PALMER has worked as an illustrator in the advertising and editorial fields, but he has spent the majority of his career in comic books. His first assignment, fresh out of art school, was on *Doctor Strange*, and he has gone on to lend his inking talents to many of Marvel's top titles, including *X-Men, The Avengers, Tomb of Dracula,* and more recently *Punisher, Hulk,* and *Ghost Rider.* He lives and works in New Jersey.

DEAN WHITE is one of the comic industry's best and most sought-after color artists. Well-known for his work on titles such as *The Amazing Spider-Man, Punisher, Dark Avengers, Captain America, Black Panther, Wolverine* and countless more, Dean's envelope-pushing rendering and color palette bring a sense of urgency and power to every page he touches.

CHRIS ELIOPOULOS is a multiple award-winner for his lettering, having worked on dozens of books during the twenty years he's been in the industry—including Erik Larsen's *Savage Dragon*, for which he hand-lettered the first 100 issues. Along with his success as a letterer, he also publishes his own strip *Misery Loves Sherman*, wrote and illustrated the popular *Franklin Richards: Son of a Genius* one-shots, and writes Marvel's *Lockjaw and the Pet Avengers* series.

MICHAEL HORWITZ's student thesis (a five minute documentary about the private lives of cabbages) was met with resounding indifference by NYU, forcing the Virginia native to realize a career in experimental film wasn't in the cards. With a résumé padded to the extreme (and omitting a regrettable excursion into the world of go-go dancing), Michael somehow fooled Marvel Comics into hiring him, where he now edits such titles as Laurell K. Hamilton's *Anita Blake* and Stephen King's *The Dark Tower*.

JOHN BARBER self-published his own comics before joining the world of webcomics, and later co-wrote a book called *Webcomics*, with Steven Withrow. In 2003, Barber joined the Marvel Comics editorial team and became editor of the Wolverine franchise, before leaving to pursue a freelance career—including a return to comics on the web (webcomicsnation.com/thejohnbarber). He stuck around on *Kick-Ass*, though, which is a hell of a way to go out, editorially speaking.

KICK-ASS'S GREATEST HITS

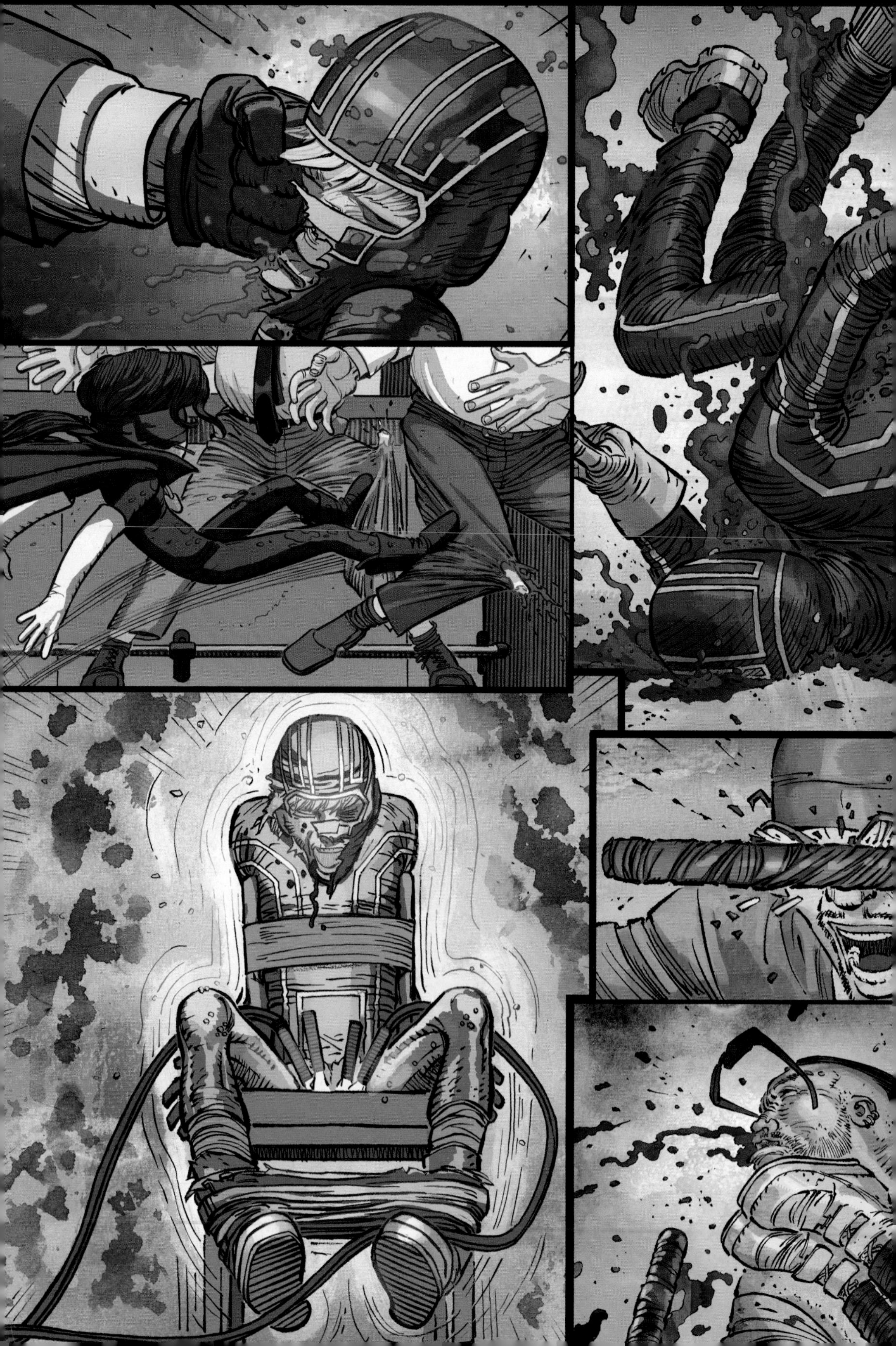

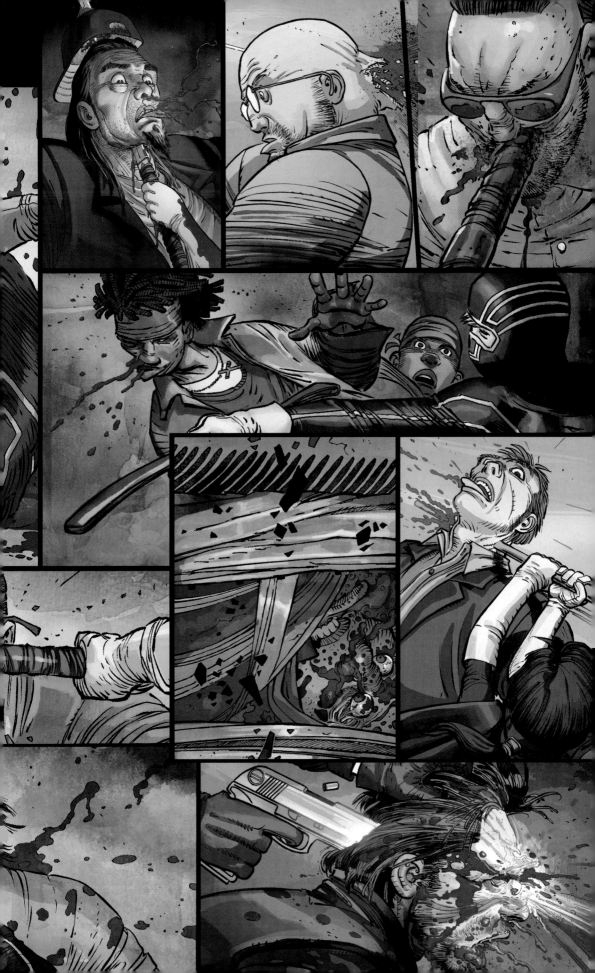

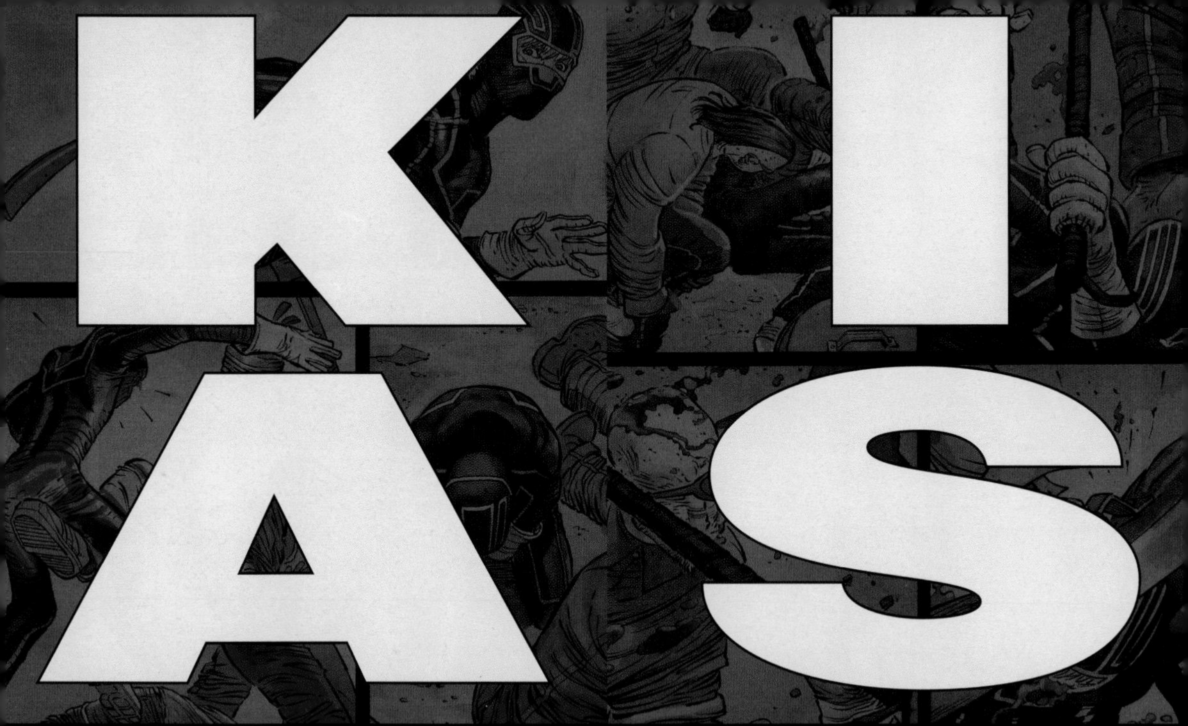
KI
AS

COMBINED COVERS FOR ISSUE #1 6TH PRINTING, #2 4TH PRINTING, #3 4TH PRINTING AND #4 3RD PRINTING

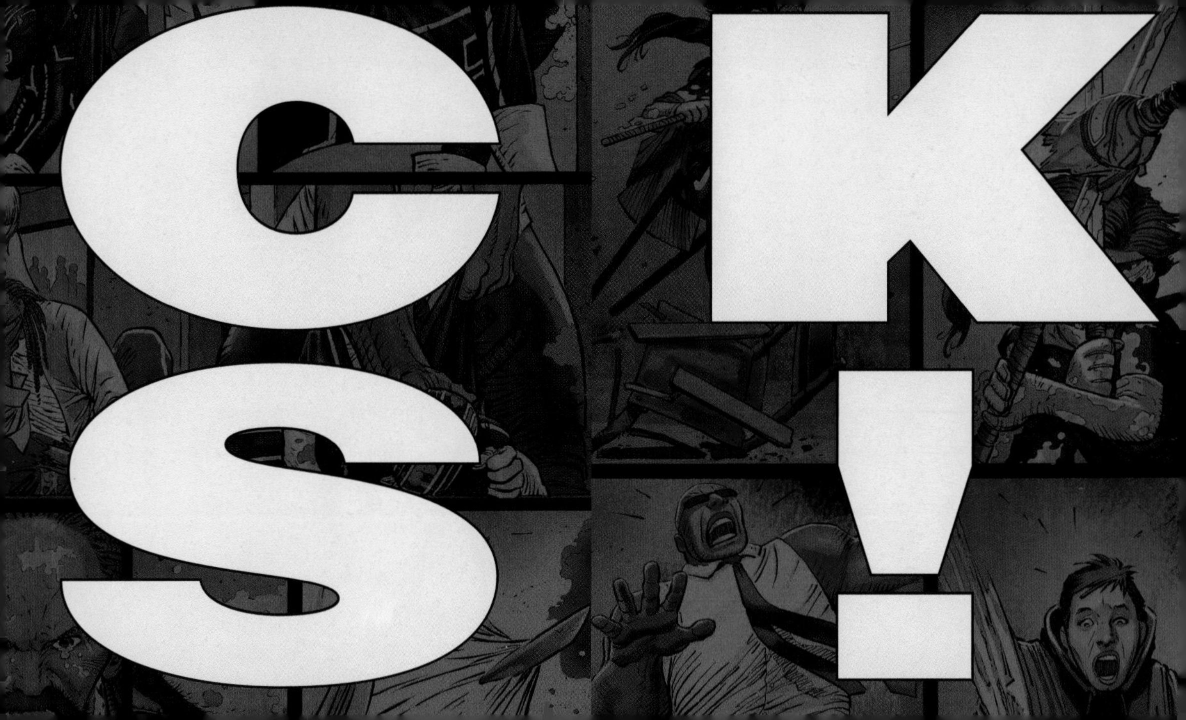
CS
K!

ONE (VARIANT BY MCNIVEN)

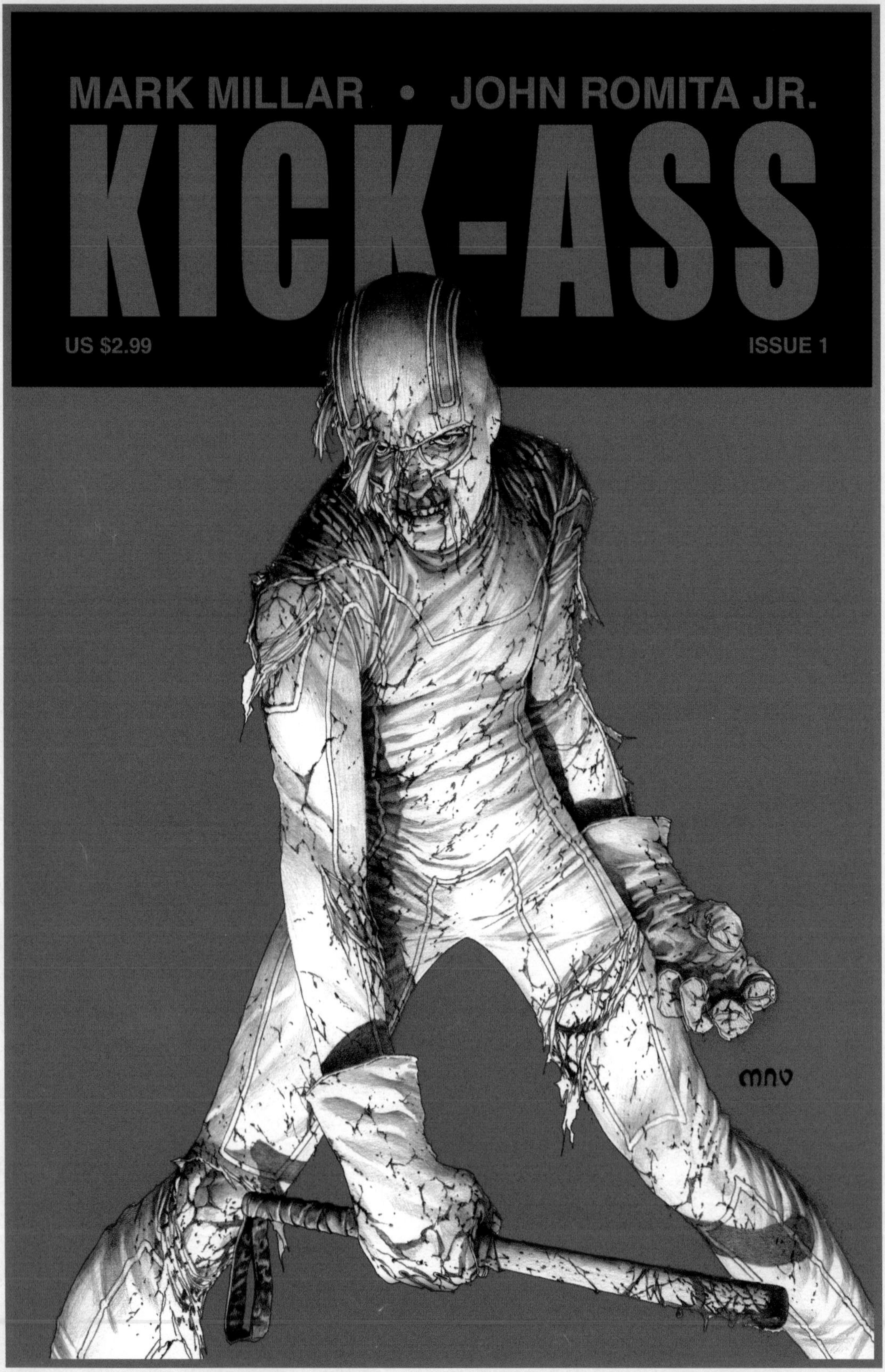
MARK MILLAR • JOHN ROMITA JR.
KICK-ASS
US $2.99
ISSUE 1
MNV

TWO (VARIANT BY JOHN ROMITA JR.)

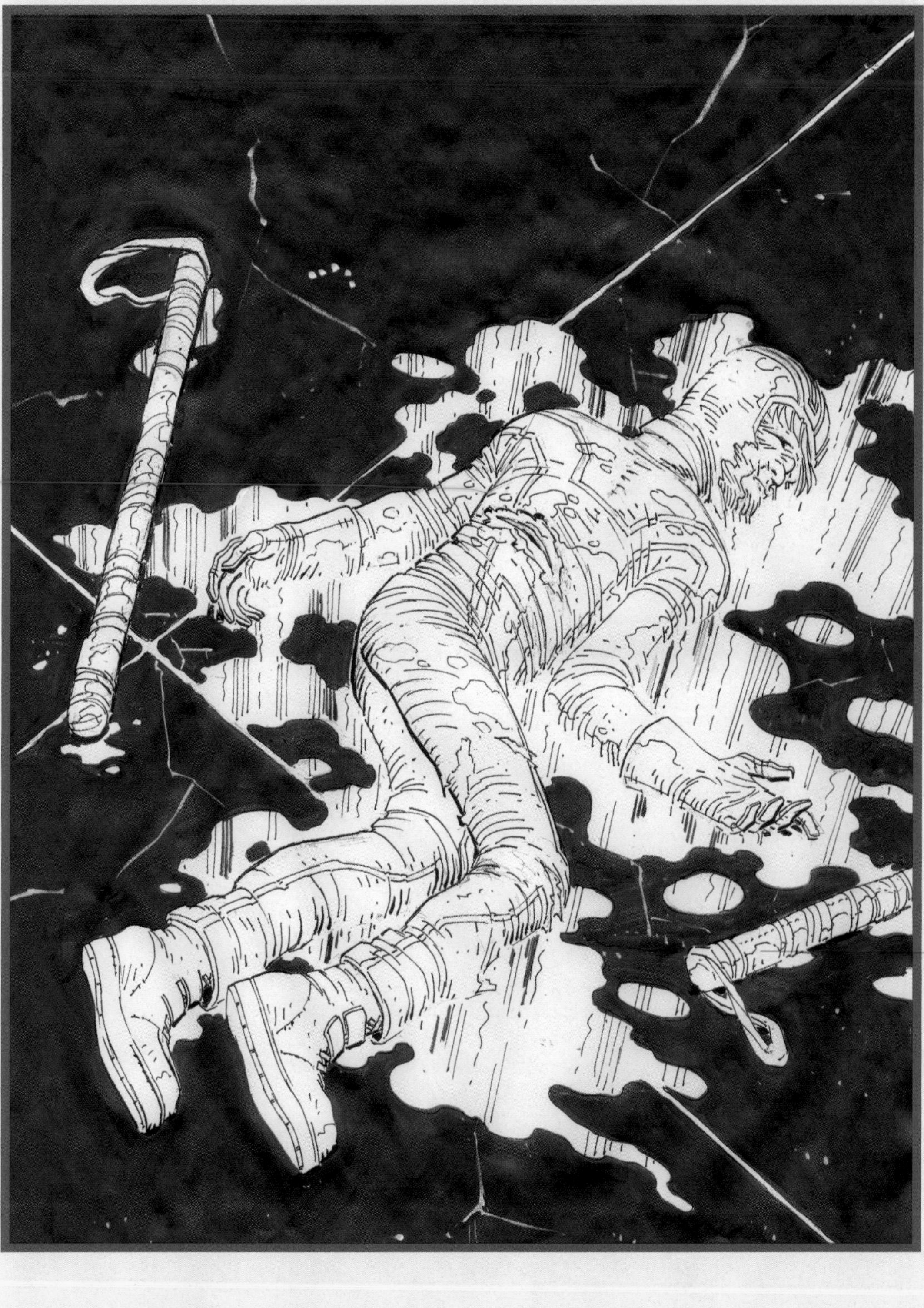

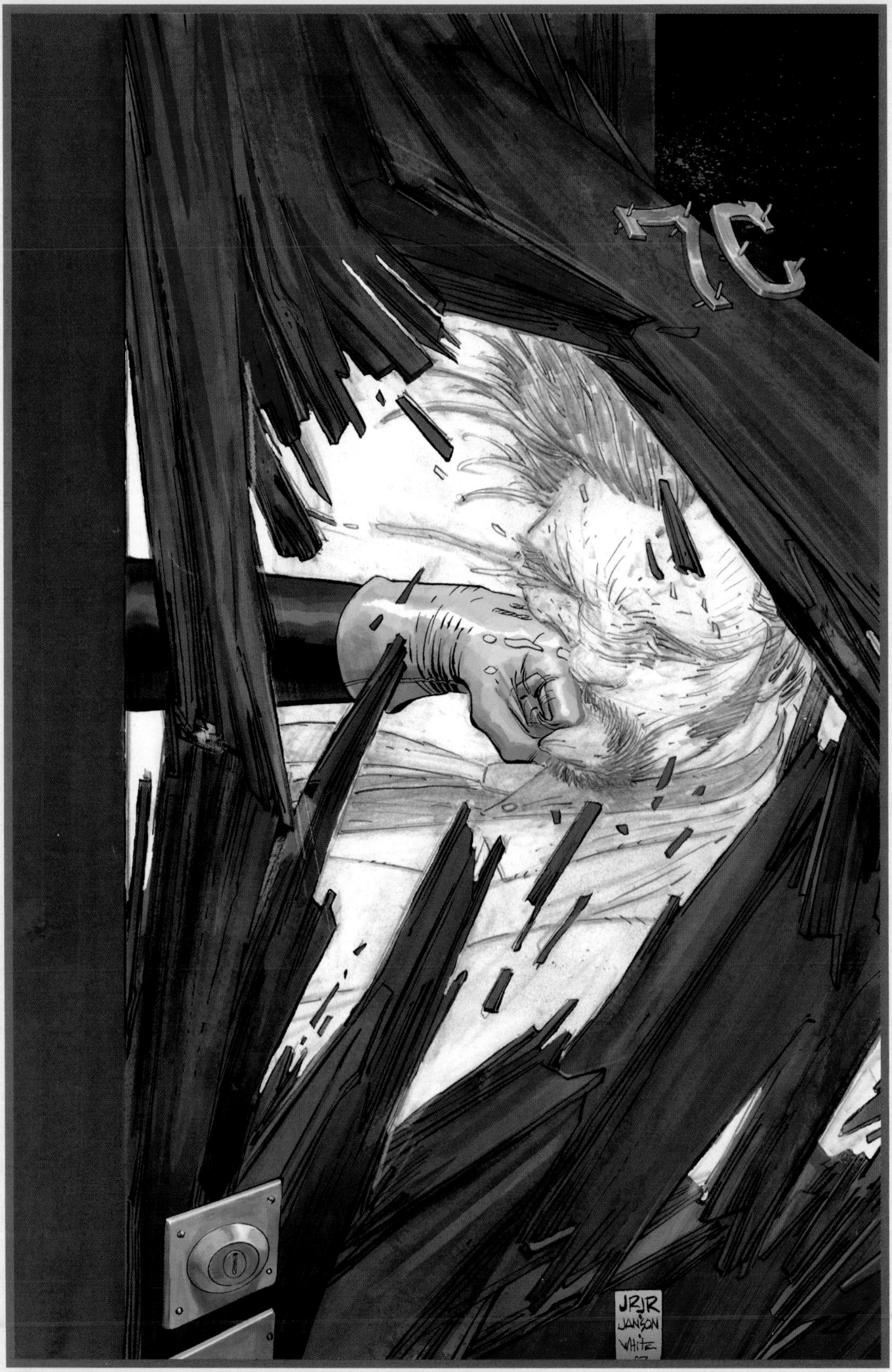
JRJR
JANSON
WHITE

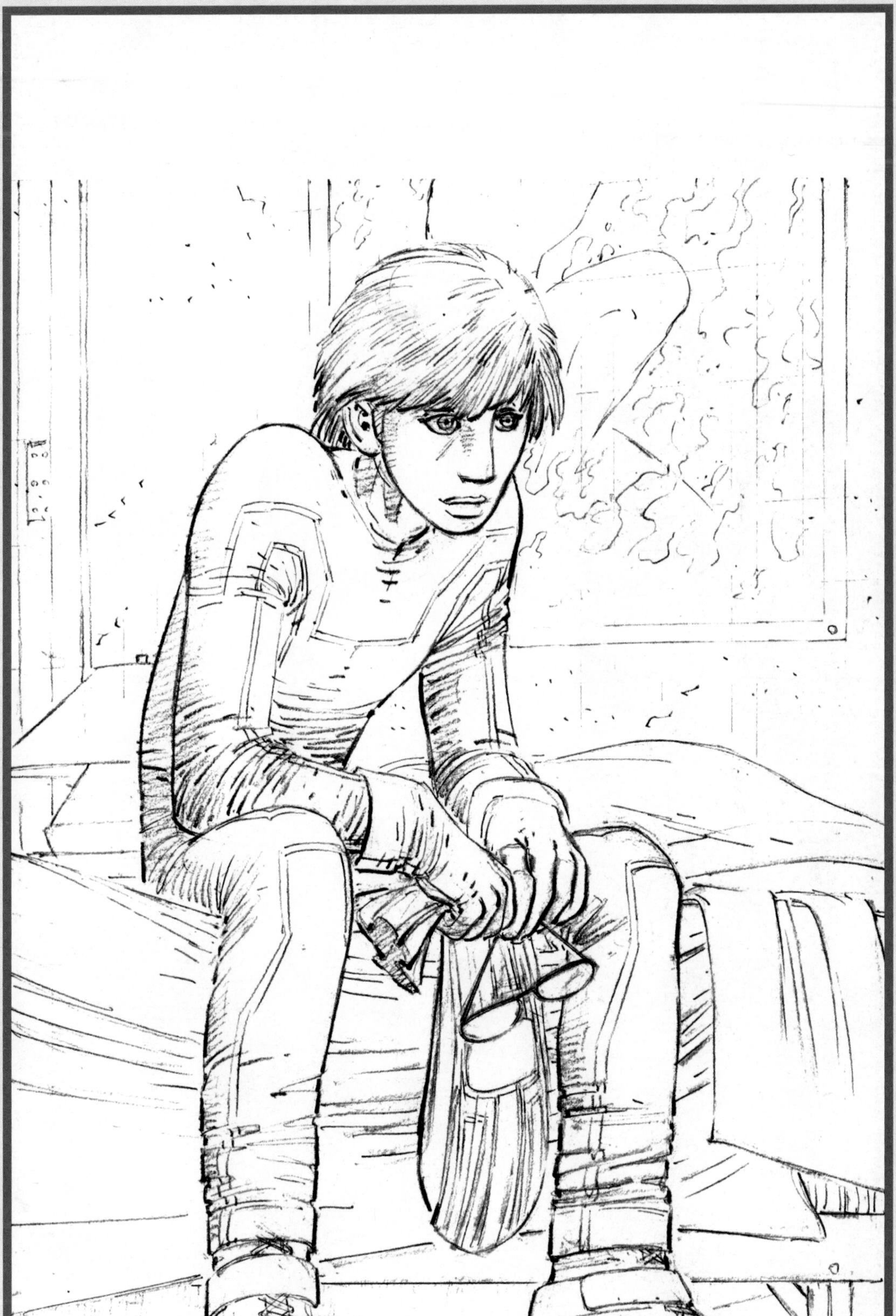

KICK-ASS
THE MOVIE

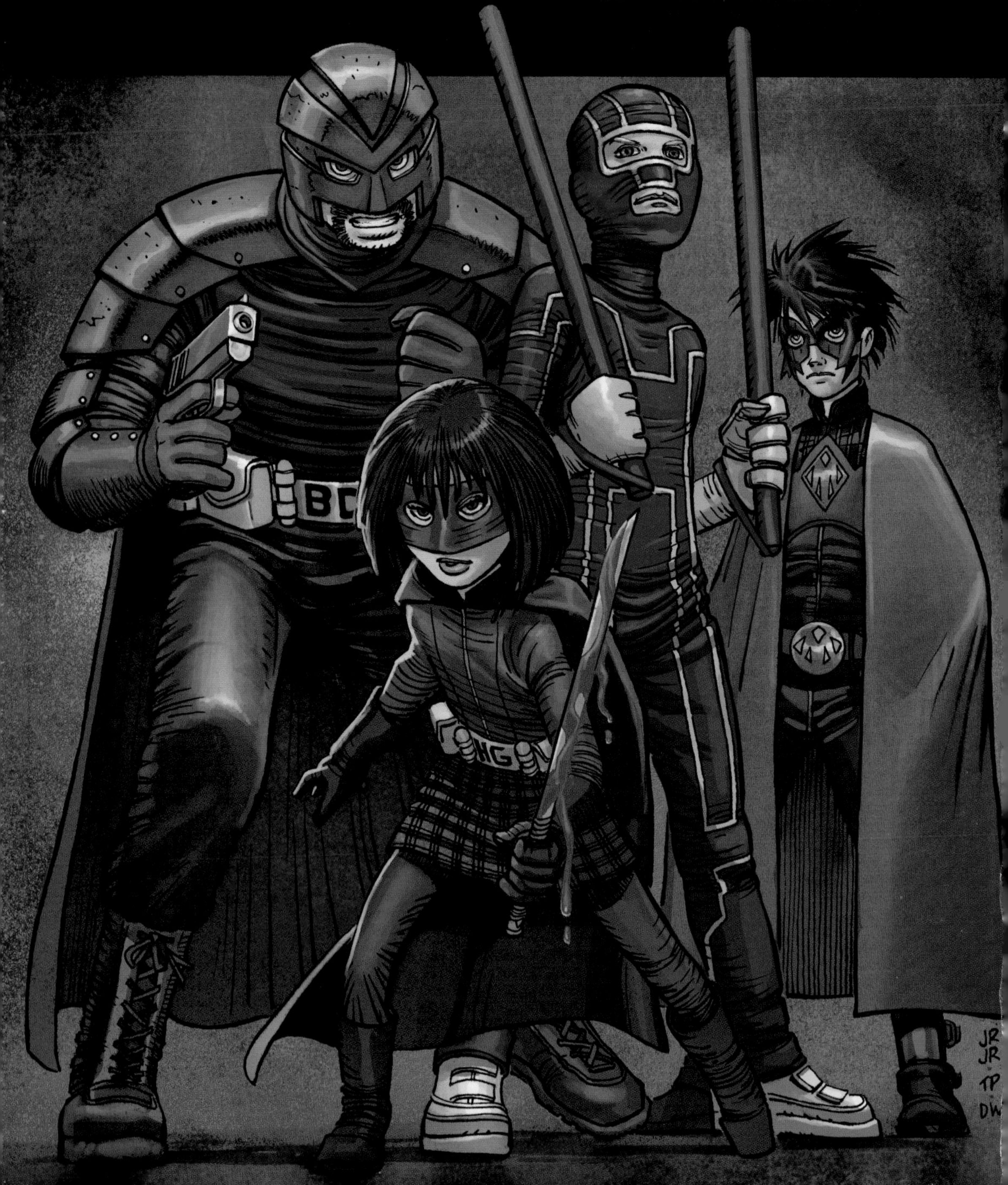
JR JR
TP
DW

COMING SOON

PENCILS-JOHN S. ROMITA INKS-TOM PALMER COLOR-DEAN WHITE